Supervision
A Guide to Practice

Jon Wiles
University of Montana

Joseph Bondi
University of South Florida

CHARLES E. MERRILL PUBLISHING COMPANY
A Bell & Howell Company
Columbus   Toronto   London   Sydney

Published by Charles E. Merrill Publishing Company
A Bell & Howell Company
Columbus, Ohio 43216

This book was set in Helvetica and Avant Garde.
Production Editor: Laura Wallencheck Gustafson.
Cover Design Coordination: Will Chenoweth.

Library of Congress Catalog Card Number: 79-90125

International Standard Book Number: 0-675-08168-8

Printed in the United States of America

1 2 3 4 5 6 7 8 9 10—85 84 83 82 81 80

We dedicate this book to Kimball Wiles, pioneer in the field of educational supervision.

Contents

Preface

Supervision is a rapidly changing role in the field of education. While supervision has historically been linked to administration, supervisors are presently mapping out new relationships and spheres of responsibility. *Supervision: A Guide To Practice* is an effort to capture the essence of this educational role in transition.

We have divided the book into four parts. Part One addresses the changing role of educational supervision and explores dimensions of supervisory leadership. Part Two describes and analyzes specific leadership roles enacted by school supervisors. Part Three focuses on methods of improving supervisory performance. Part Four outlines future options and opportunities.

Additionally there are three appendices to assist the reader in summarizing material presented in this text. Appendix A contains indices for assessing effective supervisory practice. In Appendix B, three case histories are drawn to demonstrate the application of supervisory behaviors to school tasks at the elementary, middle, and secondary levels. Appendix C is a compilation of resources useful to supervisors in meeting novel instructional problems in their work.

We wish to acknowledge the contributions of the many professional educators who allowed us to incorporate their work. We especially wish to cite our reviewers—Thomas H. Metos, Arizona State University; Dr. V. J. Kennedy, University of Houston; Dr. Thomas McGreal, University of Illinois; and Dr. Delbert K. Clear, University of Wisconsin—for their professional insights. Such sharing is essential to the improvement of education.

Thanks also to our typists, Susan Cornette and Donna Whitney, who went beyond the call of duty to help us meet deadlines on our manuscript.

Finally, we wish to thank our wives, Margaret Wiles and Patsy Bondi, and our children, Amy and Michael Wiles, and Pamela Jo, Beth Jana, and Bradley Joseph Bondi, for their support during the development of this book.

part one

Dimensions of Supervision

The Field of Educational Supervision

At this time supervision is one of the most complex and difficult leadership roles in education. It is a role with many titles, numerous functions, and an uncertain future. Supervision is, nonetheless, indispensable for the improvement of educational programs.

Educational supervisors practice their profession at many different levels of operation in school systems. While most supervisors are central office personnel or building administrators, some are university or state department of education personnel. Supervisors can be superintendents, principals, assistant principals, school coordinators, directors, department chairpersons, subject matter specialists, or a host of related professionals found in school settings. It is the role, rather than the title, that defines the educational supervisor.

In the past, supervision has been perceived in a piecemeal fashion by educational literature. There has been a distinct tendency to define supervision as a residual function, according to its relationship with oher educational roles. Overall, a false dichotomy has been drawn that distinguishes between supervision as an organizational/managerial role and supervision as a people-centered, interpersonal function. The absence of a comprehensive view of supervision has contributed to the ambiguity that surrounds its function. Supervision in school settings is in need of a more dynamic and active definition of its role.

The uniqueness of supervision in a professional setting must be recognized. Supervision in education is not the same as supervision in an industrial setting. While the problems encountered by supervisors in business and education are similar, the responses to such problems must differ. A definition of an industrial supervisor is found in the 1947 Taft-Hartley Act:

> those having authority to exercise independent judgment in hiring, discharging, disciplining, rewarding, and taking other actions of a similar nature with respect to employees.

In education, supervisors must use persuasive and professional, rather than authoritative, influence in responding to problems and needs.

The field of supervision is rapidly changing. Like all areas of education, such change in supervision is pivotal, with the ultimate direction unknown. Forces at work, both in schools and outside of schools, suggest that supervision must assume a new role and mission in the near future. We believe that the kinds of change that will occur in the field of supervision will be yavily influenced by the assumptions supervisors make about their own roles.

All supervisory behavior rests on assumptions, generalizations, and best guesses—based on theory. The assumptions supervisors make are usually implicit and sometimes contradictory. The predictive value of assumptions (if I act in this manner, these things will occur) determine behavior. To the degree that educational supervisors think through their assumptions, understand their surroundings, and comprehend the effect of their actions, they can influence their future role.

In this chapter we will review historical factors that have shaped the present role of supervision in American education. Also, the various current definitions of supervision will be outlined, and the function of supervisors will be analyzed. Finally, we will look ahead to some difficult choices confronting educational supervisors during the 1980s.

HISTORY OF EDUCATIONAL SUPERVISION

The meaning of the term *supervision* and the role played by educational supervisors in school settings have evolved over time. For the most part, supervision in schools has developed as an extention of educational administration. As we enter the 1980s, however, supervision appears on the brink of fulfilling an independent and distinct function.

During most of the eighteenth and nineteenth centuries, supervision was a form of inspection. Early schools in America utilized appointed boards of laypersons or citizens to oversee school operations. Early records indicate that these lay boards periodically reviewed school facilities, equipment, and the progress of pupils attending the schools. This early lay assistance, fashioned after lay advisement to churches, soon became a form of lay inspection and control. The relationship of the inspectors with the teachers was often stern and punitive. Characterized by directing, telling, and judging, supervisory visits sometimes led to the dismissal of teachers.

With the growth of individual schools and school districts in the late nineteenth century, the observation and the inspection functions of the lay board were taken over by an appointed supervisor. Serving as an adjunct of the superintendent and working in the schools, this individual freed the board of lay advisors to deal with more global concerns such as constructing buildings and raising money.

By the early years of the twentieth century, lay inspection of schools had given way almost entirely to supervisory inspection of teachers. The redefining of supervision to deal specifically with classroom instructional concerns resulted from the increased responsibilities of the superintendent. When the superintendent's "span of control" (the manageable scope of responsibilities) no longer allowed classroom visitations or individual teacher assessments, the supervisor, as a representative of the superintendent, assumed these duties. It was at this time that the supervisory role "crossed over" from an authoritative line position to a "staff" capacity that borrowed its authority directly from the superintendent. From about 1910 until the present, supervision has remained primarily an extension of administration.

In the first third of the twentieth century American education was heavily influenced by models of industrial mechanization and the practices of so-called scientific management. The impact of an industrial orientation in education was pervasive and dominated supervision practices for nearly a quarter of a century. Writing of the period, Callahan observes:

> The procedure for bringing about a more businesslike organization and operation of the schools was fairly well standardized from 1900–1925. It consisted of making unfavorable comparisons between schools and business enterprise, of applying businesslike criteria (e.g. economy and efficiency) to education, and of suggesting that business and industrial practices be adopted by educators.[1]

For educational supervision the impact of the business age was the emergence of bureaucratic supervision. Supervision became tied to goals, objectives, and specifications. An orientation toward efficiency

---

[1] Raymond E. Callahan, *Education And The Cult of Efficiency* (Chicago: University of Chicago Press, 1962), p. 6.

and economy led to divisions of labor, technical specialization, high organizational discipline, specific procedures for work situations, and a reliance on written communication.

Serious applications of empirical research accompanied the emphasis on rules and regulations, stratified authority, and the generation of comprehensive policy documents. Following the lead of industry, educators who served as supervisors conducted time and motion studies and looked for new ways to operate schools more efficiently. It was also during this period that instruction, and hence supervision, became specialized by subject area.

By the early 1930s educational supervision in the United States was becoming ineffective in its enforcement and inspector role. School supervisors, often called "snoopervisors" behind their backs, were able to work with classroom teachers in only the most mechanical ways due to the evaluative dimension of their observations and reports. Again, it was changes in the area of educational administration that altered the role of instructional supervision.

American education during the thirties entered a new era, a period to be labeled "progressive education" by later historians. A combination of rapid growth in school population, increasing diversity among school children, economic prosperity, mobility, and other socioeconomic factors temporarily released American education from its structured heritage. New school programs swept over the land. Schools became more personal, humane, and "child-centered."

For school administrators this new era meant increased responsibilities. Schools became more complex institutions, and even more complex management skills were needed. Early research on group dynamics indicated that a human element existed in organizations that administrators had not previously considered. School administrators, following the lead of business professionals, began to practice a more democratic style of leadership. By the 1940s such "human relations" behavior was common in schools and had become an emerging theme of educational supervision.

School supervision in the 1940s and into the middle of the next decade focused on processes rather than products. Supervisors spent more of their time helping teachers develop as instructors than judging teacher performance. Cooperative group efforts were maximized and democratic interaction practiced. During this period, supervision emerged as a recognized specialty area in education, and definitive texts were written on the subject.

The launching of Sputnik I by the USSR in 1957 altered the form and substance of American education. Overnight, old programs and goals were scrapped, and new educational plans and programs were designed. Curriculum development dominated the educational scene, and such development influenced the role of educational supervisors. In many school districts supervisors became curriculum developers and the lines of demarcation between these two specialized roles blurred.

In the early 1960s supervisors became subject matter field agents. Their roles were a combination of organizing materials, involving teachers in the production and implementation of school programs, and serving as resource persons to teachers in the field. As a collateral duty, most supervisors found themselves entering into the training and retraining of classroom teachers by organizing in-service opportunities.

By the late sixties, the goals of most school districts were no longer distinct. Too many program changes, an overextended and crowded school curriculum, and rising costs forced a reassessment of programs as a matter of necessity. Administrators, pinched by rising expectations for schools and declining resources for operating schools, returned to traditional practices of making things orderly. The evolution of schools through performance contracts, behavioral objectives, accountability programs, management schemes, and standardized graduation expectations is still evident as this book is written.

Conditions during the late sixties and administrative responses in the early seventies have had an interesting effect on the field of supervision. As supervision was fighting for an identity in a time dominated by curriculum development, there was an effort to focus on instructional aspects of schooling. The supervision literature of the late 1960s and early 1970s was focused on analyses of the teaching-learning process and the concept of "clinical supervision." Supervisors following this lead became proficient in the uses of videotaping, in assessing interaction between teachers and learners, and in using techniques such as "action research" to explore new possibilities for instruction.

By the late 1970s economic and political pressures on school systems had become so great that administrators were returning to an industrial orientation reminiscent of the first quarter of the century. Supervisors, sensing a declining interest in research and efforts to improve classroom instruction per se, also began moving toward a managerial role. Such movement can be construed as yet another attempt to perceive supervision as an extension of administration. As a result, the literature of supervision in the late 1970s spoke of behavior systems, organizational theories, and other concerns related to management. Entering the 1980s,

Table 1.1
The Evolution of Supervision Roles

1750–1910	Inspection and enforcement
1910–1920	Scientific supervision
1920–1930	Bureaucratic supervision
1930–1955	Cooperative supervision
1955–1965	Supervision as curriculum development
1965–1970	Clinical (instructional) supervision
1970–1980	Supervision as management

the role of supervision is still evolving, balanced somewhat precariously between administrative, curricular, and instructional concerns.

DEFINITIONS OF SUPERVISION

Over time the definition of what constitutes supervision in schools has evolved into a number of distinct conceptualizations. These differ in focus and in how they relate supervision to other elements in the school environment. In all, six common concepts can be identified that define supervision in terms of administration, curriculum, instruction, human relations, management, and leadership.

Some definitions of supervision follow a historic thread and link administration and supervision. Eye, Netzer, and Krey, for instance, define supervision as "that phase of school administration which focuses primarily upon the achievement of the appropriate instructional expectations of the educational system."[2] Harris and Bessent also define supervision as an administrative action:

> Supervision is what school personnel do with adults and things for the purpose of maintaining or changing the operation of the school in order to directly influence the attainment of major instructional goals of the school.[3]

Another frequent definition found in supervision literature sees the supervisor as a curriculum worker. Cogan, as an example, gives the following definition of general supervision work:

> General supervision, therefore, denotes activities like the writing and revisions of curriculums, the preparation of units and materials of instruction, the development of processes and instruments for reporting to parents, and such broad concerns as evaluation of the total educational program.[4]

Writing with the same orientation, Curtin observes:

> Curriculum practices can exist without supervision, although one would scarcely wish to vouch for their vitality. However, it is so blatantly obvious that supervision is utterly dependent on concern for curriculum that one need hardly bring up the matter at all. That is, if the newer concept of supervision is accepted. Of course, supervisors can 'do' things that are not related to curriculum and instruction, just as they have in the past. They can

[2] Glen G. Eye, Lanore A. Netzer, and Robert D. Krey, *Supervision of Instruction* (New York: Harper & Row, 1971), p. 31.
[3] Ben Harris and Wailand Bessent, *In-service Education: A Guide to Better Practice* (Englewood Cliffs, N.J.: Prentice-Hall, 1969), p. 11.
[4] Morris Cogan, *Clinical Supervision* (Boston: Houghton-Mifflin, 1973), p. 9.

gather statistics and information to no avail; they can observe teachers for no good reason; they can confer with teachers about irrelevancies; and they can conduct staff meetings that are unrelated to the imperatives of teaching. Enough of this exists today to make one uneasy. The only comfort that one can draw is that these activities are not supervisory at all. They are called 'supervisory,' and this tends to give the whole concept of supervision a bad name. Supervision must find meaning in curriculum. If it does not, it has no meaning.[5]

A third definition of supervision focuses squarely on instruction. An early example of this definition of supervision was provided by the Association for Supervision and Curriculum Development (ASCD), the major professional organization for school supervisors:

> Since the titles 'supervisor' and 'curriculum director' are often used interchangably as to function, the terms might be used to indicate a person who, either through working with supervisors, principals, or others at the central office level contribute to the improvement of teaching and/or the implementation or development of curriculum.[6]

The definition of supervision in terms of instruction continues today in the work of Marks, Stoops, and King-Stoops: Supervision is "action and experimentation aimed at improving instruction and the instructional program."[7]

A fourth definition of supervision found in the literature sees the supervisor in terms of human relations, working with all persons in the educational environment. The earliest proponent of this definition wakimball Wiles:

> They [the supervisors] are the expediters. They held establish communication. They help people hear each other. They serve as liaison to get people into contact with others who have similar problems or with resource people who can help. They stimulate staff members to look at the extent to which ideas and resources are being shared, and the degree to which persons are encouraged and supported as they try new things. They make it easier to carry out the agreements that emerge from evaluation sessions. They listen to individuals discuss their problems and recommend other resources that may help in the search for solutions. They bring to individual teachers,

---

[5] James Curtin, *Supervision in Today's Elementary Schools* (New York: Macmillan, 1964), p.162.

[6] Association for Supervision and Curriculum Development, *Role of the Supervisor and Curriculum Director in a Climate of Change*, 1965 Yearbook (Washington, D.C.: Association for Supervision and Curriculum Development, 1965) p. 2-3.

[7] James R. Marks, Emery Stoops, and Joyce King-Stoops, *Handbook of Educational Supervision: A Guide for the Practitioner*, 2nd ed. (Boston: Allyn & Bacon, 1978), p. 15.

whose confidence they possess, appropriate suggestions and materials. They sense, as far as they are able, the feelings that teachers have about the systems and its policies, and they recommend that the administration examine irritations among staff members.[8]

A definition provided by Sergiovanni and Starrett follows this same theme:

Traditionally, supervision is considered the province of those responsible for instructional improvement. While we hold this view, we add to this instructional emphasis responsibility for all school goals which are achieved through or dependent upon the human organization of the school.[9]

Finally, a draft from the 1982 ASCD Yearbook on supervision continues the human relations theme:

By 'supervisor' we mean not only those who have the word in theivitle but also principals, superintendents, department heads—all those whose responsibilities include helping other staff members improve their performance.[10]

Supervision has also been defined as a form of management. Illustrating this position is a definition by Alfonso, Firth, and Neville:

Supervision is found in all complex organizations. This is so because organizations are determined to maintain themselves and are sometimes concerned about their improvement or refinement. The connection between supervision and organizations is clear and direct. Organizational resources must be applied to the analysis of efficiency and effectiveness. . . . These descriptions of supervision within organizational production systems have implications of significant consequence to the educator engaged in instructional supervision. The school is a production system.[11]

The sixth definition of educational supervision is as a leadership function. According to Mosher and Purpel:

We consider the tasks of supervision to be teaching teachers how to teach, and the professional leadership in reformulating public education—more specifically, its curriculum, its teaching, and its forms.[12]

---

[8] Kimball Wiles, *Supervision for Better Schools*, 3rd ed. (Englewood Cliffs, N.J.: Prentice-Hall, 1967), p. 10.

[9] Thomas Sergiovanni and Robert Starrett, *Emerging Patterns of Supervision: Human Perspectives* (New York: McGraw-Hill, 1971), p. 3.

[10] Draft statement, ASCD 1982 Yearbook Committee, *Supervision* (working title).

[11] Robert Alfonso, Gerald Firth, and Richard Neville, *Instructional Supervision: A Behavior System* (Boston: Allyn & Bacon, 1975), p. 3.

[12] Ralph Mosher and David Purpel, *Supervision: The Reluctant Profession* (Boston: Houghton-Mifflin, 1972), p. 4.

We believe that all of the above definitions of educational supervision are meaningful in the context from which they are drawn. The difference in definitions results from contextual variables and the relative emphasis given supervisory functions vis-a-vis other components of the school environment. Such definitions, clearly, are influenced by social and economic conditions during the times in which they were formulated.

For reasons we give in the closing section of this chapter, we believe that supervision must assume a more focused role. Supervisors must attempt to remove themselves from the orbits of administration, curriculum, and teaching, and define supervision as a unique leadership role. We define supervision as **a leadership function that bridges administration, curriculum, and teaching, and coordinates those school activities concerned with learning.**

In Table 1.2 the major definitions of supervision, by contemporary authors, are outlined.

Table 1.2
Definitions of Supervision 1960–80

Focus	Names	Year
Administration	Harris and Bessent	1969
	Eye, Netzer, and Krey	1971
Curriculum	Curtin	1964
	Cogen	1973
Human Relations	K. Wiles	1967
	Sergiovanni and Starrett	1971
	ASCD Yearbook (draft)	1982
Instruction	1965 ASCD Yearbook	1965
	Marks, Stoops, and King-Stoops	1978
Leadership	Mosher and Purpel	1972
	Wiles and Bondi	1980
Management	Alfonso, Firth, and Neville	1975

AN ANALYSIS OF EDUCATIONAL SUPERVISION

To understand supervision we must be able to look beyond definitions and describe the individuals serving in supervisory roles. The answers to numerous questions will supply the portrait:

Who is the supervisor?
What does the supervisor do?
What does the supervisor think he or she should be doing?
How is the supervisor trained?
How *should* the supervisor be trained?
How are positions in supervision changing?

Such analyses must be preceded by recognition of the fact that there is no such thing as *the* supervisor. Rather, there are many men and women serving in roles, with a variety of functions, that are generically referred to as "supervision."

Numerous variables affect what supervisory positions are and what they can become. Of the many social, political, and economic variables shaping the role of supervision, one of the most influential factors during the past twenty years has been the increased urbanization of the United States. Urbanization has had the effect of increasing the number and scope of supervisory positions, while at the same time blurring the distinctiveness of supervision as an educational specialty.

The 1970 Census of the United States revealed that three-quarters of all Americans were living in one-third of our available spaces. About 73.5 percent of the total population was classified as "urban" dwellers. The consolidation of people and places in the United States, a trend that is projected to continue into the 1990s, meant that by 1970 nearly half of the population lived in one of eight densely populated states. Approximately 48 percent of all school children, correspondingly, attended school in one of eight states. Such population density meant, in many cases, new school districts or larger school districts and a demand for increased supervision.

With most growth in supervisory positions occurring in school districts with over 25,000 students, the role of supervisor became diversified. With diversity often came a less clear understanding of the role and function of supervision. In contrast, most schools in the latter half of the 1970s faced *declining* enrollments and staff reductions and this trend continues. Economic and political pressures on school districts threaten to eliminate, reallocate, or dilute leadership positions that are not clearly defined. This is especially true in large urban school districts. It is therefore imperative that supervision, as an independent and legitimate function in education, define itself in terms of role and responsibility. Several major studies indicate the kinds of things supervisors do and how supervisors are currently trained.

One major study of educational supervisors conducted in Florida during the late 1960s provided a data-based profile of the practicing supervisor.[13] The study involved over 60 percent of all practicing supervisors in that state and collected some 260 items of information about the educational supervisor. The following portrait is drawn from this study.

An equal number of men and women served as educational supervisors. Their average age was fifty, and 90 percent were over thirty-five years old. Their experience in education, on the average, was fifteen years, eight years having been spent as a classroom teacher, and seven in various administrative or supy positions. Only one-fourth of the 373

---

[13] Ione Perry, *A Role Study: The County Level Supervisor in Florida* (Tallahassee: Florida Department of Education, 1967).

supervisors studied had less than six years of classroom teaching experience, drawn from all levels of schooling.

Almost 90 percent of all supervisors held a master's degree, but only 10 percent were graduates of six-year programs and 6 percent held a doctorate.

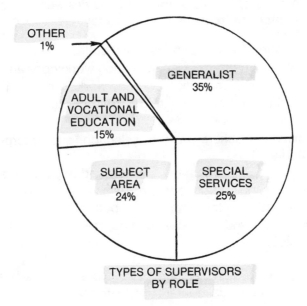

TYPES OF SUPERVISORS
BY ROLE

Figure 1.1

Source: Adapted from Ione Perry,. *A Role Study: The County Level Supervisor in Florida* (Tallahassee: Florida Department of Education, 1967).

Over one-third of all supervisors had no formal training during the past five years.

Supervisors were generally of four types: generalists, special services, subject area, and adult or vocational. Generalists, the largest group at 35 percent, spent their time coordinating instructional programs, assisting in the orientation of new teachers, and participating in in-service activities. Special service supervisors, comprising about 25 percent of all supervisors, performed routine administrative duties, participated in in-service activities, and assisted in policy formation. Subject area supervisors, at 24 percent, collected and disseminated current curriculum materials, held conferences with individual teachers, and aided classroom teachers in the interpretation of materials. Finally, about 15 percent of all supervisors served in adult education, vocational education, or other roles. Their roles included public relations, developing proposals for federal funds, and performing routine administrative duties.

Most supervisors (57 percent) did their teaching in the same county in which they served as supervisor. Such elevation from within the ranks was most typical in areas of low population mobility or small student population. Overall, half of all supervisors were found in school districts with over 25,000 students, and only 5 percent were found in school districts with less than 2,500 students. Better than 40 percent of the supervisors served on a staff with at least twenty other supervisors.

The supervisors reported that thirteen activities were performed most frequently. In order of frequency those responsibilities were:

1. Performing routine administrative duties.
2. Participating in in-service education workshops and programs.
3. Planning and arranging in-service workshops and programs.
4. Collecting and disseminating current curriculum materials.
5. Engaging in public relations.
6. Assisting teachers in the selection and interpretation of materials.
7. Assisting in the orientation of new and beginning teachers.
8. Coordinating instructional programs.
9. Participating in the formation of policy.
10. Assisting in the evaluation and appraisal of school programs.
11. Developing curricular designs and coordinating improvement efforts.
12. Assisting in the development of proposals for federal funds.
13. Holding individual conferences with teachers.

Other activities and responsibilities identified by supervisors but not performed with great frequency included visiting and observing class-rooms, conducting research studies, developing and preparing new instructional media, and teaching demonstration lessons.

Of interest is the fact that supervisors worked most frequently with individual school principals. In descending order of frequency, they also worked with other members of the district central office staff, the school office staff, and classroom teachers. Only one-fourth of the supervisors reported working regularly with the superintendent, a fact that suggests that many supervisors are not considered a part of the district "manage-ment team."

Finally, the supervisors expressed considerably similar opinions of what they thought their role *should* be: overwhelmingly, the supervisors saw themselves responsible for instructional improvement. This im-provement was to be accomplished by providing assistance where needed, providing educational leadership, and serving to coordinate the efforts of all educators in the system. Primary areas of involvement, reported the supervisors, should be in curriculum development, in-service education, and human relations/communications.

The Perry study summary observed the following about role expec-tations and on-the-job performances:

Florida supervisors, regardless of the particular positions they occupy, show considerable agreement concerning activities and responsibilities that help define the supervisory role. These role expectations frequently differ from the supervisor's role performance. There is apparently little relationship between what supervisors actually do and the activities they feel should receive priority.[14]

A major study on instructional supervisors was conducted by the ASCD in 1978.[15] This study, involving 1,000 ASCD superintendents, supervisors, and professors of supervision, attempted to distinguish between the roles of curriculum workers and instructional supervisors. The findings suggested that curriculum directors are more closely associated with "program-type" activities, while instructional supervisors are more closely associated with "people-type" activities.

All respondents in the ASCD study projected a more active role for the instructional supervisor:

The instructional supervisor should be more in the role of decision maker with authority than in an advisory one; should be more of a subject matter specialist in the supervised area than a generalist; should be more capable of planning and conducting research than merely an interpreter of research; should be more involved in the improvement of instruction than in curriculum development; should work with the teaching staff more in a directive fashion with authority than in a permissive manner; should be less involved in staff evaluation than responsible for such evaluation; and should exercise more budgetary or fiscal management control responsibility than no control over the budget.[16]

In choosing among twenty tasks and major roles typically assigned to curriculum directors and instructional supervisors, the respondents were able to distinguish between "curriculum tasks" and "supervision tasks" on some items:

Strong Supervision Tasks	Strong Curriculum Tasks
Develop standards of effectiveness	Conduct Research
Evaluate teachers	Develop materials
Observe teaching	Select curriculum content
Conduct staff meetings	Write grant proposals
Conduct in-service programs	Prepare courses of study
Evaluate instruction	Report to the Board of Education

---

14 Ibid., p. 29.
15 Allan Sturges, ed., *Certificating the Curriculum Leader and Instructional Supervisor* (Washington, D.C.: Association for Supervision and Curriculum Development, 1978).
16 Ibid., pp. 20–21.

Other tasks, such as the preparation of a budget, testing learners, negotiating with staff groups, working with community groups, evaluating programs, determining educational goals, writing policy statements, determining job descriptions, and so forth, were seen as roles played by both curriculum directors and supervisors.

The lack of clarity in role distinction between curriculum directors and instructional supervisors was recognized by the study:

> The data gathered by the survey substantitated the thesis that there was great confusion and little agreement when it comes to defining distinct roles for supervisors and curriculum directors.[17]

The ASCD study also sought to identify the kind of preparation program experienced by instructional supervisors. Twelve college courses were frequently found in preparation programs and were ranked from 1 (most important) to 12 (least important) by respondents:

1. Supervision of Instruction
2. Group Processes and Human Relations
3. Curriculum Theory and Development
4. Educational Measurement and Evaluation
5. Educational Psychology
6. Organization and Administration of Schools
7. Educational Research
8. Philosophy of Education
9. Media and Technology
10. Sociology of Education
11. History of Education
12. Anthropology of Education

Finally, the group conducting the ASCD study identified certain standards and guidelines for the training of instructional supervisors:

I. Experience
  A. Minimum of two years of classroom teaching experience
  B. Minimum of one year of leadership experience (such as department chairperson, principal, internship, laboratory school researcher)
II. Preparation
  A. Certification as a teacher (assumes competence in the science of teaching and conditions of learning)
  B. Completion or equivalent of an educational specialist degree leading to certification as an instructional leader with courses and experience in:
    1. Supervision, including:

---

[17] Ibid., p. 28. The remainder of this section has been condensed from the ASCD study with the kind permission of the association.

    a. Knowledge regarding the principles and nature of supervision, trends, and issues in supervision and models of staff development

    b. Ability to apply communication and group development skills

    c. Ability to evaluate staff personnel and to design improvement programs

2. Curriculum, including:

    a. Knowledge regarding curriculum programs and processes of curriculum development

    b. Ability to evaluate curricular programs and plan appropriate strategies for their improvement

    c. Understanding of curriculum theory and design of various curricular models

3. Instruction, including:

    a. Knowledge regarding principles and concepts, trends, issues, and models of instructional strategies

    b. Ability to design, develop, implement, and evaluate various instructional systems

    c. Understanding of instructional theory, utilization of media, and analysis of instructional factors

4. Educational psychology, including:

    a. Ability to conduct appropriate research for determining teaching and learning problems

    b. Understanding of adult learning and the teaching/learning process

5. Leadership, including:

    a. Processes and purposes of organizations

    b. Skills to organize and coordinate perceived resources for facilitating operations of and changes in curriculum and instruction

    c. Understanding of the function of supervision as provided by other educational leaders such as college professors, principals, and district curriculum leaders

POSSIBLE FUTURES FOR SUPERVISION

To project or predict the unknown is always a dangerous venture. It is possible, however, to explore variables that may have an impact on supervision and discuss their probable implications. We believe that supervisors must anticipate possible futures in order to behave effectively in the present. Supervisors should have a feel for the forces in play about them and recognize the major trends that could shape the immediate future of educational supervision. The possible futures of supervision, in turn, affect the way in which we presently perceive supervision.

It is obvious that the role of the educational supervisor is still being defined. There is a lack of clarity concerning the identity and function of the supervisor. Supervision has historically been an administrative function but is increasingly becoming an extension of curriculum and teaching. Supervisors, it would seem, must either identify with one of these groups, or develop a new role and function.

There is also a problem of autonomy for educational supervisors. One of the major criteria for achieving professional status is the degree to which a group possesses autonomy or control over the nature, conditions, and procedures of its work. In many school districts today, such autonomy is unfortunately lacking. Supervisory positions are sometimes steps in the administrative hierarchy, shelves for unsuccessful administrators, or token promotions for attractive women whose "duties" are to brighten the central office, take visitors to the airport, and organize coffee klatches for parents and teachers. All of these are dependent, nonautonomous roles.

A final problem area for supervisors in terms of role is the question of authority. The literature on educational supervision projects the position as one of leadership, as opposed to a simple administrative designation. Yet, in filling a "staff" role rather than a position of line authority, there is a problem of placement within the school organization. The authority of an instructional supervisor is borrowed authority and, therefore, not predictable authority.

These areas (identity, function, autonomy, and authority) prevent the supervisory role from being clear and purposeful. These given conditions place the supervisor in a tenuous on-the-job posture and are important in light of three major forces that may influence what supervision can become in the future.

One such force is a shrinking resource base for supporting public education and the accompanying conservative behavior of administrators. Throughout the United States, as educational costs increase due to simple inflation there is a reluctance to support new programs. The tax structure underlying educational finance is under attack; voters are rejecting bond issues that will fund building programs and support existing and new programs. This trend toward diminishing resources for education is likely to continue throughout the 1980s. In many parts of the nation conditions will probably worsen as senior citizens on fixed incomes discover their voting power. By 1978, the fifty-five-plus age group became the largest potential voting bloc in the nation: the 42 million persons over fifty-five represented one out of every three persons eligible to vote. In some states, such as Florida, over 50 percent of the voters will be in the fifty-five-plus group by 1980.

Administrators in the public schools have reacted to these pressures in a realistic manner. Their actions have become more businesslike, more managerial. The growing conservatism in administrative behavior is less philosophical than political. The relationship between "line" administrators and instructional supervisors promises to become increasingly strained in the future unless supervisors assume a managerial posture that will either serve administrative causes or forge an independent role.

Another force likely to affect the role of supervisors in the future is the increased commercialization of curriculum development in the schools. Beginning with the national curriculum projects of the 1950s, there has been a trend toward greater involvement of business in education. As Macdonald had observed:

> The prospect of publishing a whole new series of textbooks for all subjects to sell for the use of every child in each classroom in each school in the land offered more than a minimal stimulus for development.[18]

This commercialism has expanded from a textbook market into instructional "systems" including materials, machines, and media. Complete curriculum packages with books, worksheets, tapes, records, films, transparencies, and the machines for using them are available to schools in a bewildering variety.

The effect of such commercialism on educators responsible for curriculum development has been predictable. Rather than developing instructional materials, such specialists have been placed in the posture of reviewing and selecting them. It is not inappropriate to say that in many districts the process has become mechanical and reactionary.

Adding to this "reactive" role for curriculum developers has been an increased emphasis on evaluation in many districts. A by-product of a drive for economic efficiency, the concern with curriculum evaluation has forced curriculum workers to use standardized, norm-referenced, commercially prepared tests to validate curriculum effectiveness. The curriculum specialist has thus been "co-opted into the role of systems analyst" rather than that of educational planner.

These trends in curriculum, without some sort of planned intervention by a governmental or funding agency, are likely to continue. The implications for the instructional supervisor are significant. If curriculum directors are increasingly concerned with materials, per se, and see the curriculum as a system, then teaching is likely to be perceived as an extension of that system. Good teaching, from this perspective, would be defined in terms of its contribution to content mastery and achievement on standardized testing. The possibilities for conflict between this conception of the role of teachers and attempts to gear instruction to the needs of students, for example, are great. The instructional supervisor

---

[18] James Macdonald, "Curriculum Development in Relation to Social and Intellectual Systems," in *The Curriculum: Retrospect and Prospect*, NSSE Yearbook (Chicago: University of Chicago Press, 1971), p. 96.

and the curriculum director are on a collision course unless the supervisor defines his or her role according to the curriculum system.

A final force that may affect the future role of the supervisor is the rising influence of classroom teacher organizations in America. Developments during the 1970s suggest that many functions and activities currently carried out by instructional supervisors may soon become negotiable items in collective bargaining and subject to control by teachers. While professional organizations among teachers have long existed in the United States, their growth and power to influence are relatively recent phenomena. By 1976, nearly 80 percent of all teachers in the United States were unionized. Membership in the National Education Association (NEA) in 1977, for instance, reached 1.8 million members. The next largest professional organization, the American Federation of Teachers, claimed 475,000 members in 1976. In 1966 only eleven states recognized the teachers' right to enter into collective bargaining over issues relating to contracts; by 1977, thirty states recognized this right.

Early collective bargaining issues by teacher groups focused on extrinsic factors such as work conditions or salary. By the mid-1970s, however, professional groups were bargaining for input or control in areas that historically were administrative domains. Flygare explains:

> Once the exclusive bargaining representative has been selected, the union and the board are ready to begin bargaining. What do they bargain about? Potentially, the number of topics about which teachers would like to bargain is almost limitless: salaries, tenure, school calendar, curriculum, student discipline, sick leave, promotion policy, sabbaticals, clerical assistance, dues check off—to mention a handful.[19]

It is probable that collective bargaining will deal with issues of a curricular and instructional nature as soon as major extrinsic issues have been addressed by professional groups. Among the kinds of concerns that may be negotiated are teacher assignments, class size, minimum competency goals, and in-service topics. Such issues and negotiation will have implications for the instructional supervisor. As Eiken observes:

> A supervisory staff's flexibility in initiating changes is more limited as collective bargaining agreements incorporate issues directly affecting curriculum innovation.[20]

Exactly how teacher self-determination through professional negotiations affects the role of instructional supervision remains to be seen. It is obvious, however, that there is a great potential for conflicts between

[19] Thomas J. Flygare, *Collective Bargaining in the Public Schools*, Fastback Series No. 99 (Bloomington, Ind.: Phi Delta Kappa, 1977), p. 21.
[20] Keith P. Eiken, "Teacher Unions and the Curriculum Change Process," *Educational Leadership* 35 (December 1977): 174.

representatives from a particular school who speak for its classroom teachers and the instructional supervisor from the central office who is a member of the superintendent's staff.

These three forces (declining resources, increased commercialism in curriculum development, and the rising influence of teacher organizations) will all affect the supervisor in the 1980s. We believe that without a purposeful response, supervision as it has been known in American education for fifty years could cease to exist. We feel that instructional supervision is a legitimate function and area of competence in education. Schools, and schoolchildren, need the presence of a functionary concerned with increasing the quality of teaching and learning. There may be a number of responses by educational supervisors to these forces. Those responses are best understood in terms of the four areas related to the role of the supervisor.

Response 1

It may be that instructional supervisors across the United States will take no action to deal with declining resources, commercialism, and teacher organizations. Supervisors may feel that such forces will have little or no impact on their roles because the influence of the pressures has been overplayed in terms of individual positions in specific school districts.

If no action is taken, however, possible problem areas are numerous. Declining resources could lead to the abolition of positions not directly contributing to identifiable educational goals; the functions of supervision related to program development could be taken over by curriculum developers or representatives of the teacher organizations. Supervisors could be caught in the cross fire between militant teacher groups and adamant administrators. Unable to satisfy either group with neutrality, instructional supervisors could easily become scapegoats during intense negotiation sessions.

Response 2

Supervisors can continue the drift into administrative-managerial roles during the 1980s. In doing so, supervision will return to its historic posture as an extension of administration. Benefits from this response will be increased job security and the possibility of obtaining "line" authority. If supervisors choose such a posture, they will have to work very hard to develop a specific identity and will certainly have to give up whatever autonomy they may have.

By returning to the administrative camp, instructional supervisors will further remove themselves from the classroom and diminish their ability to work with teachers to improve instruction. Their relationship to teachers will be bureaucratic rather than professional, and they can expect to be the target of the teacher organization in collective bargaining sessions.

Response 3

Another possible move for supervisors in the immediate future is to become more closely aligned with the curriculum development process. Such a move would require that supervision continue to sharpen its distinctiveness from the curriculum developer and would probably prescribe a more technical role for instructional supervisors. In accepting developments in the field of curriculum (i.e., seeing instruction as part of a larger learning system dominated by packaged materials), supervisors would become more concerned with such things as testing, training, evaluation, and working with new materials under controlled conditions. It would appear that both professional autonomy and authority would be diminished, and the role of supervision considerably narrowed.

On the other hand, such a move would free instructional supervisors from the traditional identification with administration. The new posture would undoubtedly make the supervisor less suspect and more utilitarian to classroom teachers. The natural connection between curriculum development and implementation would also be strengthened.

Response 4

A fourth possible response would be for instructional supervisors to become the premier "educators" in school systems, focusing on the instructional aspects of teaching and learning. Such a role would have supervisors gaining authority by their knowledge, contributing to all members of the educational community. Such authority would be "silent power"—providing leadership by being useful and knowledgeable.

Such a role is fraught with danger for individual supervisors—the supervisor must be seen and recognized as the "resident educator" in a system where others have more dominant concerns. The supervisor must be able to deliver, through thoughts and actions, those things that administrators, teachers, and other staff members need. The supervisor must remain neutral and not be drawn into one or more opposing camps; the supervisor must display a forcefulness that will overcome undercurrents of power and influence. In short, the instructional supervisor would have to develop an identity, function, autonomy, and authority allowing him or her to practice effective supervision.

We believe that while any of the four projected responses may prove adequate in the coming years, the fourth response is the most desirable for educational supervision. Supervision is a dynamic, rather than static, role and should be so defined. We call for supervisors to assume a coordinating leadership function in schools. We think that supervisors should bridge administrative, curricular, and teaching concerns and link together those aspects of schooling that affect learning. Subsequent chapters address how educational supervisors can fulfill such a new role.

Table 1.3
Supervision in the Future

Current Supervision Needs	Reactions	Implications
Identity	No response	No major changes
		Position abolished
Clear Function		Role taken by curriculum
		Sacrificed during negotiation
Autonomy		
	Join	Job security
Authority	Administration	Alienation from teachers
		Negotiation target
Influencing Forces		
	Join	Technical support role
Shrinking Resources	Curriculum	Closer to teachers
Commercial Influences	New Role	Influence by knowledge
		Service role
Teacher Power		Possible conflict with other roles

SUMMARY

Supervision is an area of specialization in education that is in transition. At present the role and function of educational supervisors are not clearly defined and their futures are uncertain.

Historically, the role of supervisors has evolved from that of inspector to a more complex and diversified set of behaviors. At this time, supervision is defined in relation to six major roles: administration, curriculum, instruction, human relations, management, and leadership. We define supervision as a *leadership function* that bridges administration, curriculum development, and teaching, and connects those aspects of schooling concerned with learning.

An analysis of supervisors in practice shows that a common theme is fulfilling tasks related to instruction and learning. It remains to be seen whether supervisors will continue to function in such a role in the face of such pressures as shrinking resources, commercialism in education, and rising teacher power. We believe that supervisors must act in this decade to define their role more clearly.

Suggested Learning Activities

1. Identify major forces that have acted to change the definition and role of supervision in the past.
2. Develop a conceptual model that shows the relationship of supervision to persons serving in administration, curriculum, and instructional roles.
3. Develop a list of those things that make supervision unique as an area of specialization in education.

Books to Review

Alfonso, Robert; Firth, Gerald; and Neville, Robert. *Instructional Supervision: A Behavior System.* Boston: Allyn & Bacon, 1975.

Argyris, Chris. *Executive Leadership: An Appraisal of a Manager in Action.* New York: Harper & Bros., 1953.

Beach, Donald. *Managing People at Work: Readings in Personnel.* New York: Macmillan, 1971.

Bishop, Leslie. *Staff Development and Instructional Improvement.* Boston: Allyn & Bacon, 1976.

Cogan, Morris. *Clinical Supervision.* Boston: Houghton-Mifflin, 1973.

Curtin, James. *Supervision in Today's Elementary Schools.* New York: Macmillan, 1964.

Harris, Ben. *Supervisory Behavior in Education.* Englewood Cliffs, N.J.: Prentice-Hall, 1963.

Lucio, W. H., and McNeil, J. D. *Supervision in Thought And Action.* New York: McGraw-Hill, 1979.

Mosher, Ralph, and Purpel, David. *Supervision: The Reluctant Profession.* Boston: Houghlin-Mifflin, 1972.

Sergiovanni, Thomas, and Starrett, Robert. *Supervision: Human Perspectives.* New York: McGraw-Hill, 1979.

Wiles, Kimball, and Lovell, John. *Supervision For Better Schools.* Englewood Cliffs, N.J.: Prentice-Hall, 1975.

2

Dimensions of Supervisory Leadership

Supervision in a school setting is a leadership role. In general, supervisory leadership will consist of a series of actions related to the improvement of instruction and learning. The exact way in which a supervisor will exhibit leadership will depend upon local school conditions. In Chapter 1, we suggested that because their roles are in transition, it is desirable for schools supervisors to define their responsibilities clearly. While role overlap with administration, curriculum, and teaching is inevitable, the supervisor can fulfill a unique role in schools—coordinating those school activities related to learning. In assuming such a leadership posture, it is important that the supervisor understand the nature of leadership.

THE NATURE OF LEADERSHIP

Over the years, considerable research has been conducted in the area of leadership behavior. Despite such information, leadership remains one of the least understood concepts in education. Studies of leadership have evolved through three stages of inquiry: study of leadership traits, situational or environmental analysis, and study of exchange or transaction.

In early studies of leadership there was an attempt to identify the traits and characteristics unique to leaders. While many characteristics were common to leadership, no single trait withstood objective analysis as an absolute predictor of leadership ability or style. One major study of traits during the 1930s developed the following list of possible characteristics of leaders:[1]

Personality Factors	Social Factors
Knowledgeable	Tactful
Abundance of physical energy	Sympathetic
Enthusiasm	Holds faith in self and others
Originality	Prestigious
Speed of decision	Patient
Initiative	Can demonstrate submission
Imagination	
Purposeful	**Physical Factors**
Persistent	Advantaged height
	Advantaged weight
	Attractive

Various forms of the "trait approach" to defining leadership continue today, but such an avenue has been largely abandoned due to a lack of productive results. Numerous leadership trait studies show common denominators from one investigation to another.

A 1948 leadership study by Stogdill proved an important turning point in our understanding of leadership. Still following the trait approach, Stogdill catagorized personal factors associated with leadership under five headings: capacity, achievement, responsibility, participation, and status. To these five, Stogdill added a sixth factor, the situtation. Stogdill conceptualized leadership as the relationship that exists between persons in a social situation, rather than as a singular quality of an individual who serves as a leader. Stogdill concluded, "A person does not become a leader by virtue of the possession of some combination of traits, but the pattern of personal characteristics of the leader must bear some relevant relationship to the characteristics, activities, and goals of the followers."[2] With this observation, the study of leadership shifted to an environmental focus.

---

[1] Harry L. Smith and Leonard M. Krueger, "A Brief Summary of Literature on Leadership," *Bulletin of the School of Education* (Indiana University) 9 (1933): 3–80.

[2] Ralph M. Stogdill, "Personal Factors Associated With Leadership: A Survey of the Literature," *Journal of Psychology* 25 (1948): 64.

Stogdill's observations about leadership contributed to an understanding of what constitutes leadership because, by adding the situational factors, he broadened the definition considerably. A leader is a person who, due to a situation, emerges to help a group attain specific goals. Other things being equal, any member of a group with special or correct abilities can become a leader in a given situation. On the other hand, when a leader ceases the important function of facilitating the attainment of group goals, he or she may cease to function as the leader.

Further research on leadership turned up another critical factor in the leadership formula—the perceptions of the follower. The follower is crucial in determining leadership because it is the follower who perceives the leader and the situation and reacts accordingly. With the acknowledgment of the importance of the leader's characteristics, the situation in which those characteristics are displayed, and the perceptions of the follower, research on leadership emerged to the exchange stage.

Exchange theory, or transactional analysis, focuses on how leaders initially motivate groups to accept their influence, the processes that undergird the prolonged exertion of such influence, and the ways in which the leader makes contributions to group goals. In short, the analysis of exchange seeks to learn how leaders work within groups to establish and maintain influence. Thus, leadership is really an exchange or transaction that occurs in a group when needs are present. The group recognizes certain characteristics that are valuable to its members in a certain situation and "accept" the influence of the leader in satisfying needs. Leaders who know the group(s) they work with can influence the group(s) by exhibiting behaviors useful to the group(s). Because group needs in school settings are multiple, supervisory leadership behaviors are varied.

Wiles and Lovell have summarized findings of research about leadership as follows:[3]

1. Leadership is a group role.
2. Leadership, other things being equal, depends on the frequency of interaction.
3. Status position does not necessarily give leadership.
4. Leadership in any organization is widespread and diffuse.
5. The norms of the group determine the leader.
6. Leadership qualities and followership qualities are interchangeable.
7. Persons who try to persuade too much or who give evidence of a desire to control are rejected for leadership roles.
8. The feeling that people hold about a person is a factor in whether they will use his behavior as leadership.
9. Leadership shifts from situation to situation.

---

[3] Kimball Wiles and John Lovell, *Supervision For Better Schools*, 4th ed. (Englewood Cliffs, N.J.: Prentice-Hall, 1975), pp. 65–67.

There are numerous approaches to supervisory leadership, and the choice of an approach should be determined by the needs of the group being served. Examples of approaches regularly found in school settings are:

> *Authoritarian*—using power to exert influence
> *Observation*—identifying dissonance and suggesting changes
> *Planning Management*—projecting goals and evaluating progress
> *Human Relations*—building relationships in groups
> *Climate Building*—altering the perceptions of group members
> *Research*—using a trial-error format to change practice
> *Therapeutic*—serving as counselor to group members

Before the supervisor selects an approach or a combination of approaches for working with a particular group, it is necessary that the supervisor hold a theory of leadership. Without such a theory or set of ideas the leader will send ambiguous messages to the group and run the risk of being misinterpreted. Eye, Netzer, and Krey provide the following observation about the process of constructing a theory of leadership:

> Theory evolves from, or crystallizes the verbalization of, the basic assumptions, principles, observations, and notions that are held about a particular phenomenon or area of activity. When these are collated in an orderly manner so that they constitute a constellation of supporting ideas and evidence, the theory is identified. On the basis of theory, a model can be developed which will illustrate the theoretical concepts. This allows the practitioner not only to verbalize organization of ideas, but also a design for his plan of action.[4]

The working theory from which the supervisor develops an approach to dealing with a group will always have an underlying philosophical foundation. Jackson identifies two common assumptions about working with teachers in an in-service situation that illustrate the range of assumptions possible:

> The first of two perspectives from which the business of inservice training might be viewed is found in the notion of repair and remediation. For this reason I have chosen to call it the "defect" point of view. It begins with the assumption that something is wrong with the way practicing teachers now operate and the purpose of inservice training is to set them straight—to repair the defect, so to speak.

> The second approach, the "growth" approach,

> begins with the assumption that teaching is a complex and multi-faceted activity about which there is more to know than can ever be known by one person. From this point of view, the motive for learning more about teaching

---

[4] Glen G. Eye, Lanore A. Netzer, and Robert D. Krey, *Supervision of Instruction* (New York: Harper & Row, 1971), p. 48.

is not to repair a personal inadequacy as a teacher but to seek greater fulfillment as a practitioner of the art. The central goal of inservice from the growth perspective: to help the teacher become progressively more sensitive to what is happening in his classroom and to support his efforts to improve on what he is doing.[5]

To summarize, leadership is a facilitating behavior that serves the needs of the group being led. Leadership can be promoted from any number of approaches, and such approaches reflect both a theory of leadership and a philosophical orientation toward the needs of the followers.

PROMOTING DYNAMIC LEADERSHIP

While leadership is dependent on both group needs and group recognition of leadership characteristics, the process of leading is not static. By the actions they initiate, leaders can influence which group needs they can help satisfy. That is, leadership activity can be both static and dynamic, satisfying the known needs of a group or organization *and* their emerging needs. In many school districts supervisors are in the unique posture of being able to select the correct balance between these two types of leadership.

Harris has distinguished the difference between a dynamic and static leadership with his definitions of a "tractive" and "dynamic" supervisor:

> [Tractive supervision]—Activities geared to continuity are those which are intended simply to maintain the existing level of instruction, to promote minor changes in the program, to enforce or support existing relationships, and to resist pressures for change from various sources.

> [Dynamic supervision]—Activities which are designed to change the program. . . .the emphasis is on discontinuity, the disruption of existing practice and the substitution of others.[6]

Examples of static (reinforcing) or dynamic (change-oriented) activities in which supervisors might engage are:

Static

Enforcing statutory requirements
Evaluating semester course outlines
Filing lesson plans in the district office

---

[5] Philip W. Jackson, "Old Dogs and New Tricks," in *Improving Inservice Education: Proposals and Procedures for Change,* ed. Louis J. Rubin (Boston: Allyn & Bacon, 1971), pp. 21, 26, 28.

[6] Ben Harris, *Supervisory Behavior in Education* (Englewood Cliffs, N.J.: Prentice-Hall, 1963), pp. 18–19.

Holding class enrollments to correct teacher-pupil ratios
Approving daily class schedules
Final editing of curriculum guides
Enforcing legal length of the school day
Scheduling psychological services in the district
Arranging for publishing companies to display their products
Regulating visitors to school buildings

Dynamic

Planning programs for staff development
Holding conferences with individual teachers to improve instruction
Working with teachers to apply research findings
Initiating pilot projects and innovative programs
Developing long-range curriculum plans
Demonstrating new instructional methods to teachers
Designing enrichment and remedial activities for students
Leading revision of school or district philosophy of education
Circulating newly acquired professional literature
Evaluating various media

As educational supervisors select an appropriate balance between reinforcing activities and change-oriented activities, they define their role. We believe that supervisors must emphasize dynamic activities in most districts in order to fulfill the distinct role of supervision—influencing the development of quality instructional programs that promote improved learning. The role of the supervisor should be one of innovating, restructuring, and upgrading, rather than one of resisting, enforcing, and codifying.

THE DEPLOYMENT OF SUPERVISORS

To some extent the type of leadership the supervisor exhibits is dependent upon his or her position in the school district's administrative hierarchy. As noted in Chapter 1, supervisors in schools hold numerous titles including, but not restricted to, supervisor, consultant, director, and administrator. In general, some supervisors have limited responsibilities with a single task (e.g., specific subject supervisors such as math coordinator or reading consultant). Some supervisors have broad responsibilities in a single area of school operation (director of elementary programs or area head for vocational education). Finally, some supervisors have broad responsibilities spanning both supervision and general administration (assistant superintendent for instruction or general supervisor).

In the organizational chart below, (Figure 2.1) five levels of supervision are identified. Note that the relationship to other functionaries in the organization, rather than the position title, will affect the type of activities the supervisor can engage in and the type of leadership he or she can provide.

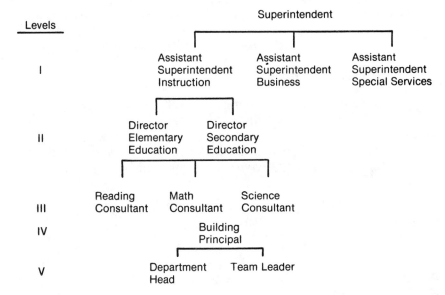

Figure 2.1
Supervisory Positions in the Administrative Hierarchy

While the level of operation has some effect on the type of leadership activities the supervisor can engage in, there is considerable latitude or flexibility for behavior at all levels. Mosher and Purpel summarize the conditions found in many school districts:

> The conflicting pressures on the school supervisor to teach; to work with student teachers and beginning teachers and evaluate experienced teachers; to supervise across subject areas; to direct curriculum projects; to discharge a host of administrative and clerical tasks, complicate the problem of defining the job. It almost becomes the case that supervision in schools is most accurately defined as what the particular supervisor does or say he does.[7]

The supervisor, by selecting the type of activities and emphasizing a style or approach, can define the job that he or she does. What is called for is an analysis of the role and a thorough study of the organization in which supervision is to be practiced. As Wilson observes:

---

[7] Ralph Mosher and David Purpel, *Supervision: The Reluctant Profession* (Boston: Houghton-Mifflin, 1972), pp. 3–4.

Without realizing it the supervisor decides: 'Teachers are like this; administrators are like that; supervisors are like neither but serve both; my job is. . . .' His logic is deductive with its anchor lodged in the assumptions he makes about the two older and more tradition-regulated roles. If his orientation is the mere accommodation of his personal services, sandwiched between two layers of rigid institutional practice, he becomes a prisoner of the past before he even starts to work. His alternative is to analyze the companion roles of teaching and administration in view of a possible reconstruction and refinement of the supervisory function wherever it finds effective expression.[8]

In summary, while the supervisor will always operate within some sort of administrative hierarchy, it is more likely that limitations on supervisory activity will be imaginary rather than real. The supervisor who can be analytic and creative can develop a leadership pattern that will allow effective practice in the various dimensions of the job.

THE DIMENSIONS OF SUPERVISION

The role of the supervisor has many dimensions and frequently overlaps with administrative, curricular, and instructional roles. Since supervision is a coordinating function concerned with the improvement of instruction and learning, such overlap is natural and should be perceived as an asset rather than a liability.

Supervisory leadership involves planning, organizing, and evaluating. The planning phase of improving instruction and learning is most often administrative in nature, the organizing function is most often curricular in its focus, while the evaluating dimension of supervision is usually directed toward instructional activity.

Administration

Among the many administrative supervision tasks usually encountered are:

1. *Setting and prioritizing goals*—Helping others in the school district focus on ends for schooling and establishing priorities among the many possible programs available to schools.
2. *Establishing standards and developing policies*—Translating goals into standardized levels of expectation, complete with rules and regulations to enforce such performances.

---

[8] L. Craig Wilson et. al., *Sociology of Supervision: An Approach to Comprehensive Planning in Education* (Boston: Allyn & Bacon, 1969), p. 14.

3. *Providing long-range planning*—Designing expectations in terms of actions and activities to be accomplished over time.
4. *Designing organizational structures*—Establishing structural connections between persons and groups within school districts.
5. *Identifying and securing resources*—Locating applicable resources and seeing that they are available to various organizaal structures.
6. *Selecting personnel and staffing*—Identifying of personnel needed to implement programs and assignment to organizational structures.
7. *Providing adequate facilities*—Matching available facilities with program needs; developing new facilities where needed.
8. *Securing necessary funding*—Raising the monies needed to adequately finance programs.
9. *Organizing for instruction*—Assigning staff and other instructional and support personnel to organizational structures.
10. *Promoting school-community relations*—Establishing and maintaining contact with those who support educational programs.

Curriculum

Curriculum-oriented supervision tasks are:

1. *Determining instructional objectives*—Translating goals into specific objectives for instruction.
2. *Surveying needs and conducting research*—Assessing present conditions to determine how school programs can effectively meet learner needs.
3. *Developing programs and planning changes*—Organizing the instructional content and reviewing existing programs for greater relevance.
4. *Relating programs to various special services*—Tying together the many instructional components both within the school and
5. *Selecting materials and allocating resources*—Analyzing available instructional materials and assigning them to appropriate programs.
6. *Orienting and renewing instructional staff*—Introducing the school program to new teachers and assisting regular staff in upgrading their capacity.
7. *Suggesting modification in facilities*—Designing a plan to restructure facilities to fit the instructional program and, where appropriate, suggesting the need for new facilities.
8. *Estimating expenditure needs for instruction*—Cost-estimating program development and making recommendations for the application of existing and anticipated funding.

9. *Preparing for instructional programs*—Forming various instructional units and teams; providing in-service opportunities for instructional development.
10. *Developing and disseminating descriptions of school programs*—Writing accurate descriptions of school programs and informing the public of successful activities.

Instruction

Some supervision tasks that are instructional in nature are:

1. *Developing instructional plans*—Working with teachers to outline and implement instructional programs.
2. *Evaluating programs*—Conducting testing and other types of evaluation to determine if instructional program is meeting standards.
3. *Initiating new programs*—Demonstrating new techniques and otherwise establishing the groundwork for new programs.
4. *Redesigning instructional organization*—Reviewing existing instructional organization for effectiveness and, where appropriate, making alterations.
5. *Delivering instructional resources*—Being sure that teachers have necessary instructional materials and anticipating future material needs.
6. *Advising and assisting teachers*—Being available to teachers in a consulting, helping role.
7. *Evaluating facilities and overseeing modifications*—Assessing educational facilities for instructional appropriateness and making on-site visits to insure that modifications are as designed.
8. *Dispersing and applying funds*—Following the flow of monies to insure their application to intended programs.
9. *Conducting and coordinating in-service programs*—Guiding in-service programs so that they are applied to instructional needs.
10. *Reacting to community needs and inquiries*—Receiving community feedback about school programs and sending information to parents of school children where appropriate.

While all of the above tasks are supervisory in nature, they do intersect with administrative, curricular, and instructional domains. The unique role of the supervisor is to initiate, plan, organize, and evaluate instructional problem solving and program development. Much like an engineer overseeing a construction project, the supervisor follows and directs the work flow from inception to evaluation. Supervisors are on-site educators who are responsible for improved instruction. Table 2.1 illustrates the flow of the instructional improvement effort.

Table 2.1

Administration Tasks	Curriculum Tasks	Instructional Tasks
1. Set and prioritize goals	Determine instructional objectives	Develop instructional plans
2. Establish standards and policies	Survey needs and conduct research	Evaluate programs according to standards
3. Provide long-range planning	Develop programs and plan changes	Initiate new programs
4. Design organizational structures	Relate programs to special services	Redesign instructional organization where needed
5. Identify and secure resources	Select materials and allocate resources	Deliver instructional resources
6. Select personnel and staff	Orient and renew instructional staff	Advise and assist teachers
7. Provide adequate facilities	Suggest modifications in facilities	Oversee modifications in facilities
8. Secure necessary funding	Estimate expenditure needs for instruction	Disperse and apply funds
9. Organize for instruction	Prepare instructional programs	Coordinate in-service activities
10. Promote school-community relations	Disseminate descriptions of school programs	React to community inquiries about school programs

⟵————— THE SUPERVISION FLOW OF ACTIVITY —————⟶

Note: Supervisory activity overlaps and coordinates administrative, curricular, and instructional concerns and tasks.

SUMMARY

Supervision in school settings is a leadership role. Research has shown that leadership is a complex phenomenon with many dimensions. Because the needs of schools are varied, many types of leadership behavior are appropriate for the school supervisor. To be effective, supervisors must display a style that accurately reflects their beliefs about schooling and the people they seek to assist. We favor a "growth" approach to supervision that assumes that all persons who teach can benefit from further understanding of the teaching-learning process.

Because supervisory roles are not clearly defined in most school districts, supervisors have latitude in establishing their role. By concentrating on dynamic activities, supervisors can emphasize the uniqueness of their global perspective of instructional improvement. While organizational structures may impose some limits on the type of activities supervisors can engage in, we feel that most limitations are more imaginary than real.

The tasks of supervision overlap with administrative, curricular, and instructional tasks. This overlap can be a benefit to the supervisor who follows the flow of activity to improve instruction and learning.

Suggested Learning Activities

1. Identify ways in which followers select a leader and enter into a "transaction" to accept his or her influence.
2. Develop a list of your own assumptions, principles, and observations about the leadership process. Can these statements be presented in the form of a theory of leadership?
3. Study a school district familiar to you to assess how supervisors are deployed in the administrative hierarchy.
4. Describe why the role of the supervisor is not more clearly defined.
5. Taking any supervisory behavior, see if you can improve the outline of supervision tasks found in Table 2.1.

Books to Review

Eye, Glen; Netzer, Lanore; and Krey, Robert. *Supervision of Instruction.* New York: Harper & Row, 1971.

Harris, Ben, and Bessent, Wailand. *Inservice Education: A Guide To Better Practice*. Englewood Cliffs, N.J.: Prentice-Hall, 1969.

Hyman, Ronald. *School Administrators Handbook of Teacher Supervision and Evaluation Methods*. Englewood Ciffs, N.J.: Prentice-Hall, 1975.

Jacobs, T.O. *Leadership and Exchange in Formal Organizations*. Alexandria, Va: Human Resources Research Organization (HumRRO), 1971.

Rubin, Louis J. *Improving Inservice Education: Proposals and Procedures for Change*. Boston: Allyn & Bacon, 1971.

Wilson, Craig, et al. *Sociology of Supervision: An Approach to Comprehensive Planning in Education*. Boston: Allyn & Bacon, 1969.

part two

Leadership Roles in Supervision

3

Leading Teachers in Planning Instruction

INTRODUCTION

Changes occurring in the role of today's teacher have dramatic and far-reaching implications for the role of the supervisor. The problems of declining test scores, increased costs, and declining resources for education have brought on demands for more efficiency and better teaching in the classroom. The public is looking to those in supervisory positions to exert greater leadership in seeking solutions to some of society's most difficult educational problems.

While our schools are now serving an increased variety of population, they have been asked, in addition, to assume responsibilities that have resulted in such programs as:

Drug education   Career education
Driver education   Law education
Sex education   Moral education
Parenting education   Citizenship education
Environmental education   Bilingual education
Consumer education

Oftentimes, these programs are incorporated into existing courses of study, creating a problem of balance and sequencing in the curriculum.

Instructional programs in our schools have been challenged as being irrelevant, too easy, or taught poorly by teachers. The supervisor's role is balanced between administrative concerns of insuring accountability for pupils and teachers, and staff functions of improving teaching and curriculum development. Demands on the supervisor to carry out one or both functions of supervision, administrative-curricular, have led to a need to focus on supervision as a coordinating leadership function

The reference point for teachers in instruction is pupil improvement The supervisor has the same reference point, but is somewhat remote from the classroom due to his or her dependence upon an intermediary the teacher, to carry out instructional plans.

Instructional improvement deals with much more than easily identifiable methods of teaching. Involved in the whole process of the teaching-learning act is formation and selection of goals and objectives, conducting of needs assessments, selection and use of teaching and learning aids, and use of techniques that will evaluate the results of teaching-learning activities. A more detailed list of teaching expectations is found in Table 3.1

The major impact on instructional improvement is found not in the materials or techniques that become a part of the instructional method, but in the processes by which the supervisor attempts to influence the instructional program There is nothing inherent in equipment or materials that will bring about improved learning The potential of such objects is realized only to the extent that a person can convert the potential into instructional possibilities. Thus, to be effective supervision must concern itself with teachers as people

HELPING TEACHERS UNDERSTAND TERMS

Teachers are often introduced to new terms in connection with curricular, instructional, and evaluative considerations. The following glossary of terms should be useful to a supervisor in working with teachers. The definitions are not complex or lengthy. Supervisors should encourage teachers to pursue more technical definitions of these terms after they become familiar with the definitions in the glossary.

Glossary of Terms

AFFECTIVE   A term describing behavior or objectives of an attitudinal emotional, or interest nature, discussed in the *Taxonomy of Educational Objectives. Handbook II, The Affective Domain* by David Krathwohl et al

Table 3.1
Becoming a Teacher—Acts and Attitudes

Primary Acts	Primary Attitudes
Knowledge of subject matter	An openness to ideas and practices
Understanding and keeping records	An experimental outlook toward teaching
Planning and preparing lesson plans	Acceptance of all students
Using instructional media and resources	Enthusiastic
Presenting prepared lessons to students	Patient and understanding
Basic classroom management techniques	Treats young people with respect
Evaluating student progress	Sees teaching as more than just a job
Supervising extracurricular events	Has a sense of humor
Assessing student needs	Sees self as worthy person
Integrating subject matter	Perceives self and world accurately and realistically
Dealing with discipline problems	Identifies with others in a positive way
Teaching for thinking and application	
Promoting affective learning in classrooms	
Designing learning environments	
Individualizing instruction	
Promoting creativity in classrooms	
Increasing student self-concept formation	
Counseling students individually and in groups	
Developing teacher-made materials	
Planning with students	
Understanding culturally different students	
Identifying persistent instructional problems	

BEHAVIOR OBJECTIVES This term describes an instructional intent in such a way that the postinstructional behavior of the learner is described: what the learner should do, or be able to do at the conclusion of an instructional sequence.

COGNITIVE An adjective referring to learner activities or instructional objectives concerned with *intellectual* activities; discussed in the

Taxonomy of Educational Objectives: Handbook I, The Cognitive Domain by Benjamin S. Bloom et al.

COURSE OF STUDY   A prescriptive guide prepared by a professional group of a particular school or school system for teaching a subject or area of study in a given grade or other instructional group.

CRITERION   The measure used to judge the adequacy of an instructional program. Ordinarily, it would be a test, broadly conceived, of the program's objectives.

CURRICULUM   A structured series of intended learning outcomes.

LESSON PLAN   A teaching outline of the important points of a lesson for a single class period arranged in the order in which they are to be presented, it may include objectives, points to be made, questions to ask, references to materials, assignments, and so forth

PSYCHOMOTOR   This refers to learner activities or instructional objectives relating to physical skills of the learner such as typing or swimming.

RESOURCE UNIT   A collection of suggested learning and teaching activities, procedures, materials, and references organized around a unifying topic or learner problem. It is designed to be helpful to teachers in developing their own teaching units.

SCOPE   The extent or range of the content/objectives covered by a course or curriculum

SEQUENCE   The order in which content or objectives are arranged in the curriculum

SUBJECT   A division or field of organized knowledge such as English or mathematics

SYLLABUS   A condensed outline or statement of the main points of a course of study

TEACHING UNIT   The plan developed for a particular class or group of learners by an individual teacher to guide instruction of a unit of work for a period longer than a single class session

CONDUCTING NEEDS ASSESSMENTS

Supervisors help teachers determine "where students are" in the classroom so teachers, as instructional leaders, can know where to expend time and energy in planning. This process of determining the gap between established aims and actual conditions in a classroom is called *needs assessment*. At the school level aims may be more general, while in a classroom they may be specific. The identification method of determining needs permits curriculum planning to be systematic rather than haphazard

A complete range of diagnostic devices may be used in identifying and clarifying needs The supervisor must know what tests and inventories to suggest, how to help teachers conduct interviews, report critical incidents, write open-ended questions, record discussions, and interpret drawings and pictures. A knowledge of sociometrics, socioeconomic analysis, and a facility for performance observation and recording are essential if supervisors are going to help teachers in collecting data useful in needs assessment.

The following outline suggests the kind of data a teacher might find useful in needs assessment:[1]

  I. Data about pupils
      A. General data about the pupil population
          1. Classification of pupils by age, sex, and grade level
          2. Pupil mobility
          3. Characteristics of students who drop out
          4. Number of students retained—reasons
          5. Composition of population by age group
      B. Data about growth and development characteristics of students
          1. Data about physical or mental handicaps
          2. Motor skills
          3. Health status
          4. Emotional and social stability
          5. Personality traits
          6. Readiness for various types of learning
          7. Creativeness—special talents
 II. Data about family, home, community
      A. Family status
          1. Nature of family—two-parent, one-parent home
          2. Socioeconomic status of family
          3. Number of siblings
          4. Occupation(s) of parent(s)—do both work?
          5. Who is at home at night? Family activities
      B. Home
          1. Conditions at home—crowded? Child has own bedroom?
          2. Amount of time allowed for TV viewing—study conditions at home
          3. Physical condition of home
      C. Community
          1. Nature of the community—urban, suburban, rural
          2. Community activities available—library, recreation, culture

---

[1] For a more complete discussion on conducting a needs assessment, see Jon Wiles and Joseph Bondi, *Curriculum Development: A Guide to Practice* (Columbus, Ohio: Charles E. Merrill, 1979), pp. 241–63.

III. Data about how pupils learn
    A. The learning process
       1. Learning theories
       2. Learning styles
       3. Factors conducive to learning
       4. The nature of learning disabilities
       5. Motivation, self-concept as factors in learning
       6. Problems of readiness
       7. Intellectual stages of development

WAYS OF GATHERING INFORMATION ABOUT STUDENTS

Informal Observation

Teachers can become more aware of a student's interests, physical and mental sets, and potential for learning by informal observations of students in instructional settings. Supervisors can sit with teachers as they observe a child and help teachers identify behaviors that will enhance or inhibit learning. Informal observation is a particularly helpful technique in diagnosis because it allows teachers to see a child as a person rather than a statistic.

Experienced supervisors can use observations to point out patterns of student behavior that teachers can use to determine readiness for learning. Teachers looking for reading readiness often rely solely on formal testing when they could just as easily determine readiness through informal observations.

Interest Surveys

Supervisors can suggest a variety of interest surveys for teachers to use in determining student interests. Most surveys utilize the "what I like most or least" technique. Students like to respond to these surveys and teachers can find the information they are seeking about student interests.

Time Samplings

Teachers can use time samplings in observing individuals or groups. In this method, teachers jot down entries on a card every few minutes during a portion of the school day. The information recorded describes the exact behavior of a student or group of students and can yield useful information about work habits and group interaction.

Anecdotal Records

A more formal record of observations of student behavior can be obtained by recording descriptions of student behavior in various situations over a number of weeks or months. Anecdotal records give important clues to a child's self-concept and personal or intellectual needs. An evaluation of the records is not made until behavioral patterns can be identified by the teacher.

Sociometric Analysis

Sociometric studies can help teachers study interpersonal relationships in a group setting. The social structure of a class can be determined by asking students to list classmates they would prefer to work with on a project or identify the students they would like for class leaders.

The teacher uses the information to plot a sociogram that graphically depicts the social pattern of a class; cliques, social stars, class leaders, and isolates can be identified. Teachers can use this information to structure situations that will allow greater student interaction. New friendships and a greater sense of belonging will hopefully evolve as students form new social relationships.

Standardized Tests

Supervisors need to help teachers understand not only the potential but also the limitations of tests in providing information about students. Group tests generally are not as definitive as tests administered individually. Students with special problems, therefore, need to be tested individually by the teacher or a specialist.

Supervisors should help teachers in interpreting test results. Many times a teacher will use test results as the sole criterion for determining a pupil's abilities. This often leads to stereotyping a child as "bright" or "not so bright." Test results should be used as information, not judgment. Information gathered through informal observations can help teachers interpret test data relating to a given student more accurately.

Files and Cumulative Records

Cumulative folders and files may contain samples of a student's work, test results, and other descriptive information. Supervisors must help teachers apply the same principles used in writing anecdotal records to these data; descriptive rather than interpretive information should be recorded. Comments that are judgmental have no place in a student's file or cumulative folder. Professional access to student files should be carefully controlled.

Teacher-prepared Diagnostic Materials

Supervisors can help teachers prepare diagnostic materials that identify a child's reading level, mastery of a math skill, or other areas of performance. Often, the best diagnostic materials are those prepared by a teacher rather than those prepared by a person unfamiliar with the student.

Parent Conferences

The parent conference can be helpful to the teacher in providing information about family expectations, home environment, and quality of family relationships. Parents many times inform teachers about unique home problems that may be affecting school work.

Pupil Conferences

Student conferences can provide teachers with information that cannot be obtained elsewhere. As with parent conferences, there must be a feeling of mutual trust during the conference. Comfortable settings and a friendly, open atmosphere contribute to that feeling of trust. Supervisors can use a variety of techniques (e.g., modeling and role playing) to help teachers develop good conference skills.

SELECTING GOALS AND OBJECTIVES

In working with teachers in instructional settings, the supervisor must be able to synthesize a number of skills in concert. The initial skill in helping teachers design instructional systems is identifying the needs of students for whom the system is intended.

A second supervisory skill is helping teachers determine learning outcomes for students. The effectiveness of teaching is measured by the degree to which students learn what is intended by the teacher. The emphasis is not merely on accountability but on student achievement. The instructional process is important in itself, but the reason for its existence lies in facilitating student achievement of the instructional objectives.[2]

Supervisors must assist teachers in distinguishing between goals, general educational objectives, and specific behavioral objectives. In

---

[2] Robert Alfonso, Gerald Firth, and Richard Neville, *Instructional Supervision: A Behavior System* (Boston: Allyn & Bacon, 1974), pp. 248–49.

addition, supervisors must be able to assist the teacher in writing behavioral objectives in proper terms and ordering objectives into performance hierarchies. Too often teachers learn to write behavioral objectives, but fail to use objectives that require thinking beyond the lowest cognitive levels of knowledge and comprehension.[3]

To help teachers distinguish between goals, general objectives, and behavioral objectives, the supervisor should train teachers to formulate learning objectives at three different levels—Level I, Level II, and Level III.

Level I objectives are sometimes referred to as "purposes" or "goals." They are usually formulated at the system level by superintendents, school board members, supervisors, community interest groups, classroom teachers, and, in some instances, students. Data sources for Level I, as well as Level II and III, objectives are the learner, society, and the disciplines. Groups that carry the title "Curriculum Council," "School Advisory Council," or "Educational Improvement Committee" write Level I objectives or goals for school systems. Often the goals are a replication of a list borrowed from some other district, school, or textbook. Level I objectives are seldom reviewed or revised. They are usually accompanied by a related or complementary policy statement describing how the objectives are to be met and upon whom the various responsibilities fall. Supervisors and teachers should review district goals to see where and how those goals affect classroom instruction. See Table 3.2 for an example of typical Level I goals.

Table 3.2
Proposed Level I Goals from an Elementary School District

PROPOSED INSTRUCTIONAL GOALS

Definition of Goal: Broad statements of purpose designed to give general direction to educational practices, programs, and services.

The Instructional Program of District One Should Enable a Student to:

1. Sustain an enthusiasm for learning now and in the future.

2. Acquire and effectively use BASIC ACADEMIC SKILLS such as:

reading	speaking	thinking
writing	listening	problem solving
spelling	computing (arithmetic)	decision making

3. Examine and evaluate information.

4. Acquire useful study habits and skills.

---

[3] D. Cecil Clark, *Using Instructional Objectives in Teaching* (Glenview, Ill.: Scott, Foresman, and Co. 1972), pp. 98–107.

Table 3.2—*continued*

5. Develop a positive sense of self-worth and self-respect and a feeling of success in relation to school experiences.

6. Recognize and weigh values and develop a commitment to act upon them.

7. Nurture creative instincts and encourage independence, spontaneity, and creativity.

8. Develop an awareness of:

family	economic systems
neighborhood	citizenship responsibilities
community	democratic ideals
national heritage and history	social change
cultures of the world	natural (physical) environment
political systems	

9. Develop an ability to get along with those with whom he/she lives and works.

10. Develop an awareness and appreciation of the fine arts.

11. Participate in fine arts activities such as music, drama, speech, and visual arts.

12. Develop practical skills for family living.

13. Be aware of a variety of career possibilities and possess general knowledge of skills needed for specific careers.

14. Develop a pride in work.

15. Understand and value the requirements for physical and mental health.

16. Understand how to effectively use leisure time.

17. Enjoy recreational activities.

18. Develop basic sports skills.

19. Acquire skills to prepare him/her for lifelong sports.

20. Develop and maintain a suitable level of physical fitness.

21. Participate in programs especially designed for "gifted and talented" children if he/she has been so designated.

22. Receive guidance and counseling services.

23. Have access to a variety of appropriate learning materials in the schools' libraries.

24. Have an opportunity to participate in co-(extra) curricular activities.

25. Have an opportunity, if he/she excels in fine arts or athletics, to participate in select groups.

26. Have an opportunity to participate in intramural activities.

Source: Goals distributed to parents by Missoula District One, Missoula, Montana, 1979. Used with permission.

Level II objectives are still stated in broad, general terms but are more specific than those of Level I. They are, however, not as specific as behaviorally-stated Level III learning objectives. Level II objectives are usually planned at a division, school, or department level. They are stated in terms that support and complement Level I objectives, and reflect the basic philosophy. These objectives include an outline process necessary to realize Level I goals and purposes.

Table 3.3
Levels I, II, and III Objectives Compared

Level of Objective	Type	Origin	Features
Level I	Broad goals or purposes	Formulated at district level by councils or school board	Seldom revised
Level II	General but more specific than Level I	Formulated at school or department level	Contain an outline of process to accomplish Level I objectives
Level III	Behaviorally-stated	Formulated by teams of teachers or single teacher	Describe expected outcome, evidence for assessing outcome, and level of performance

---

Level III objectives are behaviorally stated and are usually developed at the classroom level by the individual teacher. Mager lists three essential elements of a properly stated behavioral objective:

> First, identify the terminal behavior by name that will be accepted as evidence that the learner has achieved the objective.

> Second, the desired behavior should include the important conditions under which the behavior will be expected to occur.

> Third, specify the criteria of acceptable performance by describing how well the learner must perform to be considered acceptable.[4]

Level III objectives are planned and supported in terms that reflect Level I and II objectives. However, Level III objectives require the

---

[4] Robert F. Mager, *Preparing Instructional Objectives* (Palo Alto, Calif.: Fearon Publishers, 1962), p. 12.

following additional considerations that are not of prime importance at Levels I and II:

1. Differences in individual students in the class
2. Student needs
3. Student interests
4. Student aptitudes
5. Subject matter and available equipment facilities
6. Individual teacher competencies and skills
7. Other relevant considerations that may be unique to a given subject area and may have been overlooked by those formulating Level I and II objectives

There are at least seven considerations that must be made when selecting goals and objectives:

1. The underlying philosophy and cultural forces influencing those selecting goals and objectives.
2. The operational level at which one is working (Level I, II, or III).
3. The mechanics of writing behaviorally-stated objectives such as those stated by Robert Mager in *Preparing Instructional Objectives.*
4. The cognitive level of the objective. Refer to the levels of cognitive behavior developed by Bloom, et al. See Table 3.4 for a description of those levels.
5. The affective level of the objective. Refer to Krathwohl's *Taxonomy of Educational Objectives: Affective Domain.* See Table 3.5 for a description of affective levels of behavior.
6. The psychomotor level of the objective. Refer to the levels of psychomotor behavior developed by Harrow. See Table 3.6 for a description of levels in the psychomotor domain.
7. The financial support that is available.
8. The individual differences and peculiarities of students, teachers, and subject matter areas.

If clearly stated, objectives identify for students precisely what they are expected to learn. They also provide a guide for selection of the materials and learning activities necessary for achieving objectives. Supervisors must help those charged with carrying out instruction to understand the total instructional process. An instructional paradigm such as the one found in Figure 3.1 should prove useful in helping teachers achieve that understanding.

Developing Plans and Lessons

Teachers plan daily what they and their students will do in the classroom. After objectives are identified, plans and lessons must be developed to

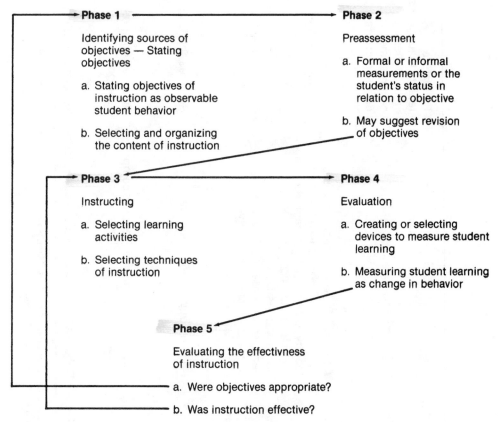

Figure 3.1
The Instructional Paradigm

achieve those objectives. Ralph Tyler, in his now classic syllabus for Education 360 at the University of Chicago, *Principles of Curriculum and Instruction*, identified four fundamental questions that must be answered in developing any curriculum and plan of instruction. They are:

1. What educational purposes should the school seek to attain?
2. What educational experiences can be provided to attain these purposes?
3. How can the educational experiences be effectively organized?
4. How can we determine whether these purposes are attained?[5]

Tyler and others identified a means-end approach to curriculum and instruction where educators identified objectives to be attained, selected subject matter and teaching methods, and finally evaluated their activities to see if they had reached their objectives .

---

[5] Ralph W. Tyler, *Basic Principles of Curriculum and Instruction* (Chicago: University of Chicago Press, 1949), pp. 1-3.

Table 3.4
Levels of Cognitive Behavior

Knowledge	Comprehension	Application	Analysis	Synthesis	Evaluation
(ability to recall; to bring to mind the appropriate material)	(ability to comprehend what is being communicated and make use of the idea without relating it to other ideas or material or seeing fullest meaning)	(ability to use ideas, principles, theories in new particular and concentrated situations)	(ability to break down a communication into constituent parts in order to make organization of the whole clear)	(ability to put together parts and elements into a unified organization or whole)	(ability to judge the value of ideas, procedures, methods, using appropriate criteria)
					Requires synthesis
				Requires analysis	Requires analysis
			Requires application	Requires application	Requires application
		Requires comprehension	Requires comprehension	Requires comprehension	Requires comprehension
	Requires knowledge	Requires knowledge	Requires knowledge	Requires knowledge	Requires knowledge

Source: From *Taxonomy of Educational Objectives: The Classification of Educational Goals. Handbook I: Cognitive Domain* edited by Benjamin S Bloom et al. Copyright © 1956 by Longman, Inc. Reprinted with permission of Longman

Table 3.5
Levels of Affective Behavior

Receiving	Responding	Valuing	Organization	Characterization
(attending; becomes aware of an idea, process, or thing; is willing to notice a particular phenomenon)	(makes response at first with compliance, later willingly and with satisfaction)	(accepts worth of a thing, an idea or a behavior; prefers it; consistent in responding; develops a commitment to it)	(organizes values; determines interrelationships; adapts behavior to value system)	(generalizes certain values into controlling tendencies; emphasis on internal consistency; later integrates these into a total philosophy of life or world view)
	Begins with attending	Begins with attending	Begins with attending	Begins with attending
		Requires a response	Requires a response	Requires a response
			Requires development of values	Requires development of values
				Requires organization of values

SOURCE: From *Taxonomy of Educational Objectives: The Classification of Educational Goals: Handbook II: Affective Domain* by David R. Krathwohl et al. Copyright © 1964 by Longman, Inc. Reprinted with permission of Longman.

55

Table 3.6
Levels of Psychomotor Behavior

Observing	Imitating	Practicing	Adapting
(watches process; pays attention to steps or techniques and to finished product or behavior; may read directions)	(follows directions; carries out steps with conscious awareness of efforts, performs hesitantly)	(repeats steps until some or all aspects of process become habitual, requiring little conscious effort, performs smoothly)	(makes individual modifications and adaptations in the process to suit the worker and/or the situation)
	Requires observation, or reading of directions	Requires imitation	Requires practice
		Requires observation, or reading of directions	Requires imitation
			Requires observation, or reading of directions

Source: *From A Taxonomy of the Psychomotor Domain: A Guide for Developing Behavioral Objectives* by Anita J Harrow Copyright © 1972 by Longman, Inc. Reprinted with permission of Longman.

Teachers determine the ends of teaching by identifying learning outcomes, but often fail to see the connections between the ends and the means necessary to achieve those ends. Supervisors must help teachers understand the step-by-step approach necessary in the instructional process. An instructional paradigm such as the one found in Figure 3.1 can be useful in helping teachers understand the means-end connection.

When a course of study is being planned by a teacher, there may be any number of resources or restrictions that influence that planning. There may be a mandate from a particular source (state department, legislature, superintendent) in the form of a particular goal or requirement for a certain level of achievement. The requirement in many states that students demonstrate certain competencies before graduation has certainly influenced instructional plans.

We define *plan* as any hierarchical process that a teacher uses to control the order in which a sequence of operations is to be performed. A plan allows a teacher to choose among alternative events or behaviors that might occur, and then helps the teacher establish priorities for events in the sequence in which they occur

SELECTION AND USE OF LEARNING MATERIALS/ MEDIA

Classroom teachers and curriculum supervisors today often find themselves drowning in a sea of learning materials. Faced with the task of selecting learning materials, the teacher and supervisor must first (1) identify the learning materials available, (2) determine the quality of the materials, and (3) choose materials that are appropriate for the learners for whom the materials are intended.[6]

Learning materials are produced by a number of sources including governmental agencies, commercial publishers, professional organizations, school districts, research and development agencies or laboratories, business corporations, individual classroom teachers, students, and parents! We use the term *learning materials* to emphasize that materials are designed for one purpose—to help students learn.

Identifying Sources of Learning Materials

There are a number of resources for identifying sources of learning materials including advertisements by publishing companies and publishers' representatives. The effective supervisor can provide

---

[6] M. Francis Klein, *About Learning Materials* (Washington: Association for Supervision and Curriculum Development, 1978), p. 1.

teachers with brochures, advertisements, and samples of publications. He or she can also arrange for demonstrations of materials by representatives of publishing or audiovisual firms. Supervisors should also be acquainted with professional journals that carry advertisements of the latest materials. Many journals provide reviews of texts and materials.

Supervisors often are able to set up displays of materials for teachers to review Publishing companies will often provide free samples and representatives will appear to answer questions about their materials Sample kits allow an opportunity for careful scrutiny of materials.

Professional organizations display learning materials at conferences. The Association for Supervision and Curriculum Development (ASCD) has a large display of materials at its annual conference. The ASCD display is particularly valuable because it contains not only commercial materials, but materials developed by governmental agencies, private organizations, school districts, schools, individual teachers, and parents.

Many times, new printed and audiovisual materials are previewed for the first time at annual conferences of professional organizations. Supervisors, because they are able to travel more often to conferences, have greater access to new materials. They must be able to judge the quality and appropriateness of materials to be introduced to teachers.

Another valuable source of materials are federally-funded agencies such as the Far West Regional Laboratory for Educational Research and Development. The National Middle School Resource Center, funded by Title III, is a particularly valuable resource for materials on the middle school. The Middle School Resource Center acts as a clearinghouse for materials produced by teachers, schools, school districts, and governmental agencies.

Determining Quality of Learning Materials

After identifying learning materials available, the supervisor and teacher must determine how good those materials are for a particular school district, classroom, and most important, for students using the materials.

It must be recognized that advertisements and representatives reflect biased opinions about the learning materials being sold. Supervisors and teachers must turn to other sources for judging the *quality* of materials. Several resources are available for teachers and supervisors in evaluating and selecting learning materials Publications such as *EPIEgram, The Educational Consumers Newsletter, Curriculum Products Review* and *Curriculum Review* not only help identify materials, but provide quality assessments

There are limitations, however, to the usefulness of evaluations published in these reviews. Often, published evaluations or reviews do not provide enough detail for making a decision about using the materials. Also, some publications provide a description, rather than an evaluation, of materials. Because different standards are used by reviewers, it is often difficult to compare learning materials reviewed in several publications.

Criteria used in evaluating learning materials have been formulated by a number of authors. The sets of criteria have been divided into two major types—procedural and substantive.[7] Procedural types include the processes of setting up committees, procedures, and responsibilities for evaluating materials, while substantive types provide the user with criteria that can be applied to the materials themselves.

Some criteria have been developed for specific types of materials such as those relating to ethic studies, humanism, or sex roles. Other criteria have been developed that are more general; they can be applied to any subject matter.

Selected Publications Having a Primary Focus
on Learning Materials

ALERT, Sourcebook of Elementary Curricula: Programs and Proj-
jects. Published by Far West Regional Laboratory for Educational Research and Development, San Francisco, 1972. This
publication includes descriptions of model projects, programs,
innovative curricula, and resources for grades pre-kindergarten
through grade six.

Curriculum Review. Published by Curriculum Advisory Service,
Chicago, Illinois. Published bimonthly, this magazine reviews
textbooks and other materials for grades K–12 in all curriculum
areas.

EPIEgram, The Educational Consumers Newsletter. Publishes
eighteen newsletters a year spotlighting news, strengths, and
weaknesses of materials and audiovisual equipment used in
schools. Published by Educational Products Information
Exchange Institute, New York, N.Y.

Games and Stimulations for School Use. Published by the Board of
Cooperative Educational Services, 1974. This publication
contains an index to games in a number of major areas including
career education, drugs, and ecology

Media and Methods Educators' Purchasing Guide Published by
North American Publishing Company, Philadelphia. This annual
guide helps in the selection process, particularly valuable
because it contains information from every known supplier of
educational materials and equipment.

Guide to Teaching Materials for English, Grades 7–12 Published by

Ibid pp 9–10

National Council of Teachers of English, 1975. Provides an index of available English materials at secondary level.

Social Studies Curriculum Materials Data Book. Social Science Education Consortium, Boulder, Colorado, 1977. Includes three volumes containing analyses of curriculum materials in the social studies.

Tenth Report of the International Clearinghouse on Science and Mathematics Curricular Developments. Joint project of American Association for the Advancement of Science and Science Teaching Center, University of Maryland, 1977. Provides a description of new science and mathematics curricula from many countries.

Publications Catalogue. Research for Better Schools, Inc., 1977. Publication of private, nonprofit educational laboratory largely funded through contracts with the National Institute of Education. Lists selected publications in a number of areas such as Social Education, Critical Thinking, and Individualized Instruction. Areas listed are results of RBS research and developmental activities.

Sources for Evaluating Learning Materials

Banks, James A. "Evaluating and Selecting Ethnic Studies Materials." *Educational Leadership* 31 (April 1974): 593–96. Provides criteria to help evaluate ethnic studies resources.

Eash, Maurice J. "Developing an Instrument for Assessing Instructional Materials." *Curriculum Theory Network*, monograph supplement (1972): 193–220. Instrument designed to help reviewer identify strengths and weaknesses of materials.

Klein, M. Francis, and Thayer, George D. *Selecting Curriculum and Instructional Materials.* Los Angeles: Regents of California, 1973. An audiovisual program designed to assist educators in the systematic selection of materials.

Tyler, Louis L.; Klein, M. Francis; and Associates. *Evaluating and Choosing Curriculum and Instructional Materials.* Glennville, Calif.: Educational Research Associates, 1976. Includes 28 recommendations to be considered in evaluating learning materials

Free Educational Materials Lists

A number of publications such as *The Instructor Magazine and Teacher* publish lists of free materials available to teachers. Supervisors can build extensive lists of such materials, as well as ordering and filing free materials for teacher use

Television as a Medium of Instruction

It has been estimated that school children spend one-third of their waking hours outside school watching television. Television, as a medium for instruction both in school and out, has had an impact on curriculum content. Who can forget Alex Haley's *Roots*? Both the novel and television production of that great story have been used in many classrooms. Television, as a medium of positive desirable learning, has been the subject of a number of groups.

1 The Agency for Instructional Television (AIT) is a nonprofit American-Canadian organization formed in 1973 from the parent organization, National Instructional Television. The stated purpose of AIT is to strengthen education through television and other technologies. The AIT, in a joint effort with state agencies, develops and distributes program projects. Schools may write to the main office to request being placed on the AIT mail list to receive the quarterly newsletter and program information.
   Agency for Instructional Television
   Box A
   Bloomington, Indiana 47401
   (812) 339-2203

2. Prime Time School Television (PTST) is a nonprofit organization dedicated to "making television work for teachers and teachers work for television." Teachers are encouraged to recommend and use evening television programming as part of their classroom resources. Guides and program materials produced through PTST are made available through the programs' commercial sponsors. PTST is funded in part by the Harris Foundation of Chicago and the Bush Foundation of St. Paul. PTST's advisory board includes parents, educators, and representatives of ACT, AASL, and television networks. The PTST guides include a self-contained booklet with single and series program listings, the Creative Handbook (every other month), units of study concerned with television, special interest subjects, and a monthly PTST calendar listing important programs for the coming months. To receive PTST materials you must make application for membership and contribute a small sum to the organization. For information, write:
   PTST
   120 South LaSalle Street
   Chicago, Illinois 60603

3 Periodicals such as *Media and Methods* (published September–May), *Instructor* (published September–May), and *Senior Scholastic* (published biweekly during school) have sections providing teachers with guides to television. *Media and*

Methods, as well as *Instructor*, provides "TV News," which describes one or more programs with suggestions for class discussion and follow-up.

4. *Teachers' Guides to Television* is a subscription booklet published in the fall and spring with the cooperation of the Television Information Office of the National Association of Broadcasters. The guides, available at a nominal cost, state the objectives of the program, gives a synopis, teaching suggestions before viewing, and ideas for further exploration. Time, date, network, and subject areas are given.

5. Action for Children's Television (ACT) began in 1968 in Newtonville, Massachusetts. It is a "national organization of parents and professionals dedicated to child-oriented quality television without commercialism." A *Newsweek* article[8] credits this group of activist parents with achieving more reform in television programming than any other group. ACT is responsible for reducing the time of commercials on children's programs from sixteen to nine and one-half minutes per hour. ACT provides information in its pamphlets concerning advertising, violence, and exploitations of children. ACT wants to use television positively. They urge parents to preview and recommend programs of value, to watch and discuss television with their children (i.e., change from passive to active participation). The quarterly newsletter includes articles on commercials, programming, a book review, materials available for order from ACT, and a list of contact people in every area.

   Action For Children's Television
   46 Austin Street
   Newtonville, Massachusetts 02160

6. *New Season: The Positive Use of Commercial Television with Children* by Rosemary Potter. Published by Charles E. Merrill, 1976. A Florida educator shows how to utilize commercial TV constructively in the classroom, with many learning exercises based on programming popular with children. All grade levels included. Available in paperbook.

   Charles E. Merrill Publishing Company
   1300 Alum Creek Drive
   Columbus, Ohio 43216

Assessing Textbooks for Readability

The textbook is still the prime source of cognitive learning in the classroom. There are a number of sources available for testing

---

[8] "What TV Does to Kids," *Newsweek* (February 21, 1977): 63–70.

appropriateness and readability of textbooks. The effective supervisor must work closely with teachers to determine if reading materials fit the particular skill level of the students for whom they are intended.[9]

Readability is the objective measure of the difficulty of a book or article, and usually involves the use of a specific formula with results reported in terms of grade level. Seven such formulas are listed below.

1. Flesch Reading Ease Score—Grades 5–12. Involves checking word length and sentence length. Source: Flesch, R. F. *How to Test Readability*. New York: Harper & Brothers, 1959.

2. Wheeler and Smith—Index Number. Involves determining sentence length and · number of polysyllabic words. Grades: Primary–4. Source: Wheeler, L. R., and Smith, E. H. "A Practical Readability Formula for the Classroom Teacher in the Primary Grades." *Elementary English* 31 (November 1954): 397–99.

3. The Cloze Technique. The readability of two pieces of material can be compared by the Cloze technique. Measures redundancy (the extent to which words are predictable) while standard readability formulas measure the factors of vocabulary and sentence structure. It can be used to determine relative readability of material, but cannot predict readability of a new sample. It does not give grade level designations. Source: Taylor, W. C. "Cloze Procedure: A New Tool for Measuring Readability." *Journalism Quarterly* 30 (Fall 1953): 415–33.

4. Lorge Grade Placement Score—Grades 3–12. Uses average sentence length in words, number of difficult words per 100 words not on the Dale 769-word list, and number of prepositional phrases per 100 words. Source: Lorge, I. *The Lorge Formula for Estimating Difficulty of Reading Materials*. New York: Teachers' College Press, 1959.

5. The Fry Graph. Method is based on two factors: average number of syllables per 100 words, and average number of sentences per 100 words. Three randomly selected 100 words samples are used. Source: Fry, Edward. "Graph for Estimating Readability." *Journal of Reading* (April 1968): 513–16, and *Reading Teacher* (March 1969): 22–27.

6. SMOG Grading Plan—Grades 4–12. Involves counting repetition of polysyllabic words. Source: McLaughlin, Harry G. "SMOG Grading—A New Readability Formula." *Journal of Readings* 12 (1969): 639–46.

7. Spache Grade Level Score—Grades 1–3. Looks at average

---

[9] For a thorough treatment of this important topic see Joan Nelson, "Readability: Some Cautions for the Content Teacher," *Journal of Reading* 21 (April 1978): 620–25.

sentence length and number of words outside Dale list of 769 words to give readability level. Source: Spache, G. "A New Readability Formula for Primary Grade Reading Materials." *Elementary School Journal* 53 (March 1953): 410–13.

SELECTING LEARNING ACTIVITIES AND TEACHING STRATEGIES

The next step in the instructional process after selection of objectives and learning materials is the selection of learning activities and teaching strategies.

The classroom teacher is much like an actor on stage, sending and receiving messages through voice, dress, and body language. Too frequently learning activities chosen in a classroom do little to convey a sense of excitement in learning. Much like the star salesman, the teacher must put color, enthusiasm, and drama into the learning experience. The teacher often turns to the supervisor for strategies and skills for teaching and selection of creative learning activities.

Selecting Learning Activities

Learning activities are designed for students, but often involve teachers in the activities. Activities are not selected as ends, but as means in the learning process. Learning activities lead to the mastery of selected objectives.

Traditionally, classrooms have been characterized by an active role for teachers and a dependent, or passive, role for students. A passive role has little potential in effecting learner change.

Learning stations, interest centers, games, problem-solving activities, field trips, and role playing are among the many learning activities used by effective classroom teachers. These activities are often introduced to teachers through instructional workshops conducted by supervisors. Many times, supervisors can introduce activities that require only everyday references as resource materials.

Selecting Teaching Strategies

The teaching strategies selected must consider the students to be taught, objectives to be mastered, and resources available.

Teaching strategies or methods are designed to enhance certain kinds of learning for specific kinds of learners, but have positive effects on several kinds of learning.

We must not forget that the student does the learning in the teaching-learning process. Intelligence, personality, motivation, and other factors, rather than the teacher, materials, or methods used, are determinants of how much a student will learn. Effective teaching can increase the likelihood that students will become more creative in their thinking as they learn facts, concepts, and interpersonal skills.[10]

Clegg listed twenty-three teaching strategies that a teacher might use for eliciting certain cognitive student responses. (Table 3.7) Even though the strategies suggest cognitive responses, they will have positive effects on affective learning.

Table 3.7
Clegg's Questioning Strategies

Teaching Strategies

NAME	MEANING
NO. 1 —PARADOXES	Situation opposed to common sense Self-contradictory statement or observation Discrepancy in belief but true in fact
NO. 2 —ANALOGIES	Situations of likeness Similarities between things Corresponding circumstances
NO. 3 —SENSING DEFICIENCIES	Gaps in knowledge Missing links in information Unknown elements
NO. 4 —THINKING OF POSSIBLES	Guessing or forming hypotheses Thinking of probabilities Constructing alternatives
NO. 5 —PROVOCATIVE QUESTIONS	Inquiry to bring forth meaning Incite knowledge exploration Summons to discovering new knowledge

---

[10] Bruce R. Joyce, *Selecting Learning Experiences: Linking Theory and Practice* (Washington, D.C.: Association for Supervision and Curriculum Development, 1978), p. 15.

Table 3.7—*continued*

NO. 6 —ATTRIBUTE LISTING	Inherent properties Conventional symbols or identities Ascribing qualities

NO. 7 —EXPLORING MYSTERY OF
   THINGS
	Detective work on unfamiliar
	   knowledge
	Examine unnatural phenomena
	Deductive thinking

NO. 8 —REINFORCING
   ORIGINALITY
	Rewarding original thinking
	Allowing opportunities to
	   think of something no one else
	   has thought of
	Strengthen unlikely but relevant
	   responses

NO. 9 —EXAMPLES OF CHANGE	Demonstrate the dynamics of
	   things
	Provide opportunities for making
	   alterations, modifications, or
	   substitutions

NO. 10—ORGANIZED RANDOM
   SEARCH
	Use a familiar structure to
	   lead at random to another
	   structure
	Case studies from which new
	   courses of action are devised

NO. 11—EXAMPLES OF HABIT	Discuss the effects of habit-
	   bound thinking
	Build a sensitivity against
	   rigidity in ideas and functional
	   fixation of things

NO. 12—SKILLS OF SEARCH	Consider ways something has been
	   done before (historical search)
	Trial and error search on various
	   methods and describe results
	   (descriptive search)
	Control experimental conditions
	   and report subsequent results
	   (experimental research)

NO. 13—TOLERANCE FOR
   AMBIGUITY
	Provide encounters which puzzle,
	   intrigue, or challenge thinking
	Pose open-ended situations
	   which do not force closure

Table 3.7—*continued*

NO. 14—INTUITIVE EXPRESSION	Feeling about things through all the senses Skill of expressing emotion Be sensitive to inward hunches about knowledge
NO. 15—PROCESS OF INVENTION	Steps of problem solving leading to invention Study the incubation process leading to insight
NO. 16—ADJUSTMENT TO DEVELOPMENT	Examine how failures or accidents have paid off Learn how to learn from mistakes Examples of process of development rather than adjustment to something already developed
NO. 17—STUDY CREATIVE PEOPLE	Analyze traits of eminently creative people Study the process which has led to creation
NO. 18—INTERACT WITH PAST KNOWLEDGE	Allow opportunities to toy with information already acquired Nurture ideas from previously stored knowledge
NO. 19—EVALUATE SITUATIONS	Deciding upon solutions in terms of their consequences and implications Extrapolate from the results of ideas and actions
NO. 20—RECEPTIVE TO SURPRISE	Alert to the significance of novel thoughts Capitalize upon unexpected ideas
NO. 21—CREATIVE READING SKILL	Develop a utilitarian mind-set for information Learn the skill of idea generation by reading
NO. 22—CREATIVE LISTENING SKILL	Learn the skill of idea generation by listening Listen for information which allows one thing to lead to another

Table 3.7—*continued*

NO. 23—VISUALIZATION SKILL

Practice describing views from unaccustomed vantage points

Express ideas in three-dimensional forms

Look at things in plan form or views

SOURCE: Ambrose A. Clegg, Jr., "Teacher Strategies of Questioning for Eliciting Selected Cognitive Student Responses" (Paper presented at the Annual Conference of the American Educational Research Association, Los Angeles, February 1969). Used with permission.

SUMMARY

Supervisors must display a wide range of behaviors in leading teachers in planning for instruction. Due to the many changes occurring in schools today, the public is looking to those in supervisory roles to exert greater leadership in instructional planning.

Among the many tasks related to instructional planning are: helping teachers develop an appropriate instructional vocabulary, conducting assessments of student needs, selecting meaningful goals and objectives, developing plans and lessons, using learning materials and media, assessing textbooks for readability, and choosing appropriate teaching strategies. Collectively, these supervisory acts can contribute to the development of effective educational planning. Such planning, when implemented, will lead to improved classroom instruction.

Suggested Learning Activities

1. The superintendent has established the first full-time instructional supervisor position in your school district. Write a job description for that position in terms of improving instructional planning.

2. You have been asked to assist elementary teachers in your district in conducting a needs assessment. What diagnostic devices and other

means would you use to gather data? What kinds of data would you suggest as most helpful to teachers in planning instruction?

3. Prepare a list of resources teachers might use in assessing pupil performance.

Books to Review

Bellon, Jerry J. *Classroom Supervision and Instructional Improvement: A Synergetic Process.* Dubuque, Iowa: Kendall/Hunt, 1976.

Bloom, Benjamin S., ed. *Taxonomy of Educational Objectives—Handbook I: Cognitive Domain.* New York: Longman, 1956.

Gronlund, Norman E. *Preparing Criterion-Referenced Tests For Classroom Instruction.* New York; Macmillan, 1973.

Hudgins, Bruce B. *The Instructional Process.* Chicago: Rand McNally, 1973.

Joyce, Bruce R. *Selecting Learning Experiences: Linking Theory and Practice.* Washington, D.C.: Association for Supervision and Curriculum Development, 1978.

Klein, M. Francis. *About Learning Materials.* Washington, D.C.: Association for Supervision and Curriculum Development, 1978.

Meyen, Edward L. *Developing Instructional Units.* Dubuque, Iowa: William C. Brown, 1976.

4

Leading Teachers in Implementing Instruction

Implementation of educational plans in the classroom calls for both understanding and skill. The supervisor can be an invaluable resource to teachers in promoting both an understanding of the instructional process and the development of teaching skills.

An initial step in implementation is to organize for effective classroom instruction. Such organization includes grouping students for appropriate learning and establishing an environment that fits the instructional plan.

To implement an instructional plan teachers must be skilled in assessing student performances. Specific skills needed include conducting testing and assessment, and developing an effective means of reporting learning progress.

A third area that contributes to successful implementation is the coordination of teaching activities among teachers. In some cases such cooperation may be focused on shared teaching, while in other cases it may center on the development of common teaching units.

Finally, teachers may need to possess the basic skills used in assessing instructional programs. A set of principles is presented at the conclusion of the chapter for study and reflection.

ASSISTING TEACHERS IN ORGANIZING A CLASSROOM FOR INSTRUCTION

Grouping

The main objective of organizing a classroom for instruction is to provide more effectively for students' individual differences. A classroom organized in this fashion will provide for several types of grouping dependent on need and purpose. Flexibility is the key in any grouping arrangement.

Supervisors can assist teachers in organizing a classroom that provides for a number of grouping arrangements.

1. *A class as a whole* can function as a group. Teachers sometimes have guilt feelings about whole class activities, but there are occasions when the teacher can address the whole class as a single group. New topic or unit introductions, unit summaries, and activities such as reports, dramatizations, and choral reading may be effectively conducted with the total class.
2. *Reading level groups* formed according to reading achievement levels are commonly found in classrooms. These groups are not static and must accommodate shifts of pupils from group to group as changes in individual achievement occur.
3. *Reading need groups* are formed to assist students in mastering a particular reading skill such as pronouncing a phonic element or finding the main idea in a paragraph.
4. *Interest groups* help students apply reading skills to other language arts and other content areas. Storytelling, recreational reading, writing stories and poems, and dramatization are activities that can be carried out in interest groupings.
5. *Practice or tutorial groups* are often used to allow students to practice oral reading skills, play skill games, and organize peer teaching situations.
6. *Research groups* allow for committee work, group projects, and other research activities. Learning centers in the classroom and research areas in the media center are often developed for research groups.
7. *Individualization* allows a student to work as an individual in selecting books and references for learning projects. Developmental programs provide for individual progress through a series of lessons.

Heterogeneous versus Homogeneous Grouping

Recently, federal acts and court decisions have added a legal dimension to the whole question of ability grouping. Tracking of elementary students on the basis of presumed ability or achievement was declared unconstitutional in the federal court of Washington, D.C. in 1976. This court decision was based on evidence that tracking practices are discriminatory and result in the denial of equal protection of the laws to children from varying racial and socioeconomic backgrounds. This decision, coupled with new federal acts relating to sex discrimination and rights of handicapped students, has put new demands on the supervisor to work with teachers in developing fair grouping practices.

Teachers who organize skill groups in the classroom are using homogeneous grouping. The key is flexibility. Students are moved from group to group as they achieve required skills. Also, the skill groups are organized only for a portion of the school day. The rest of the day students are organized into heterogeneous groups where they can interact with students of varying abilities.

A major task of supervisors in working with teachers in instructional settings is to help teachers understand and use different grouping patterns. Helping teachers see that grouping is a means and not an end in instruction will prevent abuses of student grouping.

Creating the Classroom Environment

Teachers and students need to share in the management of classroom activities—contributing ideas, planning cooperatively, implementing plans, and sharing in the evaluation process.

Supervisors play an important role in helping teachers structure warm and creative learning environments. Some of the components necessary for this kind of learning environment are:

1. A pressure-free setting
2. Multisensory experiences
3. Differentiated learning
4. A comfortable and flexible physical facility
5. Creative materials
6. Diversified activities
7. Independent learning
8. Pupil interaction and cooperation
9. Freedom for students to select alternative learning activities.

Combs, drawing from the ASCD Yearbook, *Perceiving, Behaving, Becoming*, has listed factors that hinder an atmosphere for growth and creativity in the classroom:

1. Preoccupation with order, categorization, and classifying
2. Overvaluing authority, support, evidence, and the "scientific method"—all the good answers are someone else's
3. Exclusive emphasis upon the historical view, implying that all the good things have been discovered already
4. Cookbook approaches, filling in the blanks
5. Solitary learning, discouraging communication
6. The elimination of self from the classroom—only what the book says is important, not what I think
7. Emphasis upon force, threat, or coercion. What diminishes the self diminishes creativity
8. The idea that mistakes are sinful
9. The idea that students are not to be trusted
10. Lock-step organization[1]

It is clear that a positive classroom climate can be created by varying teacher leadership style. Once created, such a climate can have a significant effect on motivation and performance.

Supervisors must work in the classroom with teachers to manipulate the environment to provide opportunities for the learner to pursue and extend present interests and purposes, and identify new interests and potentials. This professional skill of working directly with teachers in the classroom points out the need for a supervisor to maintain not only the skills necessary to be a teacher of teachers, but a teacher of children as well.

HELPING TEACHERS ASSESS STUDENT PERFORMANCE

Supervisors often assist teachers in finding better ways to assess student performance, an essential step in the instructional process. Instruction is designed to bring about the achievement of selected learning objectives. Learning other than intended learning outcomes, of course, occurs in and out of the classroom. However, the prime focus of the instructional program is directed toward specific objectives, objectives that might not be achieved in a less organized fashion.

The Concept of Mastery

The topic of learning outcomes mastery introduces a need for a change in how we think about instruction as well as assessment In conventional instruction, students and teacher expect few students to master all

---

[1] Arthur W. Combs, *The Professional Education of Teachers* (Boston. Allyn & Bacon, 1965), p. 36.

objectives so as to receive an A in a course. When test scores are plotted as frequency distributions, a "normal curve" is formed, with students ranging in grades from A to F. Such a system tends to fix academic goals of both students and teachers at low levels, thus reducing student and teacher motivation. Bloom has proposed the concept of mastery learning where 90 to 95 percent of students can actually master objectives now reached by only "good students."[2] This concept requires an effort by teachers to determine why certain students fail to reach mastery and requires teachers to remedy the situation through more time for learning, different materials, or diagnosis to determine what prerequisite skills are missing. Thus, the mastery learning concept abandons the concept of students learning more or less well.

Criterion-referenced Testing

An approach in assessing student performance that is receiving increased attention is that of criterion-referenced testing. This technique of testing involves an interpretation of test results in terms of the types of learning tasks students achieve in some clearly defined area (e.g., that a student can define 90 per cent of the terms in a social studies unit).

Supervisors must help teachers with the theory and research necessary for the preparation and use of criterion-referenced tests in the classroom.

Reliability of Objective-referenced Measures

Selecting criteria for items and tests designed to accomplish objective-referenced measurement requires standards of performance appropriate for the stated objective. The items used for assessment must also have reliability. The term *reliability* refers to consistency of measurement from one item to the next or one test to another.

Norm-referenced Measures

Tests that yield scores that compare one student's performance with that of a group are called "norm-referenced." These tests generally measure student achievement over relatively large segments of instructional content rather than specific objectives. The selection and interpretation of norm-referenced tests is a major task in instruction.

Supervisors are often called upon to answer parents' questions about results of norm-referenced tests. They must assist teachers in inter-

---

[2] Benjamin S. Bloom, "New Views of the Learner: Implications for Instruction and Curriculum," *Educational Leadership* 35 (April 1978): 563–76.

preting test results and provide guidance in strengthening segments of the instructional program where achievement is low.

Standardized Tests

Norm-referenced tests designed for large numbers of students in a region, or nation as a whole, may have norms that are standardized.

Standardized tests are not appropriate for use in assessing learning outcomes from lessons having specifiable objectives. They can be used to provide information about the effects of total instructional programs.

Teacher-designed Tests

Tests designed by teachers may be objective- or norm-referenced tests. Norms generally refer to class norms.

Objective-referenced tests allow teachers to assess for attainment of specific objectives. They are more valuable to the classroom teacher than norm-referenced measures because they can provide the possibility of diagnostic help for students in overcoming specific learning deficiencies.

Alternatives to Grades

Wherever teaching and learning go on, grades usually become the end product of assessments of student learning. Recently, alternatives to grading have been proposed by those concerned with the effects grading has had on student attitudes toward learning and self. Computerized reporting systems, contract methods, and performance evaluation have been suggested as alternatives for traditional grades.[3]

If supervisors are to help students and teachers realize the extent of their creative capacities, they must provide leadership in changing the grading game played in the classrooms.

WORKING WITH TEACHERS IN TEAMS

Changes occurring in the role of today's teacher have important implications for the role of supervisors. Teachers in many schools no longer work in lonely, professional isolation with a standard-sized group

---

[3] Sidney B. Simon and James Bellanca, eds., *Degrading the Grading Myths: A Primer of Alternatives to Grades and Marks* (Washington, D.C.: Association for Supervision and Curriculum Development, 1976), pp. 64–94.

of children, but as a part of an instructional team. Such teams utilize the talents of a broad spectrum of persons in carrying out instruction. Grouping teachers into instructional teams under the coordination of an experienced team leader, with access to supporting paraprofessionals, takes us away from the concept of the "all-capable teacher" working in an isolated classroom.

Teams encourage differences rather than narrow standardization among teachers. Staffing of teams recognizes and provides for variations in teaching and learning styles. The opportunity exists for matching teaching and learning styles.

What are the implications for the supervisor's role in assisting teaching teams? One is that teachers will become supervisors in function, if not in name. This becomes more evident where there is a differentiated staffing pattern ranging from team leaders to professional aides. This development has special merit in that it reduces the distance between the supervisor and teacher, and expands the amount of time that can be given a teacher or group of teachers.

A second implication is the teacher education dimension of the supervisor's role. All supervisors, whether they function as coordinators of classroom teachers or as district supervisors, will need to function as teacher educators. Less teacher turnover and declining enrollment that curtails the hiring of new teachers have drawn greater attention to in-service rather than pre-service, training. Pre-service education in the complex, modern teaching world is still merely an introduction to, rather than a culmination of, the teacher's preparation.[4]

The emergence of teacher education centers in the 1970s has promoted a closer integration between what is taught at pre-service and in-service levels. School district supervisors often hold adjunct professorships as cooperating colleges and universities, and college professors are assigned directly to teacher centers, schools, or school districts for a portion or all of their teaching assignments. A new teaming relationship has evolved between universities and school systems, a development teachers are viewing with great interest. They are wondering aloud whether teachers of teachers can "practice what they preach" about teaming.

WORKING WITH TEAMS TO DEVELOP INTERDISCIPLINARY STUDY UNITS

One supervisory speciality is the familiar one of subject matter coordination. Subject supervisors have the responsibility for establishing

---

[4] William H. Lucio, ed., *The Supervisor: New Demands—New Dimensions* (Washington D.C.: Association for Supervision and Curriculum Development, 1969), p. 66.

a link between scholars and elementary, middle, and high school classroom teachers.

When two subject areas are related in a study unit, as is frequent now, a need arises for a new supervisory skill of assisting teachers in developing and teaching interdisciplinary units of instruction. The middle school, through its focus on large blocks of instruction (common teacher groups teaching common student groups), has revived core instruction and emphasized this new dimension. Teachers often turn to district subject area supervisors, as well as to team leaders or instructional coordinators at the school level for help. The model in Table 4.1 should be a useful tool for supervisors to assist teachers in developing an interdisciplinary unit.

EVALUATING INSTRUCTIONAL PROGRAMS

The last step in the instructional process is to evaluate the instructional program. Were objectives realistic? Did the teacher use proper materials and strategies? Were correct measures used to assess student learning? All of these questions must be asked when evaluating an instructional program's effectiveness.

Clinical supervision allows the supervisor to work directly in the classroom and become a part of the instructional process.[5] The following considerations are proposed as guides for supervisors in helping teachers plan programs for the evaluation of instructional programs:[6]

1. *Specify the desired outcomes of instructional programs.* More than 40 years ago Ralph Tyler and his colleagues wrote of the need for educators to describe their proposed instructional goals in precise, rather than vague, language. Such goals, they contended, needed to be described in terms of the *behavorial changes* sought in learners. Only in recent years, however, have many educators seriously endorsed such a position. Now, we find most teachers stating educational goals in terms of observable learner behavior.

2. *Describe in operational terms the planned classroom transactions for a given instructional program.* Specify appropriate independent and dependent variables to be measured for evaluation purposes.

   During recent years, school systems have adopted many "new" curricular and instructional programs and practices. Yet, there is frequently little agreement among experienced educators as to the

---

[5] *Clinical supervision* refers to a five-step act: (1) preobservation conference, (2) observation, (3) analysis and strategy, (4) supervision conference, and (5) postconference analysis. This subject is treated more fully in Chapters 6 and 10.

[6] The following seven considerations were cited in materials circulated at the Annual Conference of the American Educational Research Association, New York, 1967. Author not identified.

effectiveness of adopted programs and practices; they are commonly adopted with little or no sound objective evidence to support their use. Research has helped very little to indicate the efficacy of many practices.

Table 4.1
Development of an Interdisciplinary Teaching Unit

STAGE I.   Conceptualization of the Purposes of the Interdisciplinary Approach to Instruction
    A.   Having informal dialogue about the needs of students
    B.   Organizing student needs into goal statements—expected outcomes
    C.   Selecting a unifying statement, theme, or concept
    D.   Identifying some objectives based on goals—particularly in the *affective domain*

STAGE II.   Research
    A.   Selecting curricular options and activities
    B.   Identifying and selecting resources

STAGE III.   Fusion (Discipline)
    A.   Organizing the curriculum
        1.   Developing specific learning objectives
        2.   Determining the sequence of learning experiences
        3.   Determining entry level skills along a continuum of learning experiences
        4.   Selecting and/or developing evaluative criteria
        5.   Categorizing resource materials
        6.   Developing units, and so on
    B.   Developing prototypes as flow charts to clearly determine how students will move

STAGE IV.   Programming
    A.   Organizing learning centers
    B.   Developing team schedules to include
        1.   Small groups
        2.   Large groups
        3.   Independent learners
        4.   Individuals in need of special help
    C.   Scheduling off-campus visits, guests, and so on

STAGE V.   Implementation
    A.   Pretesting
    B.   Montitoring
    C.   Posttesting
    D.   Recycling

STAGE VI.   Evaluation
    A.   Professionals
    B.   Students

Two factors seem paramount among reasons for the lack of agreement and useful data on various instructional programs. One is the frequent failure of educators to describe precisely the relevant procedures in a program or practice. For example, all of us are tempted to agree that a "problem-solving approach" is effective, just because the term sounds so good. However, until we define the procedures involved in a problem-solving approach, there is no way to determine empirically whether or not such an approach actually is effective. Different investigators studying a "problem-solving approach" may obtain strikingly different results simply because the approach studied by Investigator 1 may have been an entirely different technique than the problem-solving approach studied by Investigator 2.

A second important reason for the lack of good data on new programs and practices relates to methods employed in evaluating them. Errors are frequently made in the initial planning of comparative studies in education, and these errors seriously limit the useful information yielded by the study.

3. *Select the most valid and practical design for investigating the specified relationships.* Objective evaluation is not now and never has been a common public school enterprise. Although educators are constantly designing new methods and instructional materials, the effectiveness of these innovations is seldom objectively determined. Educators shy away from experimental research and objective evaluation for several reasons. Experimentation is typically disruptive of classroom practices. More importantly, experimental research is thought to require a level of statistical and mathematical sophistication beyond that of the typical educator, and to demand specialized training in research methodology and techniques outside the scope of the typical educator's formal training.

Experimental research and objective evaluation are thus surrounded by an aura of respect, but respect from a distance. When such an activity is attempted, it is usually under the banner of "action research," leading to the generation of much enthusiasm, but little else. Even doctoral students in the area of curriculum and instruction avoid experimental studies, preferring to determine by questionnaire procedures or subjective judgment what current practices exist or should exist.

4. *Specify appropriate independent and dependent variables and state the specific relationships to be evaluated.* Faced with the necessity of evaluating many new phases of their instructional programs, educators are probing more seriously the kinds of evaluative procedures suitable for different purposes. Phrases such as "formative evaluation," "summative evaluation," "norm-referenced measures," and "criterion-referenced measures" are becoming increasingly common parlance among school people.

5. *Identify the essential components (cause-and-effect relationships) of a sound evaluation program and describe operationally the specific conditions that each must meet.* Make careful provisions that all of the known cause-and-effect relationships are identified and described in realistic terms. Be specific with respect to a given instructional factor (a process) and a given learner factor (a product) that are known to be related. For example, spell out precisely the level of student achievement that must be met in order that a given "process" factor can be determined

to be "acceptable" or "satisfactory." Without the identification of specific relationships and their associated levels of acceptability, evaluators are in danger of making value judgments that are based on nonempirical and, therefore, subjective evidence.

6. *Specify the inferences that can be made from the results of a specific study.* Reports of educational research and evaluation abound with statements of conclusions that are not warranted by the procedures and data from the reported studies. Examination of such studies enables the knowledgeable reader to determine which conclusions are valid and which are invalid from the given data and procedures.

7. Specify and describe operationally appropriate "contingency management" procedures for a given evaluation project to determine whether the requirements of the operational procedures are met.

Even though an evaluator may specify precisely the operational procedures for a given evaluation project, he has little assurance that the procedures will be carried out in the classroom according to his or her precise specifications. Too frequently, however, programs or practices are delineated and data subsequently are collected to evaluate them with inadequate attention to the transactions that actually occurred in the classroom. Thus, the program or practice is evaluated on the basis of the specified *intended* transactions, rather than on the basis of the *observed* transactions.

SOME INSTRUCTIONAL PRINCIPLES TO CONSIDER

In providing leadership at the classroom level, supervisors must help teachers understand their roles as instructional leaders. The following instructional principles must be considered in any program of instruction:

1. One thing we are sure about in education is that no two learners and/or learning situations are alike. A learner is first of all an individual with unique needs, preferences, abilities, and so on. A teacher needs to recognize this and consider it carefully when carrying out his or her role as a "facilitator of learning."

2. The same set of stimuli is perceived differently by two different learners. Both the amount and the quality of learning that takes place are dependent upon how the learner perceives the available stimuli.

3. Learning objectives should be stated precisely and clearly so that both the learner and the teacher are aware of and in agreement with what is expected. When learning objectives are unclear and ambiguous, the learner becomes overly dependent upon the teacher. Moreover, ambiguous learning objectives create problems for the teacher when it comes time to measure the learning that has taken place—valid final evaluation may be impeded or impossible.

4. The teacher is an agent of instruction. As an agent of instruction, his or her role is one of "facilitating learning."

5. Teachers need to be capable of controlling their teaching behavior. They must learn how to plan and control their teaching behavior in order to facilitate the most effective learning.

6. It is quite likely that a teacher is unable to teach a learner anything. In all probability a teacher can only hope to aid (facilitate) the student in learning.

7. A teacher must develop a sensitivity to and an ability for assessing a given learning situation. Sensing the situation, he or she must make accurate analyses and competent judgments about instructional methods and techniques that will result in maximum effective learning. To carry out this role effectively, the teacher should have available an adequate number and variety of tested instructional methods and techniques from which to draw.

8. To create an atmosphere conducive to learning, the teacher needs to display toward the learner the personal qualities of empathy, congruency, unconditionality of regard, and a willingness to be known. In such an atmosphere both the teacher and the learner are free and better able to communicate within the learning situation at hand. The relationship now becomes one of cooperation rather than competition and/or compliance.

9. Teachers need to learn to be "good listeners." Through careful listening practices the teacher becomes aware of the learner's feelings, needs, abilities, weaknesses, and so on. This awareness of the learner's nature enables the teacher to make proper analyses and plans to aid learning.

10. Neither indirect teaching behavior nor direct teaching behavior is to be preferred over the other. Rather, the proper use of each in a learning situation for which it is best suited is the optimum choice. This sensitivity of when and how to incorporate either direct or indirect teaching behavior is termed "control" or "flexibility."

Table 4.2 outlines some supervisory concerns at the design, implementation, and evaluation stages of planning for classroom instruction.

SUMMARY

Instructional improvement deals with much more than just improving teaching methods or materials. It involves examination and strengthening of the whole teaching-learning act. From needs assessments to measurement of student performance, the supervisor must be able to synthesize a number of skills to help teachers improve instruction. The processes by which the supervisor attempts to influence the instructional

Table 4.2
Planning for Classroom Instruction

Design	Implementation	Evaluation
Lessons plans	Delivery systems	Predetermining criteria
Instructional strategies	Use of equipment	(norm- versus criterion-
Selection of materials	Integrating learning	referenced)
Establishment of	(tie to student)	Establishing medium
management system	Grouping for purpose	Student assessment
	Time management	Teaching feedback
	Establishing roles	
	Setting climates	
	Individualizing, personalizing	

program have to take into account the fact that both the teacher and learner are human beings, not inanimate objects.

If a supervisor is to be effective as an instructional leader, he or she has to be concerned with not just the instructional program, but with the people involved in the instructional program.

Suggested Learning Activities

1. Develop an outline of an interdisciplinary teaching unit using the model suggested in Table 4.1.

2. Design a workshop outline for helping teachers understand the major areas in implementing an instructional plan.

3. Summarize the responsibilities of a supervisor when working with teachers to implement an educational plan.

Books to Review

Block, James H., ed. *Mastery Learning—Theory and Practice*. New York: Holt, Rinehart & Winston, 1971.

Gagne, Robert M., and Briggs, Leslie J. *Principles of Instructional Design*. New York: Holt, Rinehart & Winston, 1974.

Harrow, Anita. *A Taxonomy of the Psychomotor Domain: A Guide for Developing Behavioral Objectives*. New York: Longman, 1972.

Kirschenbaum, Howard, et al. *Wad-Ja-Get: The Grading Game in American Education*. New York: Hart, 1971.

Simon, Sidney B., and Bellanca, James A., eds. *Degrading the Grading Myths: A Primer of Alternatives to Grades and Marks*. Washington, D.C.: Association for Supervision and Curriculum Development, 1976.

Unruh, Adolph, and Turner, Harold E. *Supervision For Change and Innovation*. Boston: Houghton-Mifflin, 1970.

5

Helping Teachers Work with Special Needs Students

INTRODUCTION

Most practicing educators would freely admit that all schoolchildren are special. Yet today, because of Public Law 94–142 and other legislation, there is a new focus on a host of special learners not previously provided for in our schools. Among those special students are the following: the visually impaired, the emotionally disturbed, the physically handicapped, the chronically ill, the disruptive, and those students suffering from specific disabilities such as the autistic and aphasic.

Another class of special schoolchildren can be drawn from those students who experience mild learning problems such as inability to read or language handicaps. In addition, there are those children who are educationally deprived or culturally different.

Still a third group of special learners exists. These are students who are academically gifted, artistically talented, or experiencing special conditions during the normal pattern of growth and development.

Collectively, these special students call for a new orientation on the part of educators. We must acknowledge the presence of such students and plan educational programs to serve them. There are many educators focusing on each of these groups of students, yet few teachers and supervisors are familiar with the range of specialness found among schoolchildren. While there are many programs and services provided for special students outside the regular classroom, the great majority of students with special problems remains in the regular classroom under the supervision of the teacher who is expected to meet their individualized needs. This chapter should prove valuable to persons charged with working directly with special students and those working with teachers to develop special programs to accommodate these students.

ACCEPTING PUPIL DIVERSITY

The programs developed for students reflect the assumptions and beliefs teachers and supervisors have about the purpose of education, the nature of learning, and the whole schooling process.

A look at the many approaches to educating children with special needs reveals different assumptions about the nature of the world and the child and teacher within it. For example, one assumption is that the world is highly mechanistic and predictable. The child is seen as a relatively passive component in a setting that is arranged so that instruction impinges on her or him in a way to trigger predictable outcomes. The teacher is the technician who engineers the environment to achieve desired results.

The contrasting position is that the world is not static or predictable, but in a state of continuous transition. Students are viewed not as passive individuals, but as active and continually changing beings. Educators holding this view of children and the world see education not as getting children to make predictable responses, but as children changed by and changing their environment.

We espouse the second view of the education of children—we believe all children are different and have particular needs.

UNDERSTANDING BEHAVIOR AND MOTIVATION

In the past, considerable attention has been given in the literature to the process of defining exceptionalities. Recently, attention has been shifted to the consequences of applying definitions to children with special needs. Public Law 94–142, the Education for All Handicapped Children

Act of 1975, has been described as a "Bill of Rights for the Handicapped."[1] Some of the same issues that contributed to the need for PL 94–142 were attributed to the role definitions played in programming for the handicapped.

Too often, educators "expect" certain behavior from students because those students have been defined as "slow," "gifted," or "learning disabled." Understanding a child's behavior and motivation sometimes becomes more, rather than less, complicated when a teacher has advance knowledge of an emotional problem, or physical or mental disability. While such advance information is valuable in differentiating instruction for special learners, it can also lead to stereotyped programs that fail to challenge students.

The effect of individual differences on motivation and the influence of motivation on behavior have been the subject of numerous research studies, yet students are still treated in many classrooms as if no differences exist among them.

Children identified as having special needs often suffer from a poor self-image. The supervisor can assist teachers in providing realistic and relevant programs for these children by helping teachers understand the development of self-concept in children. The teacher who understands himself or herself will play a significant role in the self-concept of the students he or she teaches. Witherspoon[2] has identified important questions a teacher must consider in working with children. These questions are especially important for teachers working with students with special needs. Supervisors might ask teachers to consider the following questions:

Do I see children as they really are, or are my concepts clouded by my own experiences as a child?

We know that the way a person views children comes from personal experiences, often those from childhood. The child who experiences love and acceptance most often grows into an adult who loves and accepts children.

Researchers have pointed out that nurturing is learned. For instance, parents who abuse children did not receive the kind of nurturing they needed during their own childhood to become the kind of parent who in turn has the capacity to nurture. Most often, parents who abuse their children were themselves brutalized by their own parents.[3]

Can I show kindness and affection towards others, or do I feel this is unnecessary?

Children, even more than adults, need to know that others care about

---

[1] L. V. Goodman, "A Bill of Rights for the Handicapped," *American Education* 12 (May 1976): 6–8.

[2] Ralph L. Witherspoon, "Teacher, Know Thyself," mimeograph (Tampa: University of South Florida, 1975).

[3] Mary Van Stolk, "Who Owns the Child?" *Childhood Education* 50 (September 1974): 259–65.

them. Often, the child who receives very little love at home will seek love from the teacher. It is often hard for some teachers to show affection to students who evidence unsocial behaviors or who come from a culture different from that of the teacher.

Do I feel confident that those I teach feel I am a good teacher, or do they merely tolerate me because I am their teacher?

Teachers must provide a classroom environment in which children feel wanted, are challenged, and feel respected. Those children who are experiencing social, mental, or physical problems must want to come to school in spite of their handicaps. They will want to come if they feel their teacher wants them to be there.

Do my actions and deeds reflect confidence and integrity, or are they merely an attempt to "save face" to protect me from myself?

Teachers who are unsure of themselves transfer this lack of confidence to their students. Children develop confidence only when the adults working with them radiate sincerity and confidence by word and action.

Do I recognize when I need help, or am I afraid to ask for assistance?

Supervisors must encourage teachers who are unsure of themselves when working with students with special needs to ask for assistance. Teachers will often feel they are weak if they have to ask for help. The strong teacher is one who is self-confident enough to recognize that teaching students with special needs often requires special training. We strongly feel that only when teachers understand their own behavior and motivation can they understand the behavior and motivation of the students they teach.

Teachers are presently responsible for teaching many children who are difficult to teach. It appears that, in the future, teachers will be responsible for teaching more, not fewer, of these children. Teachers will be turning to those in supervisory positions for the necessary information and skills to teach these students. The more informed and skilled supervisors are in dealing with special students, the more responsive they can be to teachers in the classroom.

CLASSROOM MANAGEMENT

Teachers working with students having special needs often have to carry out learning activities under trying conditions. Although much has been written about classroom management, few teachers possess the skills to diagnose classroom situations and improve conditions. In the face of disruptions and disturbances caused by special students, teachers often create a repressive climate where there is little cognitive or affective student growth. Teachers can develop either high (positive) growth conditions in the classroom or low (negative) conditions.

Table 5.1 suggests teacher strategies and behaviors that cause high or low growth conditions.

Table 5.1
Teaching Behaviors Leading to High and Low Growth Conditions

High Growth Conditions	Low Growth Conditions
High acceptance/respect of pupil's ideas	Low acceptance/respect of pupil's ideas
1. Pupil ideas are frequently accepted. The teacher listens to and incorporates pupil ideas in discussion and other learning situations.	1. Pupil ideas are rarely encouraged or accepted. There is little opportunity for discussion. When discussion occurs, it is highly controlled and seeks *recall* of previously learned information. Pupil contributions are frequently criticized.
High acceptance/respect of pupil's affect	Low acceptance/respect of pupil's affect
2. Pupil feelings and emotions are accepted by the teacher as long as harm to others is avoided.	2. Pupil feelings are avoided or discouraged. The teacher is unwilling to recognize expressions and discussions of feelings.
High encouragement/support of pupils	Low encouragement/support of pupils
3. Pupils are encouraged to explore, make suggestions, etc. An atmosphere of "try it and tell us what happens" pervades the classroom.	3. Pupils are discouraged from exploration. The teacher has the one right way of doing things and only that way is accepted. Alternatives are not discussed or tested.
4. The teacher is willing to "get off the subject" when an interesting event or question is raised. At times the question becomes the actual topic.	4. The teacher controls the subject at all times. Penetrating philosophical questions are discouraged. The principal aim is to teach the lesson and complete it.

Table 5.1—*continued*

High pupil individualization

5. The teacher attempts to understand and respond to each child's psychological needs. The teacher recognizes that some children may need more direction and control while others may need the opportunity to exercise greater choice. The teacher, therefore, encourages children to learn and explore in ways that each child is comfortable with.

High pupil involvement

6. A continuing dialogue with pupils is maintained to involve children in making decisions about their learning (e.g., individual and small group projects, work contracts, etc.), and to help children further clarify what they are learning.

High teacher genuiness/realness

7. The teacher is genuine, willing to express ideas, feelings, experiences and be a real person rather than play a role. Where appropriate, the teacher allows students entry into his/her private world of feelings, ideas, needs, and concerns.

Low pupil individualization

5. The teacher denies individual differences and needs and demands conformity. The teacher who demands that every child participate in an "open" classroom may produce the same low growth conditions as the teacher who provides a "lockstep" classroom atmosphere. Both strategies are authoritarian, and demand conformity at the possible expense of pupil feelings of esteem, control and connectedness.

Low pupil involvement

6. The teacher always tells pupils what and how they are to learn. Little room is left for pupil choice and expression.

Low teacher genuiness/realness

7. The teacher plays a role and presents a facade that conceals feelings. The teacher acts in a confined, prescribed manner revealing little of own uniqueness and inner thoughts. A wide emotional gap is maintained between teacher and pupil and little of the common bonds, needs and feelings that the two may actually possess is explored.

Source: J.D. Wiggins and Dori English, "Affective Education: A Manual for Growth" (Dover: Delaware Department of Public Instruction, 1975), pp. 4–6. Used with permission.

Classroom management must involve organizing and coordinating the children's efforts to achieve their own educational goals. The instructional tasks students must perform in the classroom are generally spelled out by the teacher, school, or district; management tasks are not. The teacher must again turn to someone in a supervisory position to strengthen the management dimension of teaching.

Supervisors must help teachers understand that even when instruciton is individualized, the cooperation of all students is necessary because students work on their own assignments in the midst of others. Teachers must be competent to handle classroom management problems. Beginning teachers especially are fearful that they cannot manage or control disciplinary problems. The move to mainstreaming exceptional children has created doubts in the minds of new and experienced teachers alike about their abilities to manage classrooms.

The following concepts constitute a framework for improving classroom management positions.

1. Classroom management involves the individual group, school, and environmental factors which each influence each other.
2. Teachers cannot assume they are always dealing just with individuals. They must carry out practices consistent with a realistic view of the group to which the individual belongs.
3. Although many problems in a classroom are caused by individuals with emotional problems, much behavior perceived as individually caused is, in reality, individuals acting as agents of the group.
4. Members of the group attempt to shape the classroom environment. If teachers restrict communication and employ practices that reduce self-esteem of students, management problems will greatly increase.
5. The formally organized classroom group tends to develop and maintain itself. Teachers must learn to deal with not just individuals, but the collective behaviors of the group organization. Management practices, for the most part, involve group methods rather than individual techniques.
6. Accepting management as a specific dimension of the total teaching act and analyzing behavior patterns of classroom groups make it possible to determine the management functions required for a particular group.[4]

DEALING WITH DISRUPTIVE STUDENT BEHAVIOR

Disruptive behavior refers to those overt acts by students that interfere with the ongoing instructional processes in the classroom and the disruption of learning activities of other pupils. These behaviors cover a broad range of acts, from restlessness and minor "misdemeanors" to

---

[4] Lois Johnson and Mary Bang, *Classroom Management Theory and Skill Training* (New York: Macmillan, 1970), p. 39.

indicate behavior directed against self, others, and inanimate objects.

School supervisors and administrators regard the maintenance of discipline as the greatest problem of inexperienced teachers.[5] Supervisors are often called upon to assist new teachers in developing techniques for classroom management. In the previous section we outlined teaching strategies for creating positive growth conditions in the classroom. If teachers are to meet their professional responsibility to provide a proper learning environment, they must be able to control unwilling and sometimes disruptive students in the classroom. This is not always easy.

Jacob Kounin has made a major contribution to our understanding of discipline and group management in the classroom. Kounin suggests a number of techniques teachers can use to maintain classroom discipline. He maintains that teachers who want to have classrooms that operate smoothly must watch the flow of activities in the classroom. Although it seems obvious, teachers govern the flow of activities in the classroom. If they become good classroom managers, they can learn to deal with disruptive students and keep pupils working and behaving. The following are examples:

> GROUP ALERTING   The teacher notifies pupils of an imminent change in activity, watches to see that pupils are finishing the previous activity, and inititates the new one only when all of the class members are ready. In contrast, *thrusting* is represented when the teacher "bursts" in on pupil activity with no warning and no awareness, apparently, of anything but his own internal needs.

> STIMULUS BOUNDEDNESS is represented by behavior in which the teacher is apparently trapped by some stimulus as a moth by a flame. For example, a piece of paper on the floor leads to interruption of the ongoing activities of the classroom while the teacher berates the class members for the presence of the paper on the floor or tries to find out how it got there.

> OVERLAPPINGNESS is the teacher's ability to carry on two operations at once. For example, while the teacher is working with a reading group, a pupil comes to ask a question about arithmetic. The teacher handles the situation in a way which keeps the reading group at work while he simultaneously helps the child with his arithmetic.

> A DANGLE occurs when the teacher calls for the end of one activity, initiates another one, then returns to the previous activity. For example, "Now pupils, put away your arithmetic books and papers and get out your spelling books; we're going to have spelling." After the pupils have put away their arithmetic materials and gotten out their spelling materials the teacher asks, "Oh, by the way, did everybody get problem four right?"
> If the teacher never gets back to the new activity which he initiated (for

---

[5] Harvey F. Clarizo, *Toward Positive Classroom Discipline* (New York: John Wiley & Sons, 1971), p. 1.

example, if he had never returned to the spelling in the previous example) this would be a *truncation*.

WITH-ITNESS is the teacher's demonstration of his awareness of deviant behavior. It is scored both for timing and for target accuracy. Timing involves stopping the deviant behavior before it contages, and target accuracy involves identifying the responsible pupil. If, for example, an occurrence of whispering in the back of the room spread to several other children, and at this point the teacher criticizes one of the later class members who joined in, this would be scored negatively for both timing and for target accuracy.[6]

Kounin and associates have also reported the results of studies to discover techniques teachers can use to control the overt behavior of emotionally disturbed children in regular classrooms.[7] Results from these studies indicate that teachers who are successful in managing a classroom are also relatively successful in managing the emotionally disturbed children present in the classroom. Children's deviant behavior varies with changes in the classroom setting.

Teachers usually have little pre-service training in dealing with disruptive students. They complete their practice teaching under the direction of a supervising teacher who handles discipline problems. Disciplinary strategies for teachers are most often learned by trial and error and are applied in a similar pattern. We believe that a prime role of supervisors is to help teachers develop the proficiencies necessary for maintaining proper classroom discipline.

A philosophy of supervision associated with helping teachers with classroom discipline is that there are not bad teachers who dislike children, but there are teachers whose skills in training children need improvement. We believe there are two definite steps a supervisor can take to assist teachers in becoming more skilled in working with disruptive students.

The supervisor can help teachers focus on students' specific, rather than general, behaviors. For instance, in setting objectives for improving discipline teachers often use statements such as "getting Jimmy to behave." They leave out the specific behaviors such as "getting out of his seat," "talking out of turn," or "fighting with John." The teacher can avoid a global approach to behavioral problems by pinpointing the behaviors causing problems.

---

[6] From notes of presentation by Dr. Robert Soar at conference, "The Planning and Analysis of Classroom Instruction," University of South Florida, November 1975, pp. 7–8. For further details of Kounin's work see Jacob S. Kounin, *Discipline and Group Management in Classrooms* (New York: Holt, Rinehart & Winston, 1970), p. 79.

[7] Jacob S. Kounin, Wallace V. Friesen, and A. Evangeline Norton, "Managing Emotionally Disturbed Children in Regular Classrooms," *Journal of Educational Psychology* 57 (February 1966): 1–13.

After specific behaviors are identified, the supervisor should be able to help the teacher plan ways to weaken undesirable behaviors and strengthen desirable ones. The analysis of behavior and subsequent intervention to modify or replace undesirable behavior require teachers to be keen observers and behavioral technicians in the classroom. Supervisors must be aware of the latest and best scientific information about behavior if they are to be able to help teachers fulfill their role as facilitators of learning.

In numerous surveys, practicing teachers have indicated that teacher education institutions have been negligent in helping them attain needed proficiencies in handling classroom discipline.[8] Teacher training must become less general and more specifically targeted to special problems of students in schools. An extended field experience in which pre-service teachers have a chance to develop needed competencies to deal with disruptive behavior in real classrooms will do much to strengthen teacher education programs. Until that goal is achieved, the focus must be on in-service training of teachers, especially new teachers, to help them achieve the competencies needed for maintaining order in a classroom and helping students in the development of self-discipline.

There has been a growing emphasis in school districts on setting stricter standards of behavior for students. Suspensions and expulsions of students who violate school rules are seen as deterrents to disruptive behavior. Court decisions on student rights have provided procedural safeguards for school exclusions, and school officials may be liable for damages if they violate these or other rights of students.

Alternatives to external suspension from school such as the "time-out room," a room staffed with counselors to help students work out problems, have been instituted in many secondary schools. "Internal suspension" requires students to attend school, but be isolated from their regular classes. Such suspensions are usually given students for minor offenses such as smoking, skipping classes, or failing to serve detention. One high school adopted such a plan after an analysis of data on suspensions indicated that a student body of 1676 students lost 3500 student days to suspension, the equivalent of *19* school years.

One important action a supervisor can take in helping a teacher deal with disruptive behavior in the classroom is to provide an organized way of viewing the problem. Because the causes of disruptive behavior are multiple and because each student has an individual reason for being disruptive, it is unlikely that student behavior will reflect a coherent pattern. We suggest that the supervisor can be most helpful by assisting the teacher in comprehending the "pattern" of teacher response to disruptive behavior.

---

[8] Fred Pigge, "Teacher Competencies: Need, Proficiency, and Where Proficiency Was Developed," *Journal of Teacher Education* 29 (July–August, 1978): 70–76.

Modern supervisors must function as behavioral consultants to classroom teachers as they deal with day-to-day discipline problems. They must also help plan alternative programs for working with disruptive youth such as the time-out room or internal suspension. Helping teachers find positive rather than punitive methods of modifying student behavior remains an important task of the supervisor. Supervisors cannot make discipline problems vanish from the classroom, but they can help teachers improve their effectiveness and thus help students achieve their full potential.

While teacher responses to disruption are diverse, they are not nearly as numerous or unpredictable as student behaviors and, therefore, can be classified into a conceptual model. One attempt to construct a model of teacher responses to disruption categorized such actions into four groups: (1) avoid, (2) suppress, (3) defuse, and (4) restructure. According to this model, when teachers take action to respond to disruptive student behavior, the intention of the action is either to avoid the problem, suppress it, defuse it, or change the environment in an attempt to deal with the problem.

Examples of avoidance responses are ignoring student disruptive behaviors altogether, or responding in ways that are purposefully unrelated to the exhibited behavior. For example, a teacher observing a student punching another student across the aisle might request that everyone open the textbooks and begin answering the odd questions at the end of the chapter.

Teacher responses that attempt to defuse disruptive behavior also deal with effects, but are slightly different from avoidance and suppression responses. Here, the teacher is attempting to take the steam out of the situation causing the disruption. Behavior modification "economies," for instance, seek to lessen the problem by altering the reward pattern of the offender, rather than by dealing with the problem itself. In the example of the "puncher," the teacher might attempt to take the students outside the classroom and get them involved in a different activity as a diversion. It is hoped that by defusing the problem, behavior will return to acceptable limits.

Finally, teachers may seek to meet problems of disruptive behavior by restructuring or manipulating the environment. With this response, the teacher is directly concerned with causation. The student who is punching the other may be doing so because he is a frustrated nonreader or because he does not have physical education until the last period of the day. The only solution seems to be to restructure the situation or tolerate the behavior.

In its most basic form such a response model is immediately useful to teachers in analyzing classroom disruption/response interaction in their learning spaces and in plotting comprehensive strategies to meet various forms of student disruptive behavior. The model serves as a way of seeing what is going on.

Such a paradigm might also be useful to entire schools as they seek to systematize and coordinate their collective response to major types of disruptive behavior. Are there behaviors, school personnel might ask, that are of the nuisance variety, unworthy of an institutional response? Are there behaviors that the teaching staff agrees are near "sins"? Are there types of behavior in the school that might be best handled by diversionary tactics? Are there problems so basic that the learning environment itself must be altered to change the disruptive behavior?

Viewing disruption through the lens of the teacher's response might also be valuable to educators in assessing their "pattern" of behaviors to meet disruptive student behavior. Is every teacher or school response, for example, a restructuring strategy or a strategy of the suppression variety?

Through such a model the supervisor may help the teacher study classroom interaction that relates to discipline events. Over time, by cross-referencing teacher behaviors with student behaviors, the supervisor and teacher may be able to identify some global strategies to deal with disruption. Not only would the definition of disruption be sharpened, but major contradictions in teacher response to disruptive students would also be illuminated. Beyond a simple model suggested by the supervisor lies the complex task of categorizing, referencing, and testing combinations of responses to meet the challenge of student disruption. The supervisory contribution would the initiation of an organized inquiry by the classroom teacher, rather than a "bag of tricks" that cannot meet every contingency.

AVOID	SUPPRESS
RESTRUCTURE	DEFUSE

Figure 5.1
Teacher Responses to Student Disruption

WORKING WITH HANDICAPPED STUDENTS — IMPLICATIONS OF PL 94-142

The 1970s represented an era of significant progress for handicapped students. Public concern has resulted in new laws and a major investment of public dollars directed toward handicapped persons.

Although some 195 federal laws specific to the handicapped were enacted between 1927 and 1975, the National Advisory Committee on the

Handicapped reported in 1975 that only 55 percent of handicapped children and youth were being served appropriately. Of the 195 acts passed, 61 were passed between March 1970 and November 1975. Public Law 93–380, passed in 1974, was the most important of the laws passed; it extended and amended the Elementary and Secondary Education Act of 1965 and established a national policy on equal educational opportunity.

The most far-reaching and significant federal act passed affecting the handicapped was Public Law 94–142, the Education for All Handicapped Children Act of 1975, which was an amendment to Public Law 93-380. PL 94-142 has been described by many educators as a "Bill of Rights for the Handicapped." This law sets forth specific procedures that school districts must carry out to establish due process for handicapped students. The most important feature of the law is that all handicapped students between ages three and twenty-one must have available to them a free and appropriate public education. That includes an emphasis on the regular class as the preferred instructional base for all children.

It is the feature of reversing the historical method of referring handicapped *out* of regular classes that makes PL 94-142 unique. It also has major implications for classroom teachers and supervisory personnel who implement the act.

The right to education means that children with handicaps are eligible for all programs and activities sponsored by the school. This includes cheerleading, athletics, and other extracurricular activities. Children with handicaps can no longer be excluded from course offerings, most notably vocational courses.

PL 94-142 also prohibits discriminatory evaluation. Testing and evaluation materials must be selected and administered so as to not be culturally discriminatory. No single test or procedure can be used as the sole criterion for determining educational placement in a program.

Abeson and Zettel[9] outlined the history of PL 94-142 and pointed out what we strongly believe, namely, that handicapped children are first children, and second, children with special needs.

Working with children with handicaps requires an individualized instructional plan much like a plan used for all children in a regular classroom. It requires a substantial amount of diagnostic information about present and past academic and social performance. Finally, it requires teachers and supervisory personnel to project what specific needs each handicapped child may have and prescribe special programs to meet those needs.

The Individual Education Plan (IEP) provision of PL 94-142 that became practice on October 1, 1977 was really a model for instruction

---

[9] Alan Abeson and Jeffrey Zettel, "The Quiet Revolution: Education for All Handicapped Children Act of 1975," *Exceptional Children* 44 (October 1977): 115–28.

that all good teachers should follow.[10] Collecting diagnostic data, setting goals and objectives, selecting instructional materials, and evaluating student performance are all steps in the instructional process. There are in the instructional process important activities teachers must consider for handicapped students. Table 5.2 illustrates these considerations. (The reader may wish to contrast this table with the model for instructional development in Figure 3.1, p. 53.)

Table 5.2
Developing IEP for Handicapped Students

SETTING GOALS

> Basis, life-oriented, attainable goals are more important than global, unrealistic goals.

SELECTING SPECIFIC OBJECTIVES

> Teachers should take into consideration such factors as the child's attention span, level of cognitive functioning, level of written and verbal communication, and ability to participate in various academic and nonacademic activities of the school.

SELECTING INSTRUCTIONAL MATERIALS

> A variety of curriculum materials are needed for handicapped children—both teacher-made and commercial. Those materials must be appropriate if they are to help implement the objectives set for each child. Materials should be selected or constructed to fit the child's level of proficiency.

EVALUATING STUDENT PERFORMANCE

> Models of norm-referenced tests rarely apply to handicapped students. Evaluation should be skill based and continuous. A diagnostic profile of skills should be used to determine whether or not a student should move on to the next objective or receive further instruction on the same objective.

MAINSTREAMING

Mainstreaming has been defined in many ways, most of which center on moving handicapped children from segregated special education classes

---

[10] L. Jay Lev, "Public Law 94–142: The Challenge for Individualized Instruction of Handicapped Students in the Public Schools," *Impact* 13, (1978): 21–23.

into "normal" classrooms. Since the implementation of special education classes in the United States, segregated classroom environments have been the most popular method of educating handicapped children. Because children were labeled according to the severity of their handicaps and grouped into uniform categories in special classes, they were removed from what educators titled the "mainstream."

PL 94–142 mandates that the most appropriate education for handicapped children should be the least restrictive setting. This means that handicapped students should be integrated into, not segregated from, the normal program of the school. It does *not* mean the wholesale return of all exceptional children in special classes to regular classes.

Mainstreaming means looking at educational needs and creative programs that will help general educators serve handicapped children in a regular setting. It does not imply that specialists will no longer be needed, but that they and other classroom teachers must be willing to combine efforts and work cooperatively to provide the most appropriate program for all children.[11]

The supervisor who works with teachers to implement mainstreaming must help those teachers acquire the necessary knowledge and skills to successfully carry out the concept's components. Planning must precede implementation of mainstreaming programs. Classroom teachers must be able to carry out the steps in developing individual education plans for handicapped students. They must also overcome fears that they cannot teach handicapped children. Specialists must work with teachers to provide clear descriptions of children's problems and guidelines for handling them. Teachers must become acquainted with materials and techniques that fit handicapped students. Supervisory personnel should be able to provide direct assistance to both children and teachers if necessary with follow-up programs to check on student progress.[12]

Legal decisions and legislation have made it clear that the rights of all children must be respected in our schools. Unfortunately, legal decisions and legislation won't insure the development of adequate or appropriate programs. In-service education will be necessary to provide teachers with more specialized skills to deal with specific behavioral and academic problems. Mainstreaming can succeed only with a strong partnership of specialists, teachers, and supervisory persons working cooperatively to provide the most appropriate education for all children.

DEVELOPING PROGRAMS FOR THE GIFTED

It has been estimated that over 2.5 million young Americans are endowed with academic, artistic, or social talents far beyond the talents of their

[11] Pamela Cochrane and David Westling, "The Principal and Mainstreaming: Ten Suggestions for Success," *Educational Leadership* 34, (April 1977): 506–10.

[12] Ellen Kavanagh, "A Classroom Teacher Looks at Mainstreaming," *The Elementary School Journal* 77 (March 1977): 318–22.

peers. These "gifted" children come from all levels of society, all races, and both sexes.[13]

Until recently, gifted children received little attention in public schools. Parents had to seek out costly private schools, which many parents could not afford. Most American educators and the supporting public felt the poor and handicapped desperately needed extra attention and balked at singling out an "elitist" group of bright children in public schools.

In 1972, Congress established the Federal Office for the Gifted and Talented. That office was charged with helping identify and develop talented youngsters. With funding increased in 1978, the Office for the Gifted and Talented has fostered a resurgence of interest in gifted children.

All fifty states have programs for the gifted, but there are still problems of identifying and providing for talented youngsters. For instance, many gifted children cannot be identified by just IQ tests. New yardsticks for identifying the gifted have to be used including creativity, advanced social skills, and even exceptional physical aptitude such as the kind that marks fine surgeons, watch repairers, or engineers.

As a group, talented and gifted children tend to learn faster and retain more than their peers. A gifted child is also a divergent thinker. All of these characteristics can be unsettling in a class, and sometimes gifted and talented children have been seen as "troublemakers." Other gifted children are turned off by boring classes and become alienated from school.

Teachers, faced with increased demands to improve low achievers' basic skills and to also provide for handicapped and special education students, often find little time to work with the gifted and talented.

A number of instructional models have been proposed for helping classroom teachers develop curricular plans for gifted students in regular classrooms. Two of these are the Enrichment Triad Model[14] and the Self-Directed Learning Program.[15]

In addition, an exemplary longitudinal research study has been conducted at Johns Hopkins University dealing with mathematically gifted junior high school students. The results of this study have provided information on facilitating the learning of gifted students in the areas of creativity, achievement, productivity, and motivation.[16]

The models and research on the gifted and talented have helped provide a sound basis for differentiating instruction and evaluating programs for the gifted.

---

[13] Merrill Sheils et al., "The Gifted Child," *Time Magazine* 92 (October 23, 1978): 108.

[14] Joseph Renzulli, *The Enrichment Triad Model: A Guide for Developing Defensible Programs for the Gifted and Talented* (Wetherfield, Conn.: Creative Learning Press, 1977).

[15] Donald Treffinger and J. F. Feldhusen, *Teaching Creative Thinking and Problem Sovling* (Dubuque, Iowa: Kendall/Hunt, 1977).

[16] J. C. Stanley, D. P. Keating, and Lynn Fox, *Mathematical Talent: Discovery, Description, and Development* (Baltimore, Md.: Johns Hopkins Press, 1974).

Differentiating instruction, fostering creativity, allowing for independent study, and encouraging peer learning are all important tasks of teaching. They are especially important for nurturing the diverse aptitudes and abilities of gifted and talented children. Organizational procedures such as cluster grouping, mainstreaming, and part-day grouping have all been used with the gifted and talented.

Supervisors must work closely with teachers to provide them with skills for identifying gifted and talented students. They must also help them organize materials and activities to foster a climate of creativity for those students. Indeed, if a climate for creativity exists in classrooms, all children—not just the gifted and talented—will be the benefactors.

In Table 5.3 some well-known gifted persons are identified as they were originally perceived by parents, teachers, and other adults.

ACCEPTING CULTURAL DIVERSITY

By design, our schools are the melting pot of our society. Court decisions and legislation have mandated that children of different races and cultures be provided with the opportunity to learn with those of other races and cultures. While different cultures mix in our schools, we are at the same time committing ourselves as educators to cultural diversity through multicultural education.[17]

The move toward multicultural education has brought on new demands for supervisors and teachers. Recognizing cultural pluralism and the need for creating school environments that radiate cultural diversity is but the first step in building school programs that will maximize individual opportunity. Classroom teachers must be trained to examine text materials for racism, class prejudice, and sexism. They must also get help in developing new curricula to enhance and promote cultural diversity.

Organizing time, space, resources, and personnel in a school or school system to facilitate maximum alternative experiences for all children demands that a supervisor understand staffing patterns that reflect our culturally pluralistic society. It also demands that a supervisor be able to design and implement in-service programs to train staff to successfully implement multicultural education.

Developing an in-service program that will help teachers teach in a culturally pluralistic school involves three important steps:

1. Teachers must understand the concept of culture. They must be able to examine a variety of cultural traits and be able to

---

[17] Carl A. Grant, ed., *Multicultural Education: Commitments, Issues, and Applications* (Washington, D.C.: Association for Supervision and Curriculum Development, 1977).

emphasize similarities and differences among and within cultures.
2. Teachers must teach the United States ethnic and cultural experience. Too often units and lessons are prepared that deal

---

Table 5.3
Gifted and Talented?

1. YOUNG NEW JERSEY LAD—Grade school teacher wrote his mother that he should be switched to remedial school because he was inattentive, indolent, and his brain was seriously "addled." Student's name: THOMAS ALVA EDISON.

2. SON OF A GREAT AMERICAN DOCTOR—Went to medical school but dreamed of playing second base for the Boston Red Sox. Nearly signed baseball contract before his father coaxed him back to medicine. Became world's greatest brain surgeon. Ballplayer's name: DR. HARVEY CUSHING.

3. YOUNG DANE BORN IN 1805 NEAR COPENHAGEN—In early years he wasn't worth the powder to blow him to Helsinki. Nearly starved as a ham actor. At age 30 wrote a book titled "Eventyr" ("Fairy Tayles"). Ham actor's name: HANS CHRISTIAN ANDERSON.

4. FRENCH LAD—Family in despair, all he ever did was go fishing. Never studied science till he was in his 20s. French kid's name: LOUIS PASTEUR.

5. LITTLE GERMAN "DUMMKOPF"—Born 1879. Parents worried that he was seriously stupid because he couldn't speak till he was over three. At 20, got a job as a grubby little office worker and spent a lot of time scribbling mathematical doodles. At 30, his doodles caught on in the scientific world. Little dummkopf's name: ALBERT EINSTEIN.

6. A DRIFTER—Turned down by West Point, he got a job as a soda jerk. Improved his lot at a bottling works. Finally reached the top as a haberdashery salesman. Name: HARRY S. TRUMAN.

7. A FAILURE IN SCHOOL—In April, 1881 the parents of a small English boy were dismayed to read a report card from St. George's School in Ascot. Among other remarks were these:
   Diligence: "He is not to be trusted to do any one thing."
   Times late: "20. Disgraceful."
   General conduct: "A constant trouble to everybody, always in some scrape or other."
   Student's name: WINSTON CHURCHILL.

8. SCHOOL DROPOUTS—

   HENRY KAISER—President, Kaiser Industries
   RICHARD DEUPREE—President, General Electric
   ERNEST NORRIS—President, Proctor and Gamble
   H. L. HUNT—One of the world's richest men, dropped out in 4th grade.
   TRUMAN CAPOTE—Author
   WILLIAM FAULKNER—Author, Nobel Prize Winner

with particular countries such as Japan, Mexico, or Spain. Although the study of cultures of other countries is important, the ethnic experience in the United States is unique. For instance, the growing number of Hispanic Americans makes it important that we study this group within the setting of the United States if we are to understand this group's importance and impact in our society.

3. Ethnic and cultural content should be integrated throughout the curriculum, not just in social studies or special courses such as Black Studies. All disciplines can be used to stress the importance of different cultures and to dispel myths and stereotypes about certain groups.[18]

SUMMARY

Who are special needs children? The United States Office of Education has identified them as children who fall within the following twelve major categories:

Mentally retarded	Hard-of-hearing
Speech impaired	Multiple handicapped
Orthopedically impaired	Specific learning disabilities
Visually handicapped	Seriously emotionally disturbed
Deaf	Other health impaired
Deaf-Blind	Gifted or talented

We have also identified another group of children, the culturally different, as children with special needs. Disruptive youngsters are yet another group of children with special needs.

Accepting pupil diversity is a major theme of this chapter. Teachers must see children as they are and provide positive growth conditions for them. This is not always easy, and assistance must often come from those in supervisory positions.

With the passage of PL 94–142 and other legislation, handicapped youngsters now must be taught in regular classes rather than isolated in special classes away from the mainstream of the school. Legal decisions, as well as legislation, have made it clear that the rights of all children must be observed.

Diagnosing needs, developing new materials and programs, differentiating instruction, and changing organization structures for special students require that teachers in regular classrooms receive extensive in-service training. Supervisors must work closely with teachers so they can effectively organize time, space, resources, and personnel to provide the

---

[18] Gwendolyn Baker, "Instructional Priorities in a Culturally Pluralistic School," *Educational Leadership* 32, (December 1974): 176–78.

learning experiences needed by students with special needs. Table 5.4 provides a list of organizations that deal with children with special needs. Selected periodicals with a special needs emphasis appear in Table 5.5.

Table 5.4
National Organizations and Agencies
Concerned with Special Needs Children

ACLU Juvenile Rights Project
22 East 40th Street
New York, NY 10016

American Academy for Cerebral Palsy
University Hospital School
Iowa City, IA 52240

**American Association for the
   Education of Severely and
   Profoundly Handicapped**
1600 West Armory Way
Garden View Suite
Seattle, WA 98119

**American Association
   for Gifted Children**
15 Gramercy Park
New York, NY 10003

American Epilepsy Society
Department of Neurology
University of Minnesota
Box 341, Mayo Building
Minneapolis, MN 55455

American Foundation for the Blind
15 West 16th Street
New York, NY 10011

American Medical Association
535 North Dearborn Street
Chicago, IL 60610

American Psychological Association
1200 17th Street, NW
Washington, DC 20036

**Association for Children with
   Learning Disabilities**
2200 Brownsville Road
Pittsburgh, PA 16210

**Association for the Aid of
   Crippled Children**
345 East 46th Street
New York, NY 10017

**Association for Education of the
   Visually Handicapped**
919 Walnut
Philadelphia, PA 19107

**Bureau for Education of the
   Handicapped**
400 6th Street
Donohoe Building
Washington, DC 20202

Council for Exceptional Children
1920 Association Drive
Reston, VA 22091

**Institute for the Study of Mental
   Retardation and Related
   Disabilities**
130 South First
University of Michigan
Ann Arbor, MI 48108

**Muscular Dystrophy Association
   of America**
810 7th Avenue
New York, NY 10019

**National Association for
   Retarded Citizens**
2709 Avenue E, East
P.O. Box 6109
Arlington, TX 76011

**National Association of
   Social Workers**
2 Park Avenue
New York, NY 10016

Table 5.4—*continued*

National Committee for Multi-Handicapped Children
239 14th Street
Niagara Falls, NY 14303

National Institute of Health
United States Department of Health, Education, and Welfare
Washington, DC 20014

National Rehabilitation Association
1522 "K" Street, NW
Washington, DC 20005

President's Committee on Employment of the Handicapped
U.S. Department of Labor
Washington, DC 20210

President's Committee on Mental Retardation
Regional Office Building #3
Room 2614
7th and D Streets, SW
Washington, DC 20201

Table 5.5
Periodicals Dealing With Students' Special Needs

AAESPH Review (American Association for the Education of the Severely and Profoundly Handicapped)

American Educational Research Journal

American Journal of Mental Deficiency

American Journal of Psychology

Aviso (Journal of Special Education)

Childhood Education

Child Welfare

The Deaf American

Developmental Psychology

Exceptional Children

Gifted Child Quarterly

Harvard Educational Review

Journal of Abnormal Child Psychology

Journal of Abnormal Psychology

Journal of Child Psychology and Psychiatry

Journal of Creative Behavior

Journal of Learning Disabilities

Journal of Negro Education

Journal of Nervous and Mental Disease

Journal of Psychology

Journal of Social Psychology

Journal of Special Education

Journal of Teacher Education

Perceptual and Motor Skills

Personnel and Guidance Journal

Phi Delta Kappan

Psychology in the Schools

Rehabilitation Digest

Review of Educational Research

Teacher of the Deaf

Suggested Learning Activities

1. Write a "Bill of Rights" for students with special needs in your school district.
2. Develop a teaching unit on traditional Indian life in America past to present.
3. Prepare a list of creative activities classroom teachers could use with gifted students in an elementary, middle, and high school.
4. With the help of colleagues, develop an alternative plan for dealing with disruptive youth that would not include suspension or expulsion from school.
5. Prepare a plan for mainstreaming handicapped students into the extracurricular activities of a school.
6. Compile a list of community resources available for students with special needs.

Books to Review

Goldstein, Herbert. *Mainstreaming.* Guilford, Conn.: Special Learning Corporation, 1978.

Grant, Carl A., ed. *Multicultural Education: Commitments, Issues, and Applications.* Washington, D.C.: Association for Supervision and Curriculum Development, 1977.

Hammill, Donald, and Bartel, Nettie. *Teaching Children with Learning and Behavior Problems.* 2nd ed. Boston: Allyn & Bacon, 1978.

Kounin, Jacob S. *Discipline and Group Management in Classrooms.* New York: Holt, Rinehart & Winston, 1970.

Madsen, Charles, and Madsen, Clifford. *Teaching/Discipline Behavioral Principals Toward a Positive Approach.* Boston: Allyn & Bacon, 1970.

Meyen, Edward L. *Exceptional Children and Youth.* Denver: Love Publishing, 1978.

Stephens, Thomas M. *Teaching Skills to Children with Learning and Behavior Disorders.* Columbus, Ohio: Charles E. Merrill, 1977.

Worell, Judith, and Nelson, C. Michael. *Managing Instructional Problems.* New York: McGraw-Hill, 1974.

6

Leading Effective In-service Programs

INTRODUCTION

Today's educational community faces important challenges associated with both stabilization and change. Declining enrollment; reduced public support for public education along with a continuing tax revolt; changing pupil, parent, and social needs; and pressing affirmative action initiatives all require a level of responsiveness and creativity rarely demanded of a social institution.[1]

There have been numerous conferences, papers, and models outlining changing needs and priorities of in-service education. Many individuals representing a variety of special interest groups have looked to new support systems, such as teacher renewal centers and teacher education centers, as alternative paths to traditional graduate courses and in-service workshops for teachers.

---

[1] Ronald Crowell and L. Richard Harring, "Teacher Education Faculty Development," *Journal of Teacher Education* 29 (May–June, 1978): 7–8.

The need for teacher renewal activities that will enhance the quality of teaching is hardly unknown. In spite of that expressed need, in large measure teachers are masters of their own destinies. After finishing an undergraduate teacher education program and entering the profession, there are no formal sanctions for teachers who fail to become better practitioners. If teachers fail to see a need for continued professional growth, they may be destined to a career of limited skills, closed minds, and slight knowledge of children or the discipline they teach.

Since a prime purpose of supervision is to provide the leadership necessary to promote a continuing climate of improvement, it is vital that supervisors be able to plan and conduct effective in-service programs.

There are essential steps in developing an in-service plan (Table 6.1). Table 6.2 outlines a survey of in-service needs for a school while, Table 6.3 reports on a survey of training needs for all teachers in a state.

Table 6.1
A Model for In-service Education

Conduct an Assessment of Need
   A. Identify the target learners.
   B. Determine a strategy for learner needs assessment—goals and objectives, test data, survey data, nature and degree of involvement in in-service project.
   C. Conduct learner needs assessment.
   D. Assign priorities to identified learner needs—tasks.
   E. Collect baseline data regarding target learners.

Make Policy Decision to Initiate an In-service Project
   A. Involve target learners, administrators, supervisors in identifying program objectives.
   B. Designate supervisory personnel (leadership agents) and support personnel to provide leadership for the project.
   C. Develop budget and process guidelines.
   D. Set a time frame for the project.
   E. Design in-service activities, materials, resources.

Develop Evaluative Measures to Assess Developed In-service Program Objectives and Related Activities
   A. Design evaluative measures to assess competencies of leadership staff.
   B. Institute monitoring and formative evaluation regarding in-service project objectives and activities.
   C. Develop evaluative measures to assess support elements, resources.
   D. Conduct summative evaluation of in-service objectives, activities, leadership and supportive staff.

Table 6.2

SURVEY OF IN-SERVICE NEEDS

I. I would be willing to participate in the following (check one or more):

_____ Workshops on listening skills—Interpersonal relations
_____ Interdisciplinary teaming
_____ Curriculum development in my subject area—Scope and sequence—Skills checklists—Writing a base or life skills curriculum
_____ Classroom management—Motivational techniques—Classroom interaction

II. I would like to participate in clinical in-service sessions (consultant in the classroom with me) where I could get help in the following areas:

_____
_____
_____

_____
_____
_____

_____
_____
_____

III. I would like to visit certain programs such as:

_____
_____
_____

IV. I would be willing to participate in workshops (check one or more):

_____ After school hours and evenings
_____ Friday evening—Saturday morning
_____ In-service days only
_____ During released time when provided substitute
_____ One–two weeks in summer

V. I'd like to receive the following if possible:

_____ In-service points
_____ Course credit
_____ Released time substitutes
_____ Trade-off time
_____ Stipends for summer writing

Table 6.3

SUMMARY OF NEED FOR TRAINING, AVAILABILITY OF TRAINING, AND TRAINER

Teaching Skills Ranked by Need for Training

Population Sampled: All Teachers, Statewide

Teaching Skill (Ranked by need for training)	Weighted percentage of teachers indicating need for a moderate or substantial amount of training in each teaching skill	Weighted percentage of teachers indicating that training was occasionally or frequently available to them during the past two years	Weighted percentage of total respondents who indicated that a particular trainer performed training in a particular teaching skill area					
			College or University Staff	Teacher Ed. Center Staff	Educational Service Agency Staff	State Department Staff	County Staff	Other
Identifying and working with exceptional students	69.9%	65.0%	23.2%	3.0%	4.6	3.6	22.8	5.0
Prescribing individualized learning activities	68.4	77.5	33.8	5.6	3.9	4.5	30.3	6.1
Teaching students to read	66.3	72.2	28.9	3.7	3.3	2.1	27.5	6.6
Identifying student needs	61.8	81.6	34.1	5.7	4.2	4.1	30.4	6.2
Increasing self-knowledge in content area	58.8	80.8	42.0	3.8	3.5	5.4	23.0	8.4
Providing multicultural activities in the classroom	55.9	49.7	14.4	2.3	1.2	4.1	15.0	4.9
Planning instructional activities	55.8	83.5	35.2	5.3	3.6	6.0	33.6	6.2
Conducting learning activities	52.5	82.5	33.5	4.9	4.2	5.2	32.9	5.9
Evaluating student performance	52.4	74.1	29.9	3.8	2.0	2.6	25.8	5.9
Using instructional media	50.9	79.9	26.2	6.5	4.0	3.6	34.8	8.2
Planning instructional objectives	47.3	79.5	35.9	4.2	2.4	4.4	28.1	5.4
Developing a plan for self-improvement	46.5	57.4	19.2	3.6	1.3	2.5	17.9	7.0
Managing the classroom	44.6	61.0	23.5	3.4	1.5	1.4	19.8	6.6
Interacting with students	40.9	62.1	21.0	3.3	1.6	2.1	15.4	6.3
Maintaining a positive personal and professional attitude	37.4	58.3	16.0	3.0	1.3	2.6	18.6	7.3
Working with other teachers	33.3	56.6	14.3	4.1	0.9	2.3	22.2	6.6

SOURCE: Adapted from JoAnn Hall, chairperson, "A Systematic Program of Continuing Education for West Virginia" (Paper prepared by the Continuing Education Task Force, Charleston, West Virginia, May 1977), p. 9.

CLINICAL METHODS OF STAFF DEVELOPMENT

Micro-teaching

Micro-teaching is a process that makes it possible for teachers to participate in an actual teaching situation and receive immediate feedback on their performance. Teaching behavior is defined in terms of specific skills or techniques so that a specific lesson might focus on a single skill. Often, observational systems are utilized to help identify particular teacher behaviors. Other systems are used to look at such teaching skills as the effective use of classroom questions and classroom management.

Micro-teaching, as a procedure, gives teachers and supervisors the opportunity to identify, define, describe, analyze, and retest certain teaching skills in a lab setting. Teachers can try out lessons on students, other teachers, and supervisors. Through the use of such techniques as films or videotapes, teachers can teach and reteach until a skill is mastered.

Clinical Supervision

The aims of traditional supervision and clinical supervision are the same—to improve instruction. In traditional supervision, however, the supervisor is the instructional expert. In clinical supervision, both the supervisor and teacher are assumed to be instructional experts. The teacher and the supervisor communicate as colleagues, with the teacher identifying concerns and the supervisor assisting the teacher in analyzing and improving teaching performance.

Morris Cogan[2] and colleagues, in the 1950s, initiated a study of supervision that led to the process of clinical supervision. Through a study of graduate students, Cogan found that suggestions on improvement of teaching coming from supervisors often fell on deaf ears. Students were not listening to supervisors because they felt supervisors were not concerned with the same problems the graduate students were experiencing in their classrooms.

In the clinical approach the teacher is not the passive recipient of supervision, but is an active partner whose participation and commitment are critical to the success of the supervisory process. Clinical supervision emphasizes teacher growth and assumes teachers possess the drive and personal resources to improve their teaching. The system is "clinical" because it depends upon direct, trained observation of classroom behaviors.[3]

As a process, clinical supervision helps the teacher to identify and

---

[2] Morris Cogan, *Clinical Supervision* (Boston: Houghton-Mifflin, 1972).

[3] Jerry Ballon et al. *Classroom Supervision and Instructional Improvement: A Synergetic Process* (Dubuque, Iowa: Kendall–Hunt, 1976), p. 8.

clarify problems, receive data from the supervisor, and develop solutions to problems with the help of the supervisor. Clinical supervision involves more supervisory time than one or two visits to a classroom.

Clinical supervisory techniques offer a number of advantages over traditional methods of supervision. They include:

1. Supervisors and teachers work together toward common objectives.
2. Supervisors can influence teaching behavior to a greater degree.
3. Teachers and supervisors have positive feelings toward the supervisory process.

Clinical supervision involves a five-step process. These five steps are discussed below.

Preobservational Conference

The preobservational conference between supervisor and teacher helps establish rapport between the two, allows the supervisor get an orientation toward the group of students to be observed, provides an opportunity for the teacher and supervisor to discuss the lesson to be taught and observed, and finally, provides a time for the supervisor and teacher to develop a contract outlining on what aspects of teaching he or she would like feedback.

Observation

The supervisor enters the classroom quietly and tries to avoid eye contact with students or teacher. The observer takes notes during the observation, particularly noting behaviors or teaching methods discussed during the preobservational conference. After the observation, the observer slips out of the classroom as quietly and unobtrusively as he or she entered.

Analysis and Strategy

At this step, the supervisor reviews her or his notes in respect to the contract, analyzing the teaching patterns and crucial incidents observed during the lesson. Often if an observational system has been used, the supervisor can refer to specific verbal behaviors, levels of questions, or classroom management techniques. (Refer to Chapter 10 for a thorough discussion of the use of observational systems.)

After the analysis, the supervisor must consider how to approach the teacher with the suggestions he or she may have developed. The supervisor must consider how defensive the teacher is and how best to approach the conference with the teacher.

Supervisory Conference

During the supervisory conference the teacher obtains feedback on those aspects of teaching that concerned her or him. Specific contract items are reviewed first, with additional feedback on other behavioral patterns later. As a final step in the observational conference, the supervisor may help the teacher plan the next lesson. The new lesson will incorporate the improvements identified during the conference.

Postconference Analysis

The final step in the clinical supervision process is a postconference analysis of the total clinical process. This step is really an in-service process for the supervisor. The supervisor can check to see if the teacher's professional integrity was respected during the conference, if the teacher had time to fully discuss specific contract items reviewed, and if the contract was satisfactory.[4]

The combination of micro-teaching in a lab setting with clinical analysis of a live classroom holds promise for improving teaching. There are limitations in both the clinical and micro-teaching designs. The one-to-one relationship between supervisor and teacher is time-consuming and expensive; videotaping equipment is costly. There are also valuable group interaction opportunities that may be lost. Finally, the focus on self found in the clinical design may retard looking outward for new ideas and advice.[5]

COMPETENCY-BASED STAFF DEVELOPMENT

Another approach to professional development with a focus on the individual is the competency-based staff development model. In this approach no attempt is made to impose any particular instructional strategy or technique as best for everyone. There are five characteristics of the competency-based model:

1. All staff development efforts focus on the learner (teacher or administrator). Each learner is involved in designating the strategy necessary to develop a specific competency.
2. Instructional modules are prepared to help the teacher or administrator reach his or her professional objective. The instructional objectives are

---

[4] See Charles A. Reavis, *Teacher Improvement Through Clinical Supervision*, Phi Delta Kappa Fastback Series no. 3 (Bloomington, Ind.: Phi Delta Kappa, 1978) for an thorough discussion of the clinical supervision process.

[5] Ben Harris, *Supervisory Behavior in Education*, 2nd ed. (Englewood Cliffs, N.J.: Prentice-Hall, 1975), p. 99.

criterion referenced so that the competence attained by a particular participant is independent of reference to performance of others. Competencies are developed or assessed on three types of criteria: knowledge, performance, and consequences.

3. Each participant sets a target date for attainment of a particular objective view as essential to the achievement of a stated competency.
4. Developmental activities occur in a field setting. Simulated conditions are sometimes used to reduce the risk element.
5. Emphasis is placed on exit rather than entrance requirements. Objectives are clearly defined so that all parties know when the objective has been attained.[6]

There have been a number of approaches for identifying both pre- and in-service teacher competencies. Depending on what study the reader reviews, the competencies may be listed as general, specific, or sometimes "critical."

Many states have moved toward competency-based certification for initial certification as well as recertification of teachers. Florida has been a leader in developing competency tests for teachers and demanding mastery of identified teaching competencies. Effective July 1, 1980, applicants for initial regular certification must pass a comprehensive written examination based on Florida's essential competencies. Those competencies were identified by various professional specialization organizations (i.e., Florida Council of Teachers of English, Florida Council of Teachers of Mathematics) under studies coordinated by the Council on Teacher Education.

In making the transition from staff development for renewal credits to staff development for professional growth, one would assume that all teaching personnel would be motivated to acquire new competencies or refine present ones. Unfortunately, some teachers do not want to disrupt the status quo. They see change as a threat. Other teachers simply do not have the time or energy to spend time in developmental activities. Roth[7] concluded from a study of teachers that teachers are busy people. Primary teachers work an average of 43.9 hours a week, intermediate teachers, 47.8 hours; middle school teachers, 47.1 hours; and high school teachers, 51.1 hours per week. With family and other out-of-school obligations, there remains little time for professional development.

Clinical supervision and other supervisory processes, where informative (not judgmental) feedback is provided participants, are helping teachers and administrators become more supportive of professional development.[8]

---

[6] Phyllis D. Hamilton, *Competency-Based Teacher Education* (Menlo Park, Calif.: Pacific Coast Publishers, 1973), p. 4.
[7] Robert Roth, "A Study of the Use of Teacher Time in Oregon Public Schools," *Bulletin of the Oregon School Council* (March 1965): 22.
[8] Charles Beegle and Roy Edelfelt, eds., *Staff Development: Staff Liberation* (Washington D.C.: Association for Supervision and Curriculum Development, 1977), pp. 83–84.

To overcome the problem of lack of time for professional development, many school districts are providing an afternoon a week where students are dismissed early or permanent substitutes are hired to relieve teachers of classroom duties. The Stamford Comprehensive Plan for Middle School Development, discussed later in this chapter, has a provision for two afternoons a month where students are dismissed early so teachers can participate in in-service activities.

Those who work with clinical supervision and competency-based staff development recognize that good human relations are the key to the success of both processes. Supervisors must spend considerable time establishing rapport with teachers and administrators. Chapter 7 will explore in detail the ways supervisors can foster effective human relations.

SCHOOL-BASED STAFF DEVELOPMENT PROGRAMS

School-based staff development programs operate on the following premises: (1) teachers should be involved in the identification and articulation of their own training needs; (2) growth experiences for teachers, as well as for children, should be individualized. If such growth experiences are to be meaningful, they should belong to the learner, not be imposed by someone else; and (3) the single school is the largest and proper unit for educational change.

Florida has been a leader in legislating school-based staff development programs. Gordon Lawrence, in a paper prepared for the Florida Department of Education, presented many findings that support the establishment of school-based staff development programs. Nine of his findings are listed below:

1. Teacher attitudes are more likely to be influenced in school-based than in college-based inservice programs.
2. School-based programs in which teachers participate as helpers to each other and planners of inservice activities tend to have greater success in accomplishing their objectives than do programs which are conducted by college or other outside personnel without the assistance of teachers.
3. School-based inservice programs that emphasize self-instruction by teachers have a strong record of effectiveness.
4. Inservice education programs that have differentiated training experiences for different teachers (that is, "individualized") are more likely to accomplish their objectives than are programs that have common activities for all participants.
5. Inservice education programs that place the teacher in active roles (constructing and generating materials, ideas, and behavior) are more likely to accomplish their objectives than are programs that place the teacher in a receptive role (accepting ideas and behavior prescriptions not of his or her own making).

6. Inservice education programs that emphasize demonstrations, supervised trials, and feedback are more likely to accomplish their goals than are programs in which the teachers are expected to store up ideas and behavior prescriptions for a future time.
7. Inservice education programs in which teachers share and provide mutual assistance to each other are more likely to accomplish their objectives than are programs in which each teacher does separate work.
8. Teachers are more likely to benefit from inservice education activities that are linked to a general effort of the school than they are from "single-shot" programs that are not part of a general staff development plan.
9. Teachers are more likely to benefit from inservice programs in which they can choose goals and activities for themselves, as contrasted with programs in which the goals and activities are preplanned.[9]

PEER SUPERVISION

Peer supervision as a concept implies that teachers can supervise each other and provide observation, analysis, and feedback to their peers. Peer supervision is still a disturbingly slippery concept for many leaders in the field.[10] In reviewing the term, one does not know whether it is describing a system in which teachers are organized into helping teams under the direction of a supervisor, or whether the total teacher team has the responsibility for the improvement of instruction.

Teacher militancy in recent years has led teachers to demand greater control over their own teaching. Unions have pressed for more responsibility for teachers in providing in-service education, evaluation, and other supervisory tasks. Teacher education center councils, where teachers have majority voting rights, have given rise to renewed efforts to give teachers more control over their own destinies. Indeed, teacher organizations have lobbied for controlling access to the profession, selection, and retention of staff members. Because of confusion about the roles of supervisors, evaluation of teachers has become a dilemma for teachers and supervisors. For instance, teachers do not know whether a supervisor's visit is for instructional improvement, administrative evaluation, or both.

There are several drawbacks to peer supervision. As it is defined in many districts, teachers do not know if peer supervision is designed for improvement of instruction, evaualation, or both. Supervisors are also reluctant to share part of their domain of teacher evaluation with teachers. Finally, teachers must have an openness and trust among peers that exist in few places. Tenure laws and declining enrollment mean the

---

[9] Gordon Lawrence, "Patterns of Effective Inservice Education," monograph (Tallahassee: Florida State Department of Education, 1974).
[10] Robert J. Alfonso, "Will Peer Supervision Work?" *Educational Leadership* 34 (May 1977): 594–601.

prospect of increased numbers of senior teachers. With the security of tenured positions, such teachers may be resistant to supervisory efforts to upgrade instruction. Will peers be able to effect changes on those persons?

Peer supervision does hold promise as an adjunct to a broadly based program for instructional improvement. It is clear that the influence of supervisors in the instructional improvement process can be enhanced by the legitimate involvement of teachers in that process. However, supervisors must provide the linkage necessary between self-directed improvement and improvement that results from formal, organizationally-directed supervision.

TEACHER EDUCATION CENTERS

The teacher education center concept is a unified approach to the study of teaching and supervision. It is a coordinated program of pre-service and in-service experiences planned and administered cooperatively by universities, unions, private firms, governmental agencies, and public school systems.[11]

The teacher center is an approach to in-service education, but not the only approach. Teacher centers supported by federal funds must be governed by a board composed of a majority of classroom teachers. In 1978 the federal government appropriated $8.25 million to create and support teacher centers. Fifty-five local school districts and five universities were awarded grants. Additional funding for teacher centers continued in the years after 1978.

Both the National Educational Association (NEA) and American Federation of Teachers (AFT) have received National Institute of Education (NIE) grants to assist members with teacher center projects. NEA took a different approach than AFT in establishing teacher centers.[12] NEA began teacher center projects in 1977 at fifty-two sites in twenty-five states. AFT did not select sites and develop programs, but chose instead to work through its local affiliates providing help and assistance when requested.

In 1975, a national clearinghouse for teacher centers, the Teachers' Centers Exchange, was funded by NIE and housed in the Far West Laboratory for Educational Research and Development in San Francisco.

---

[11] Roy Edelfelt and Tamar Orvell, *Teacher Centers—Where, What, Why?* Phi Delta Kappa Fastback Series, no. 117 (Bloomington, Ind.: Phi Delta Kappa, 1978).

[12] "Teacher Centers," *Instructor Magazine* 88 (November 1978), pp. 32–36.

The clearinghouse has contact with over 350 teacher centers around the country.

Teacher centers can be placed in one of five categories: school district, independent, consortium, legislative, or union. Even though many centers have elements of more than one of these categories, there are unique characteristics of each of the five.

School district centers usually avoid accepting funds from sources outside the district. They remain "close" to the teachers and conduct workshops, offer graduate courses, and help develop materials for teachers in the district.

Independent teacher centers until recently comprised over 50 percent of all teacher centers; today less than 10 percent are independent. Independent centers receive funds from foundations, business donations, and earned income including that from workshops and sale of teaching materials.

Consortium teacher centers are based on cooperation of a number of groups both in and out of education. Consortium centers operate on the premise that professional growth of teachers involves pre-service, in-service, and the surrounding community, and all of those elements are incorporated in consortium teacher centers.

Legislative teacher centers are those established by legislation in a state. Florida is unique in that the Florida Teacher Center Act of 1973 mandated that each of Florida's sixty-seven school districts help sponsor a teacher center. The state legislature set aside five dollars per student to be spent on staff development, with three of those dollars going directly into teacher centers. Several legislative acts after the 1973 Teacher Center Act provided further aid and direction to teacher centers including the sharing of a portion of funds between colleges of education and teacher centers. Florida's teacher centers have been models of cooperation between school districts and the state university system.

Union teacher centers are supported and controlled by an organization representing teachers in collective bargaining. In New York City 95 percent of teachers belong to the AFT and participate in the David Wittes Education Lounge. This center is supported by union dues, and policy is dictated by the union.

Workshops, pre- and in-service courses, studies of teaching and supervision, special programs for paraprofessionals and teachers, development of materials, developing programs for children with special needs, bookmobiles, libraries, and personal tutoring are some of the services provided through teacher centers. Through centers, teachers are being offered a chance to take an active role in decisions affecting their professional growth. Teacher education centers offer a promise for professional growth and improvement of teachers, as well as a challenge to those in supervisory positions to provide new kinds of services in different settings.

IN-SERVICE FOR SUPERVISORS

The focus of this chapter has been on the leadership roles supervisors assume in developing effective in-service programs. However, supervisors themselves need professional development. Supervisors have assumed responsibility for their own development by attending seminars, conferences, summer programs, and graduate classes. Professional associations, state departments, and school districts have established supervisory development programs to help supervisors improve their own performance.

Oftentimes, without feedback, supervisors may feel they *are* providing the services teachers desire. A survey of teachers in Tennessee indicated that over 50 percent of teachers surveyed responded that the following services were not usually provided when needed:

1. Involving teachers in district-wide instructional programs.
2. Assisting in developing effective disciplinary techniques.
3. Planning inservice activities.
4. Providing teaching demonstrations.
5. Consulting with teachers on instructional problems.
6. Serving as a two-way communications link with the central office.
7. Helping describe and analyze instructional objectives.
8. Helping define instructional objectives.
9. Helping select appropriate instructional activities.
10. Helping choose methods for evaluating student progress.
11. Aiding in development of curricula.
12. Conducting or directing research.
13. Acting as a change agent.
14. Providing psychological support.
15. Suggesting new ideas and approaches for instruction.
16. Assisting in classroom organization and arrangement.[13]

When supervisors were surveyed, 82 percent of those surveyed reported heavy involvement in most teacher support services such as those listed above. It is interesting to note that supervisors had little involvement in teaching demonstrations, helping with student evaluation, or helping with discipline. A large majority of supervisors indicated a desire to increase those services where they had so little involvement.[14]

As supervisory roles change, supervisors must be keenly aware of the leadership roles they must play in the professional growth of teachers. To be effective leaders, supervisors must have both the knowledge and skills necessary to change the behavior of others. They must be able to engage

---

[13] John Lovell and Margaret Phelps, *Supervision in Tennessee* (Knoxville: Tennessee Association for Supervision and Curriculum Development, July 1976), p. 9.

[14] Ibid., pp. 14–15.

the teacher in a discussion of how the teacher perceives the supervisor-teacher relationship before supervisory strategies are selected. The need to grow professionally must not be limited to teachers, but must include those in supervisory positions.

In the following section we present a number of in-service structures that have proven effective in intersecting teacher instructional needs. These models illustrate the variety of approaches that can be designed and utilized by instructional supervisors in working with classroom teachers to improve learning.

IN-SERVICE MODELS

District Models

Teacher Orientation/Renewal Center (TORC) Pinellas County Florida School District.

Rationale:[15]
The emergence of middle schools in recent years has been, in many cases, in name only. The purpose of TORC is to introduce teachers to alternative methods of classroom management and skills development, with strategies for meeting the needs of the middle school learner. One way to involve teachers in the development and implementation of a learner-oriented classroom is to establish a center at which they can experience modeling of teacher behaviors, explore a variety of techniques of child-centered classroom management, and earn staff development component points for middle school certification or teacher certificate renewal.

In the teacher center, TORC participants explore such areas as individualization, behavior modification, behavioral objectives, diagnosis and prescription, classroom organization, classroom management systems, flexible scheduling, and student participation in planning. Work in these areas is integrated with the content in the various disciplines. Strong emphasis is placed on the techniques of building good remedial programs.

History:
When Pinellas County reorganized grade arrangements and grouped grades 6–8 together in middle schools, teachers and administrators sought to make the change mean more than just a rearrangement of grades to ease crowded schools. While adjusting the curriculum to the younger school population, a renewed desire surfaced to modify the program to meet the unique needs of this age group. This emphasis shifted the focus of

---

[15] Teacher Orientation/Renewal Center, Pinellas County Schools, Florida. Used by permission.

instruction from the subject area to the child and the learning environment—a *child-centered program.*

Middle school students enter the sixth grade with a wide variety of backgrounds. Differences in learning ability are apparent when these students enter first grade. Instruction during grades 1–5 has widened the gap between the highest and the lowest students as the highest students continually learn more, and faster. The middle school teacher must deal with all students; some need remedial work in basic skills areas, and some are capable of working with quite sophisticated skills and concepts.

The **T**eacher **O**rientation **R**enewal **C**enter is a teacher training program designed to help middle school teachers deal with students' varied instructional needs. TORC is the brainchild of a group of middle school teachers, guidance counselors, supervisors, and resource teachers.

TORC is based on the educational principle "learn by doing." The way to involve teachers in the development and implementation of a learner-centered classroom is to have teachers experience a learner-centered classroom as a learner. Teachers better understand varied classroom management systems and teaching strategies by experiencing them. The trainer models the role of the teacher while the participants evaluate the usefulness of the various systems and strategies.

Content:

Individualization, behavior modification, behavioral objectives, diagnosing and prescribing, remediation techniques, classroom organization, classroom management systems, flexible scheduling, learning centers, student participation in planning, applying TORC concepts to the content areas are skills learned in the TORC session.

Design:

Teachers may volunteer to attend a three-day training session in a center designed to model various management systems. Teachers may then sign a contract with a resource teacher and their principal to continue study of the TORC content or to implement TORC ideas in their classrooms. They may earn staff development component points for this work. Resource teachers provide follow-up support which includes:

1. Keeping the TORC center open Wednesdays from 4:00–9:00 P.M.
2. Helping teachers obtain instructional materials, supplies, and equipment.
3. Pooling materials and ideas from various schools and making them available to share.
4. Writing a newsletter to TORC graduates offering suggestions and encouragement.
5. Working in classrooms to help teachers introduce students to new classroom procedures.
6. Helping teachers make instructional materials, such as audio tapes, kits, and games.
7. Helping teachers redesign their classrooms.
8. Serving as a contact person with content supervisors.

9. Offering to TORC graduates a one-day "renewal" workshop called FOCUS (Focus On Classroom Use of Strategies—an opportunity for indepth study of a particular interest area previously experienced at TORC.

Participation is on a voluntary basis. Those teachers interested in a learner-centered classroom may receive direct help and support to put their ideas into operation. Materials are pooled and shared among schools so that successful programs throughout the county can be shared by all Pinellas County middle school students.

TORC Results:

These proposals and alternatives offer a way to put the learner-oriented school into practice. They give the teacher concrete methods and support in implementing the middle school program. Teachers working together and sharing ideas and materials, with follow-up support from the resource teachers and supervisors, will improve morale, as well as enhance the educational experiences of students. Following their attendance at the center, teachers can better determine which style, or combination of styles, of classroom management and techniques best suit them and their students. Enabling teachers to feel competent in the selection of alternative strategies is a plus for the entire instructional program.

Comprehensive Plan for Middle School Development
Stamford Connecticut School District.

The sections that follow are part of the comprehensive plan. Other sections include Philosophy, Goals, Recommendations, and Evaluation.

Preface:

In 1969, the Board of Education accepted a document entitled *"A Master Plan for Implementation of the Middle School in Stamford."* This master plan was the result of committee work involving professionals from the school system.

During the intervening six years, the middle schools of Stamford made steady progress in implementing the organizational patterns detailed in the master plan. Also, at the direction of the Board of Education, a middle school committee composed of lay and professional individuals was formed to study the middle school program. This committee's report was submitted to the Board of Education.

In the spring of 1975, at the conclusion of a workshop directed by Dr. Joseph Bondi, the middle school principals decided to assume the responsibility themselves of forming a central committee to further the implementation of the middle school concept in Stamford. Subsequently, a workshop was held during the early summer of 1975 to review the initial master plan. What follows is the report of that review in a form of philosophy, recommendations, and time frames for the accomplishment of specific objectives as established by the Middle School Coordinating Committee.

Needs Identification:
The following needs have been identified:

1. Better communication lines between district personnel, principals, and staffs of the middle schools concerning goals and purposes of the middle school in Stamford.
2. A comprehensive plan to fully implement the middle school as originally proposed in 1969 and revised in 1975.
3. Teachers more aware of the unique needs of the middle school child.
4. Better ways of diagnosing and monitoring skills in the subject areas, especially the 3 Rs.
5. The middle school program be better articulated in subject areas to provide more continuity between grade levels.
6. Classroom instruction reviewed and updated as necessary in all subject areas. Teachers to use varied and current methods of instruction for middle school youngsters.
7. An expanded program (including special interest courses) in all schools in balance with a strong academic program including the basics and the unified arts.
8. Emphasis on the interrelationship of subject matter.
9. Close identification of students with teachers; a more flexible schedule and program.
10. Better continuity of programs, sharing of materials, and curriculum articulation between the middle schools.
11. The middle school program better articulated with the elementary and senior high school programs.
12. Long-range goals for middle schools in Stamford and a system to sustain positive curriculum changes in the middle schools.

School Model

Lakeshore Elementary School Study
Palm Beach Florida School District

Purpose:
The purpose of the Lakeshore Elementary School Study is to explore the organization, curriculum, and instruction within the elementary school with special emphasis on:

1. The rationale of the elementary school.
2. The nature of the elementary school child.
3. The elementary school teacher.
4. Program of the elementary school.

Table 6.4

Timetable for a Comprehensive Plan
PERT Chart

Task	Responsible Agent	1975 June	July	Aug.	Sept.	Oct.	Nov.	Dec.	1976 Jan.	Feb.	March	April	May	June
Middle School Design Review Workshop	MSCC**	6/30 – 7/2												
Middle School Coordinating Committee: Sub Groups—														
1. PERT Chart	G. Roman			8/27										
2. Philosophy	C. Robinson				9/10									
3. Design	J. Markiewicz				9/14									
Comprehensive Middle School Plan: final review	MSCC				9/24									
Comprehensive Middle School Plan: to Superintendent	C. Robinson				2:30pm 9/30									
Middle School Project Inservice Workshop	SDC & Dr. Bondi			8/26 –29										
1. Awareness of middle school child														
2. Orientation of staff														
3. Curriculum develop.														
4. Team building														
Middle School Project Workshop (1–3 p.m.)*	SDC & Dr. Bondi					10/14 10/15								
1. Awareness of middle school child														
2. Orientation of remaining staff														
3. Curriculum needs														
4. Team building														

Table 6.4—*continued*

Activity	Responsible	Sept	Oct	Nov	Dec	Jan	Feb	Mar	Apr	May	Jun
Curricular Assessment by Principals, Coordinators a. Lang. Arts e. Art b. Soc. Stud. f. Math c. Science g. Guid. d. Music h. Phys. Ed.		a9/18 b9/16 c9/23 d9/25 e9/30	f10/1 g10/2 h10/7								
In-School Staff Development 1. Team building 2. Instruct. strategies 3. Block time scheduling	SDC, Dr. Bondi, et al.	9/8 –11	10/14 –15	11/10 –14	12/2 –5	1/12 –16	2/2 –5	3/1 –4	4/12 –15	5/10 –13	
Project Assessment and Planning (Mon., 9 a.m.)	MSCC		10/15	11/10	12/8	1/12	2/2	3/1	4/12	5/10	6/21 →
Up-date Information Sessions with M.S. Study Committee	MSCC chairman		10/1		12/10		2/3		4/7		
Staff Development Workshops (1 Wed./month)* a. Instruct. strategies b. Team building c. Expanded program refinement d. Interrelating unified arts program	SDC, Dr. Bondi, et al.			11/12	12/10	1/14	2/4	3/3	4/14	5/12	
Departmental Workshops (1 Wed./month 1–3 p.m.)* a. Curriculum assessment b. Skills continuum c. Profile charts d. Vertical articulation	Coordinators			11/19	12/17	1/28	2/25	3/24	4/28	5/26	
Middle School Project Workshop	SCD & Dr. Bondi										
Middle School Instructional Associates (4)	SDC										
1976–77 Schedules: block time for all COGS	Principals										Due 6/10

Table 6.4—*continued*

Responsible Agent	1975 June	July	Aug.	Sept.	Oct.	Nov.	Dec.	1976 Jan.	Feb.	March	April	May	June
1976–77 Physical Plan: clustering all COG rooms — Principals													Due 6/10
Family Group COGS: fully functioning — Principals													
District Ad Hoc Committees (for articulation in each curriculum area) Elem.-Middle School Middle-High School — Coordinators													
Buildings: modify and/or replace as dictated by program — Central Adm. & MSCC													
Planning for inclusion of 6th grade students — Central Adm. & MSCC													
Continuation of a. Team building b. Instructional strategies, etc. — SDC, et al.													
Building Curriculum Bank— materials, units, strategies for working with middle school students — SDC, Dr. Bondi, et al.								Start 1/76 →					
Refined Expanded Program: full implementation — Principals													
6th Grade Students included in middle schools — Central Adm. & Principals													

* released time

** Middle School Coordinating Com.

5. Organization of the elementary school.
6. Implemention and evaluation the elementary school.

This study is designed to meet the specific needs of Lakeshore Elementary School teachers, children, and the community the school serves. It will provide time to develop a total elementary school program by participants.

Objectives:
Major objectives of the study are:

1. To examine the rationale of the elementary school and to identify its goals and purpose.
2. To study the nature of the elementary school child and, in particular, the characteristics of Lakeshore children.
3. To establish a program that includes:
   A. An emphasis on diagnosis and prescription in the skills areas, building towards a continuous progress plan for students.
   B. A broad enrichment program.
   C. Wide use of media other than textbooks.
   D. A scope and sequence in each subject area.
4. To study organizational plans that have been identified with the concept of the open elementary school.
   A. Cooperative teaching.
   B. Flexible use of time and space.
   C. Schools within a school concept.
   D. Better utilization of administrative and service personnel.
5. To develop strategies for implementing and evaluating a revised program.

Evaluation:
1. Since the study will concentrate on innovative use of human resources, self-evaluation to measure change will be a significant part of the evaluation.
2. Informal evaluations will take place on a continuous basis throughout the study.
3. A subjective study will be made of comments and summarizations of the participating teachers before, during, and at the close of the study.

Expectations:
A written Lakeshore Elementary School Guide will result from the study that will outline in detail a program that can be implemented at Lakeshore Elementary School. Major sections of the guide will be the six areas listed under items 1–6 of the Purpose section. Staff members will be expected to work on one or more committees in addition to participating in horizontal and vertical team planning.

Tentative Meeting Dates:

January 4	1. Vertical planning in math and communication skills with district consultants. 2. Six major committees organize and assign responsibilities.
January 16	1. Afternoon meeting—meet in vertical math and communication skills groups. 2. During the day meet with Dr. Bondi on procedures to use in six major committees.
January 23	1. Afternoon meeting. 2. Meet with Dr. Bondi during the day.
February 8	Major committees meet, vertical groups meet—morning session.
February 18	Status report major committees; final reports math and LA groups.
February 25	Afternoon session—science and social studies vertical planning morning.
March 4	Final reports: A, B, C major committees.
March 18	Final report D (program committee including science and social studies reports, enrichment committee program).
March 25	Final reports E (organization committee) and F (implementation and evaluation committee).
April 1	1. Visitations to other elementary schools. 2. Editing and printing final report. 3. Presentation of final report to superintendent.
June 1	4. Implementation of selected areas.

Multi-School Model

Implementing the Middle School Concept:
Sample Announcement of Workshop:

TO: Middle School Principals
FROM: Dave McCauley
RE: Middle School Interdisciplinary Teams—Summer Workshop

To assist interested middle school teachers in the development of interdisciplinary teaming skills before the 1978–79 school year begins, a special 5-day summer workshop has been planned. The workshop is scheduled to be held at the Staff Development Academy during the week of 19–23 June. Participants would include 3–4 person teacher teams who have indicated an interest in becoming a part of an interdisciplinary team in their assigned middle schools. The workshop content will be very practical and structured to promote the development of necessary team skills. A required product from each team will be the development of an interdisciplinary unit which can be used in the middle school during the 1978–79 school year.

To insure the best instruction available in the United States, the services of highly competent and experienced middle school educators will be utilized. The following outline provides information of value to interested teachers.

Implementing the Middle School Concept: Workshop
Fresno, California
June 19–23

Workshop Goal:
Designing strategies for implementing a middle school curriculum.

Objectives:

1. To identify elements of the middle school curriculum.
2. To explore the concept of "team" and practice the team-building process.
3. To facilitate development of leadership skills.
4. To look at ways of "how to get people to change."
5. To establish alternative patterns of discipline and motivation.
6. To develop interdisciplinary teaching skills and develop inter-disciplinary units.
7. To participate in a variety of learning center activities:
   A. Setting up learning centers.
   B. Designing creative instructional activities.
   C. Building interdisciplinary units.
   D. Examining skill-building techniques.
   E. Facilitating leadership skills.
   F. Dealing with reluctant learners.
   G. Reviewing grouping techniques.

Prescriptive Needs-based Model

Project Point-Waxahachie Independent School District,
Texas Rationale for Change:

In order to be effective, all staff development activities must be directed toward improving professional competencies. Staff development programs are meaningful only when they have immediate relevance to the individual's everyday experiences or when they serve to increase the individual's skills in doing the job. Thus, all school personnel need to be involved in the identification, and articulation, of their own needs as those needs relate to specific teacher competency skills.

School personnel with highly developed professional competencies in a given area should be utilized to provide in-service to their peers. Additionally, individual needs can best be met by allowing all school personnel to select from a variety of learning activities provided throughout the school year. This type in-service can only enrich the quality and content of professional growth activities and opportunities.

A prescriptive needs-based model, such as Project Point, has significant implications for replication in other districts throughout the state. It is evident that if we are to individualize instruction for our students, it is essential that we do the same for both our professional and paraprofessional instructional staff.

The in-service experience in Waxahachie has been to provide some flexibility and alternatives for elementary level teachers through the local advisory center, while traditional in-service has been the norm at secondary levels. Generally, staff development programs have been prepared by the central staff for the consumption of the faculty. Past experience has allowed for minimal teacher input either in the identification of needs for in-service or in the alleviation of teacher concerns through the staff development programs. The Waxahachie administration, however, did not feel that this experience was adequate nor successful and, therefore, has rejected it as the future course of action. A definite need to coordinate and expand the staff development design and offerings at all levels has been seen as a priority in the local district.

In response to this rationale, the Waxahachie administration has felt a need for change in the direction, implementation, and application of in-service offerings.

Supervisory Models

Instructional Associates/Staff Developers
Stamford Connecticut School District.

Instructional Associates will provide peer support at the building level for teachers and/or school units via the goals and objectives of the IA program.

IAs will be appointed on a three-year rotating basis. Each IA will be identified with particular school units, to serve as the contact link in order to identify and respond to needs, and to encourage and initiate requests. Requests will be responded to by the assigned IA (or other IAs) with the appropriate expertise.

130

Figure 6.1
Prescriptive Needs-based Model, Project Point

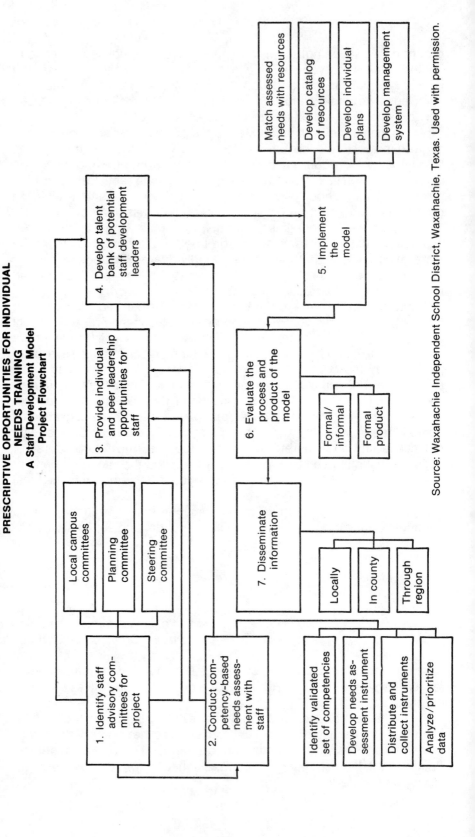

PRESCRIPTIVE OPPORTUNITIES FOR INDIVIDUAL
NEEDS TRAINING
**A Staff Development Model
Project Flowchart**

Source: Waxahachie Independent School District, Waxahachie, Texas. Used with permission.

IAs will inform school unit and/or individuals of teacher center offerings, and also act as the advocates for the school unit/individual requests for staff development assistance.

Goals and Objectives:

1. To assist in the actualization of the educational philosophy of the Stamford school system, by assisting the staff in:
   A. The application of the humanistic approach to all student learning experiences and needs.
   B. The comprehension and implementation of the process approach.
   C. The identification and implementation of ways to meet the objectives of the curricula.
   D. The exploration, utilization, and assessment of alternative methods of dealing with various learning styles.
   E. The development and implementation of teaching strategies, techniques, and skills.
2. To act as change agent(s) for the professional growth of the staff, by assisting in:
   A. The application of district and school goals in the classroom situation.
   B. The establishment of a professional climate favorable to the utilization and self-evaluative techniques.
   C. The identification and extension of professional expertise.
   D. The development and implementation of long-term planning.
   E. The dispersion and dissemination of ideas, techniques, and materials.

Steps in Organizing an In-service Program
to Develop a New Comprehensive High School

Role of Supervisor:

1. Meet with the principal. Define any county limitations; project any county directives. The principal will call a meeting of department heads and chairmen, and of other key personnel. He will set up from this group a steering committee for planning, chaired by a faculty member. Administrators will act as advisors to the committee, which should be expanded to include members-at-large from the faculty, plus student advisors and community advisors.
2. Provide information that committee members might need to consider.
3. Provide funds for resources giving background information.
4. Help principal and steering committee chairman arrange for visitations, speakers, consultants.

5. Act as advisor at meetings when decisions are being made.
6. Support decisions of steering committee.
7. Once the program has been established, provide funds, resources, and other aid in setting up activities for in-service education. Steering committee will determine needs for in-service training, and establish an agenda. Both principal and supervisor should be available to suggest effective personnel, media, activities for fulfilling those needs.

State Models

As discussed earlier in this chapter, the Florida Teacher Education Act of 1973 provided a state in-service model that is exemplary.

Although other states have reviewed their in-service programs, few have had such a thorough review as those in the State of West Virginia. An excellent source is *A Systematic Program of Continuing Education for West Virginia*, published in May, 1977 by the West Virginia Department of Education. This document is the report of a Continuing Education Task Force that was charged with preparing a recommended statewide program of continuing education for all educational personnel in West Virginia.

The West Virginia State Department of Education has also published in April, 1977 *Indicators of Effective Inservice Instructional Packages*. This document provides a checklist for developing and evaluating in-service instructional packages. Both documents can be obtained from the West Virginia Department of Education in Charleston.

SUPERVISION—A PROCESS MODEL

During the process of significant instructional improvement, such as restructuring student-centered educational programs, the act of supervision can become a high-risk situation. Building trust and clear communication are essential to continuous change. The traditional model of supervision, because of its judgmental quality and normative overtones, can make assessment of instructional improvement activities a subjective, artificial, and nonproductive experience. Supervision can become, in effect, a retarding influence on instructional improvement.

What is needed in an uncertain educational environment is a form of classroom supervision that is positive in its orientation, nonthreatening in its manner, open in its communication, and continuous in its application. Only through real involvement of concerned parties and a clearly understood operating procedure can the act of instructional supervision contribute to program development.

A model that borrows heavily from management-by-objectives procedures suggests a promising process. The model rests on the assumption that the system to be supervised is rational, that the goals of the system can be identified and described through open communication, and that the final product will be contributed to by those who will conduct the activities. The model is participatory in nature; therefore, the participants must have relatively equal status. It focuses on areas of exceptional need jointly perceived and agreed upon.

Six Major Steps

The Alternative Supervision Model consists of six major steps that lead to the activation of a supportive system of instructional assessment:

1. During released time within the school day, staff members collectively identify key performance/problem areas in instruction according to the goals of the system in which they work. These areas are then ranked by the staff as to importance. Supervisors might use a "ranking" device to identify the "key" areas.

2. Staff members collectively describe behaviors which, as a composite, indicate the optimal (desired) performance or solution in each area from item 1. The descriptions, as a whole, form an exemplary instructional profile. This profile is disseminated to all persons affected by the supervisory process.

3. At an agreed upon time, the supervisor observes the instructional performance of the classroom teacher to record and assess the current condition of instruction in each of the teacher determined areas from item 1. The observation period is followed by a conference between the supervisor and teacher during which an agreement is reached concerning present "realities" in each area and the method of observation. The product of the conference is a shared perception of "what is" by both teacher and supervisor.

4. Viewing the instructional pattern of the classroom teacher as a totality, the supervisor and teacher conduct a "discrepancy analysis" to identify those areas where performance deviates most from desired conditions. At this point, the behaviors which mediate between the actual and desired state in "priority" categories are identified. Accuracy of both teacher performance *and* observer viewing are discussed.

5. In the "priority" areas the teacher, with the assistance of the supervisor, sets improvement goals. The supervisor sets observational goals at the same time. These goals describe anticipated changes in behavior on the part of the teacher and the supervisor, the evidence which will be accepted as proof of improvement by both, and a time by which the desired changes will occur.

6. On the date identified in item 5, the supervisor returns to the classroom to observe and "validate" the progress of instructional improvement and observation. At this time, also, new improvement goals are set (Figure 6.2). By this means, classroom instruction and observational technique are continually being upgraded toward the ideal profile with emphasis directed toward eradication of the greatest deficiencies.

The supervision-by-objectives model has any number of distinct advantages over the predominant pattern of supervision found in most school districts. Primary among these advantages is that the model constrains the supervision process toward the improvement of classroom instruction by focusing on jointly agreed upon performances rather than intangibles. Not only does this method give the supervisor and teacher a common language for discussions, but it also allows for communication outlets in case of superordinate-subordinate role impediments.

The model is also advantageous because it directly involves the supervisor *and* teacher in defining and monitoring the growth of each. Such an internal, normative change strategy should significantly lower the threat level normally associated with supervision.

For the supervisor, the method can be a manager of time and resources, and a useful device for identifying common staff points of insecurity and development needs. The process is continuous and therefore should be relatively nondisruptive in nature. Where fully implemented, the model could stimulate the sharing of expertise among system teachers and supervisors in a self-reinforcing manner.

The supervision-by-objectives model is most appropriate for supervisory activity in rapidly changing instructional environments. Beyond assisting teachers who are struggling to master new techniques and educational approaches, the model has potential as a communication device with utility in the classroom with students. At the district level, the supervision-by-objectives model may prove useful for a superintendent working with building principals who have different needs and concerns.

To be effective during instructional improvement, supervision must promote both trust and clear communication about directional progress. The supervision-by-objectives model offers an objective, fair, and productive means of assisting instructional improvement. That, in turn, means an improved program of education for students.

SUMMARY

A prime role of the supervisor is to provide the leadership necessary to promote a continuing climate of improvement. To carry out this role, supervisors must be able to plan and conduct effective in-service programs.

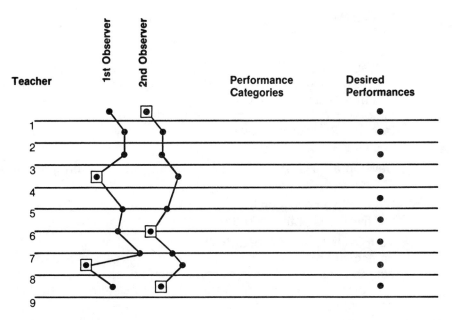

Figure 6.2
Supervision-by-Objectives

Note: At the conclusion of the first observation period, the teacher and observer plan strategies in the priority categories, 4 and 8, which represent the greatest discrepancy between the actual and desired profile.

During the second observation period, it is found that progress has been made in the previous priority areas, and attention is now directed to finding ways to correct the new priority areas, 1, 6 and 9.

By concentrating on the greatest discrepancies, the teacher instructional profile is brought closer and closer to the exemplary condition identified by the teachers.

A model for in-service education includes conducting an assessment of need, making policy decisions to initiate an in-service project, and developing evaluation measures to assess developed in-service programs.

Two promising methods of staff development are micro-teaching and clinical supervision. Both methods place an emphasis on supervisors and teachers cooperatively identifying, describing, and analyzing individual teaching skills.

Another approach to professional development with a focus on the individual is competency-based staff development. In this approach, strategies are developed to help a teacher attain specific competencies.

Peer supervision and school-based staff development programs are attempts to give teachers more control over the identification and articulation of their own training needs. An extension of this concept is the teacher education center. Teacher education centers have taken a number of forms, but all focus on the premise that teachers themselves should be responsible for their own professional growth. We offer a number of examples of in-service models for consideration.

Suggested Learning Activities

1. The superintendent has asked you to begin an extensive in-service plan to "improve teaching skills." Many teachers resent the implication that their teaching skills need improvement. You as a supervisor have the task of carrying out the superintendent's order in the face of open teacher dissatisfaction. What steps would you take to overcome hostile teacher feelings?

2. Develop an assessment of need for an in-service program at your school.

3. Work with a colleague in a clinical supervision setting going through the five steps outlined in the chapter.

4. Your district school board has mandated that middle schools be implemented in your district. You are charged with developing a comprehensive plan for converting four junior high schools to middle schools within the next two years. Outline the steps you would take in developing such a plan.

5. You have been elected to the advisory board of a teacher education center in your state. List the goals you would have for that center and the role you would play to help achieve those goals.

Books to Review

Beegle, Charles, and Edelfelt, Roy. *Staff Development: Staff Liberation.* Washington, D.C.: Association for Supervision and Curriculum Development, 1977.

Bellon, Jerry, et al. *Classroom Supervision and Instructional Improvement: A Synergetic Process.* Dubuque, Iowa: Kendall/Hunt, 1976.

Davis, Larry, and McCallon, Earl. *Planning, Conducting, and Evaluating Workshops.* Austin, Tex.: Learning Concepts, 1974.

Harrison, Raymond. *Supervisory Leadership in Education.* New York: Van Nostrand Reinhold, 1968.

Lewis, Arthur, and Miel, Alice. *Supervision for Improved Instruction: New Challenges, New Responses.* Belmont, Calif.: Wadsworth Publishing, 1972.

Lucio, William, and McNeil, John. *Supervision: A Synthesis of Thought and Action*, 2nd ed. New York: McGraw-Hill, 1969.

Sergiovanni, Thomas, ed. *Professional Supervision for Professional Teachers.* Washington, D.C.: Association for Supervision and Curriculum Development, 1975.

Wiles, Kimball, and Lovell, John. *Supervision for Better Schools*, 4th ed. Englewood Cliffs, NJ: Prentice-Hall, 1975.

Unruh, Adolph, and Turner, Harold. *Supervision for Change and Innovation*. Boston: Houghton-Mifflin, 1970.

7

Effective Human Relations Through Supervision

INTRODUCTION

The term *human relations* has taken on many meanings for those working in educational settings. Group processes such as T-groups, intergroup relations, group dynamics, transactional anaylsis, problem-solving training, and others have been associated with human relations. We choose to define human relations as more than just a single group process. We agree with Birtha that human relations are

> individual behaviors and institutional practices that affect the extent and ability of persons to 1) understand and obtain knowledge about themselves and others, and 2) use knowledge and understanding to interact productively with others.[1]

---

[1] Cheryl Birtha, "Philosophy of the Human Relations Department," (Madison, Wis.: Madison Wisconsin Public Schools 1974), p. *i*.

Dirlam and Buchanan have grouped all of the processes equated with human relations under two basic headings: (1) interpersonal relations, and (2) intergroup relations.[2]

Effective human relations through supervision involves helping students and teachers become aware of self so they can better relate to and communicate with others. The supervisor, to be effective, must have those same personal skills he or she is trying to build in others. Supervisors must be able to understand dimensions of leadership behavior, overcome resistance to change, be able to assess the climate of a school, develop a climate for change, and analyze and plan strategies to solve human relations problems in classrooms. They must also be able to work with large and small groups at the school and district levels and in the community. Finally, supervisors must be able to work directly with parents to help them become partners in the educational process.

OVERCOMING RESISTANCE TO CHANGE

Supervisors planning a program of organizational change have to take into consideration the possibility that resistance will develop among the people affected by the proposed change. Supervisory leaders must have an understanding of not only the resistance, but also of ways to deal with the resistance when it occurs.

All behavior that opposes change is not resistance. Some opposition to change is perfectly logical and supported by good reasons. There are conditions supervisors can recognize that are conducive to resistance.[3]

1. Resistance can be expected when the nature of the change is not clear to the persons expected to be influenced by the change.
2. Resistance can be expected to occur when those infiuenced are caught between forces pushing change and those resisting change.
3. Resistance will occur if the change is made on personal grounds rather than impersonal sanctions or requirements.
4. Resistance will be less where those persons influenced by the change have some say in the nature or direction of the change.
5. Resistance to change will be less likely to occur if the facts which point to the need for change are gathered by those persons who must make the change.
6. Resistance to change will be less if the group participates in

---

[2] Karen Dirlam and Roland Buchanan, "Human Relations: These Approaches Can Succeed," *Educational Leadership* 32 (October 1974), p. 22.

[3] Alvan Zander, "Resistance to Change—Its Analysis and Prevention," *Advanced Management Journal* 15 (January 1950), pp. 9–11.

making decisions about how change is to be implemented and what the change should be like.

DEVELOPING A CLIMATE FOR GROWTH

Supervision is the act releasing human potential. The supervisor who wishes to release human potential and promote professional growth must be able to create a working environment with the following elements:

1. All persons have a sense of belonging. Every person wants to belong. Teachers must feel that they belong to the group with which they work. Sub-groups exist within a faculty and a teacher feels closer to that group than the total faculty. Examples of sub-groups are grade-level groups, departmental groups, or teacher teams. Supervisors have to be careful that in promoting change and innovations that they don't destroy the psychological support of the sub-groups that exist within a faculty.
2. Many stimuli are available. Because not all people have a common readiness for change, the supervisor must be able to create an environment that will enable each teacher to move at the speed he or she wishes. Every setting then must provide many challenges and opportunities for teachers so they can find stimuli to stimulate them and release their potential.
3. Encouragement to explore. A supervisor in an official leadership role must make judgments about the readiness for change in the members of a teaching staff. The supervisor must help those who are not quite ready to change to explore various options being proposed. Opportunity to explore must include funds for research, field trips to examine programs like the one being advocated and organization of study groups with common interests.
4. Individual interpretations valued. If a supervisor wants to promote a climate for professional growth, he or she will encourage questioning of existing practices, value professional judgment, and recognize the diversity of opinion that is the product of differing backgrounds. Teachers are professionals and their professional education is similar to that of the supervisors with whom they are working. Their education has prepared them to make professional decisions and their ideas and judgments should be valued by a supervisor. If a heterogeneous community is more conducive to change, then the supervisor should seek teachers, parents, students, and administrators with different backgrounds, education, and ways of looking at educative change. A climate for staff growth will occur through interaction, and the potential of both teachers and the supervisor will be released if the difference is valued and used.
5. The organizational structure and process promote communication. Human potential will be released only when the organizational structure provides for extensive communication and interaction.
6. Counseling is provided. If it is accepted that a function of supervisory leadership is to set the emotional tone of the school, then counseling

becomes a basic responsibility of supervision. Supervisors cannnot hope to be effective when working with a teacher on the improvement of teaching if the teacher is deeply troubled with personal problems.[4]

Teachers are hampered by the same fears and anxieties that plague workers in other professions. Since they are "on stage" most of the day, they are under emotional tension much of the time. Specialized behavior standards for teachers and lack of appreciation in the community serve to aggravate existing mental or emotional disturbances of educational professionals. Supervisors can help decrease tension by listening to teachers' concerns and serving as informed counselors. Although supervisors are not trained as counselors, they can practice effective techniques of counselors such as listening to teachers and helping them work out solutions to problems.

The supervisor must be able to develop a climate for growth and devise strategies for releasing human potential. Teaching groups will grow in unity, strength, and effectiveness as individual members find satisfaction in themselves and the work they do.

DIMENSIONS OF LEADERSHIP ABILITY

Leadership is a central concept in educational research, theory, and practice. The literature in the field of supervision is filled with reference to leadership ability, leadership styles, and the selection, retention, and training of supervisory leaders.

Much of the early literature dealt with studies of leadership traits. It was assumed that leaders possessed certain special traits or characteristics. Most social scientists today view leadership traits as inadequate bases for explanations of leadership behavior.[5]

What is leadership? In basic terms, leadership is helping others toward common goals or purposes. Leadership may be regarded as a series of functions that (1) builds and maintains the group, (2) gets the job done, (3) helps the group feel comfortable and at ease (looking after physical settings, acquaintanceship, etc.), (4) helps set and clearly define goals and objectives, and (5) cooperatively works toward those goals and objectives.[6]

---

[4] Kimball Wiles, *Supervision for Better Schools*, 3rd ed. (Englewood Cliffs, N.J.: Prentice-Hall, 1967), pp. 23–26. Adapted by permission.

[5] Phillip Schlechty, "The Concept of Leadership," in *Teaching and Social Behavior—Toward an Organizational Theory of Instruction* (Boston: Allyn & Bacon, 1976), pp. 30–36.

[6] Michael C. Giammatteo, "Training Package for a Model City Staff," Field Paper No. 15 (Portland, Oreg.: Northwest Regional Educational Laboratory, 1975), p. 30. Used with permission.

Supervisory leadership is much more than routine role performance. If all a supervisor does is what is written in a job description, then that supervisor is not exercising leadership. The supervisor must develop the potential of position-related authority beyond the mechanical compliance with routine organizational directives. In viewing supervision as human endeavor, we believe that the leader is one person who can release the creative talents of those with whom he or she works. That definition of the leadership role, as opposed to the mechanistic power position role, views supervisory leadership as involving and motivating, rather than directing and controlling.

The ability of a supervisor to work effectively with groups is a leadership role that can be learned through conscientious effort, study, and practice. Leadership is dependent not only on knowing leadership principles, but on how they are applied. There are skills of leadership that have been identified by students of human relations. The following are some skills that are important to learn and practice:

1. *Skill of personal behavior.* The effective leader:
   A. Is sensitive to feelings of the group.
   B. Identifies self with the needs of the group.
   C. Learns to listen attentively.
   D. Refrains from criticizing or ridiculing members' suggestions.
   E. Helps each member feel important and needed.
   F. Should not argue.
2. *Skill of communication.* The effective leader:
   A. Makes sure that everyone understands not only what is needed, but why it is needed.
   B. Makes good communication with the group a routine part of the job.
3. *Skills in equality.* The effective leader recognizes that:
   A. Everyone is important. Everyone needs recognition.
   B. Leadership is to be shared and is not a monopoly.
   C. A leader grows when leadership functions are dispersed.
4. *Skill of organization.* The effective leader helps the group:
   A. Develop long-range and short-range objectives.
   B. Break big problems into small ones.
   C. Share opportunities and responsibilities.
   D. Plan, act, follow-up, and evaluate.[7]

Types of Leadership

Three types of leadership may be identified in educational settings.

1. The autocratic leader. He or she functions as the boss and tells group members what they may or may not do. There is little room for choices by members of the group.

---

[7] Ibid., pp. 36–37. Used with permission.

2. The laissez-faire leader. In this type of leadership the group is free to do what they want to do. No person appears in charge, and there appears to be little group discipline.
3. The democratic leader. In this setting the leader functions with the group. Members of the group share in decision making.

Table 7.1
Types of Supervisory Leadership

Type	Disadvantages	Advantages
Autocratic		
Does everything	More hostility	More production while
Manipulates others	More dependence	leader watches
Gets own way	More apathy	Quicker decisions
Pushes group	Slower action	
Laissez-faire		
Does nothing	Less satisfaction	No work for leader
Ignores others	Less production	
Lets each go own way	Poorer quality of work	
Just sits	Job falls back on someone	
Democratic		
Does something, not everything	Slower decisions	More individual responsibility
Helps group get its way		More friendliness
Pulls with group		More personal growth
Respects others		Better implementation
		More motivation

SOURCE: Michael C. Giammatteo, "Training Package for a Model City Staff," Field Paper No. 15 (Portland, Oreg.: Northwest Regional Educational Laboratory, 1975), p. 39. Used with permission.

A further explication of the relationship between leader authority and group freedom is seen in Figure 7.1.

The left side of the illustration represents autocratic leadership, while the right side represents democratic leadership. The diagonal line from left to right represents a progression toward democratic leadership. For example, the autocratic leader simply tells members of the group what to do. As the leader relinquishes more authority, he or she may try to "sell" the group on what needs to be done or even indicate what must be done if there are no objections (testing). The democratic leader consults members of the group before acting and finally joins with them in a course of action. Although there are times when a supervisor leader may want or have to "tell" or "sell" the group on an idea, group freedom will produce the best results over a period of time.

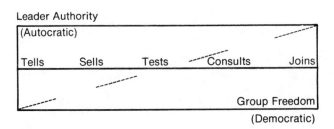

Figure 7.1

Source: Michael Giammatteo, "Training Package for a Model City Staff," Field Paper No. 15 (Portland, Oreg.: Northwest Regional Educational Laboratory, 1975), p. 48. Used with permission.

Shared Leadership

Shared leadership is one of the most effective types of leadership. The supervisor who is a democratic leader will have the skills of bringing each member of a group into a leadership role. Shared leadership involves (1) pooling the skills and abilities of the entire group, (2) promoting a feeling of group unity, (3) insuring that each group member feels a responsibility for group maintenance, (4) fostering individual interest and ownership in clearly defined goals and objectives established by the group, (5) providing an atmosphere where group members are free from fear of ridicule, and (6) providing a comfortable setting where group members are physically and socially at ease.

Today's supervisory leaders must be increasingly aware of the wide variety of interests, styles of learning, and levels of motivation of students, teachers, administrators, and community persons with whom they work. Effective leaders are those who can challenge, stimulate, and free the persons around them to perform at their highest level of competence. Only mutual respect and sharing between the supervisor and his or her colleagues can create such a productive performance climate.

In Table 7.2, an information form used in Pinellas County, Florida, schools to identify leadership behavior is shown.

Table 7.2
Dimensions of Leadership Behavior

Individual Being Rated _____

This form has been designed to give information to the individual named above that might assist him or her to focus more clearly on those things which will help the individual become more effective.

Instructions: For each numbered item, select two statements:
- (M) Place an M before that statement that seems *most like* this individual's typical behavior.
- (L) Place an L by the statement that is *least like* the person's typical behavior as you know him/her.

Please give examples to clarify your selections.

Items   **Examples**

LISTENING:
- _____ Draws other people out
- _____ Gives no indication that he/she hears what is said
- _____ Hears content but not feeling
- _____ Blocks people out
- _____ Hears and interprets communications from sender's point of view
- _____ Hears words but does not comprehend them

EXPRESSING IDEAS TO OTHERS:
- _____ Comes across clearly to individuals
- _____ Comes across clearly to both individuals and groups
- _____ Uses words well but doesn't convey ideas clearly
- _____ Is not easily understood
- _____ Conveys ideas but does so awkwardly
- _____ May not try sufficiently hard to get ideas across

INFLUENCES:
- _____ By weight of ideas and logic
- _____ By force of personality
- _____ By being friendly
- _____ By scheming and manipulation
- _____ By involving others in the issue
- _____ By status and/or position

DECISION MAKING:
- _____ Focuses primarily on keeping people happy
- _____ Tries to get job done by getting people involved
- _____ Believes in making important decisions by himself/herself
- _____ Works for compromise between productivity and morale
- _____ Focuses primarily on getting job done
- _____ Follows leads of other people

Table 7.2—continued

Items   **Examples**

RELATIONSHIPS WITH OTHERS:
_____ Harmonizes and compromises differences in the group
_____ Doesn't see need for supporting others
_____ Keeps others involved
_____ Insensitive to feelings of others
_____ Supports associates right or wrong
_____ Tolerant of differences in others
_____ Doesn't support things in which he/she doesn't believe
_____ Puts others down with value judgment

TASK ORIENTATION:
_____ Works on task only if he/she is personally interested
_____ Procrastinates in getting job done
_____ Works on task only in spurts
_____ Encourages involvement of others in work tasks
_____ Works equally hard on important and unimportant tasks
_____ Constantly presses to get job done

HANDLING OF CONFLICT:
_____ Readily engages in conflict when it presents itself
_____ Doesn't recognize any conflict
_____ Tends to smooth or gloss over conflicts
_____ Stirs up conflict for its own sake
_____ Uses and works through conflict openly
_____ Goes out of way to avoid conflict

WILLINGNESS TO CHANGE:
_____ Defends his ideas against all comers
_____ Mulls ideas over thoroughly before committing self to
         something new
_____ Values change for change's sake
_____ Quick to utilize new ideas
_____ Will try new things only if he/she thinks of them
         himself/herself
_____ Usually thinks things through until it is too late to change

PROBLEM SOLVING:
_____ Sets goals and keeps them in mind
_____ Slows down groups by going off on tangents
_____ Considers all pertinent information
_____ Jumps to conclusions quickly
_____ Doesn't recognize existing problems
_____ Utilizes resources of others

Table 7.2—*continued*

Items   **Examples**

SELF-DEVELOPMENT:
_____ Understands why he/she does what he/she does
_____ Is not critical of self
_____ Blames others for his/her own shortcomings
_____ Encourages comments on own behavior
_____ Doesn't realize how others see him/her
_____ Is growing and developing in work effectiveness

EXPRESSING EMOTIONS TO OTHERS:
_____ Clearly and frequently verbalizes emotions
_____ Acknowledges emotions only when asked by others
_____ Has difficulty stating emotions clearly to others
_____ Uses emotional words but does not act/live out feelings
_____ Uses only global words ("good", "comfortable", etc.) to
          describe emotions

Name of person doing the rating _____
Date _____

INTERPERSONAL SKILLS OF SUPERVISION

A substantial amount of behavioral research exists on interpersonal relations, yet not enough of this knowledge has been translated into a form that is useful to practitioners who work with people in educational settings. Because supervisors function in formal organizational systems, we tend to focus on skills of group productivity rather than individual growth. Effective supervisory leadership depends primarily on mediating between the individual and the organization in such a way that both obtain maximum satisfaction. The supervisor must constantly be aware of the relationship between the individual and his or her fulfillment and the demands and constraints of some supraindividual entity.[8]

Interpersonal Relations

Researchers have contributed insights into the relationships that develop between two or more individuals. The following summaries are particu-

_____

[8] Warren Bennis, "Revisement Theory of Leadership," *Harvard Business Review* 39 (1961): 26–36, 146–50.

larly useful in presenting practical techniques supervisors might use in achieving healthy relations.

Arthur Combs and other perceptual field psychologists have contributed valuable theories about human behavior. Combs has identified characteristics of a truly adequate or self-actualized person. They include:

1. The self-actualized person has a positive view of self that is learned from the ways in which he or she is treated by those in his or her environment.
2. The self-actualized person has the capacity to identify with fellow human beings.
3. The self-actualized person has a rich and extensive perceptual field that provides an understanding of the events in which he or she is involved.[9]

Rogers, in describing the fully functioning person, has identified three principles:

1. Individuals move toward being open toward their experience.
2. Each person moves toward a more acceptant and existential being.
3. The individual increases trust in his organism as a means of arriving at the most satisfying behavior in each existential situation.[10]

Gordon[11] provides a number of conflict management methods that parents and teachers can use to get children to accept responsibilities for their own behavior.

Harris[12] clarifies and extends the concept of transactional analysis that Berne presented in his book, *Games People Play*.[13] He discusses three active elements that make up an individual's personality role: The Parent, the Adult, and the Child (PAC). Harris and Berne state that through transactional analysis one can move to a more mature adult in his or her behavior.

Robert Carkhuff[14] has created a model for effective helping relations programs. Carkhuff found that there are two dimensions in the helping process: the ability to respond accurately to another person's experience, and the ability to initiate effectively from one's own experience. Carkhuff's helping process is guided by the "four R's for helping,": (1) The

---

[9] Arthur Combs, Don Avila, and William Purkey, *Helping Relationships: Basic Concepts for the Helping Professions* (Boston: Allyn & Bacon, 1972), p. 6.

[10] Carl Rogers, *Client-Centered Therapy: Its Current Practice, Implications, and Theory* (Boston: Houghton-Mifflin, 1951), p. 44.

[11] T. Gordon, *P.E.T.—Parent Effectiveness Training* (New York: Peter Wyden, 1970).

[12] T. Harris, *I'm OK—You're OK: A Practical Guide to Transactional Analysis* (New York: Harper & Row, 1969).

[13] Eric Berne, *Games People Play* (New York: Grove Press, 1964).

[14] Robert Carkhuff, *Helping and Human Relations*, vols. I and II (New York: Holt, Rinehart & Winston, 1969), p. 114.

right of an individual to intervene in another person's life; (2) The responsibility the helper has to assume when he or she intervenes; (3) The role a helper plays in the process of helping; and (4) The realization by a person of his own resources for helping.

Supervisory Skills for Improving Communication

There are a number of basic skills supervisors can utilize in communicating with teachers, students, and parents.[15] Supervisors can teach these skills to others so they can improve their own communication skills.

Listening is the first important skill in communication for supervisors. Unless teachers perceive that the supervisor is listening to them, there will be little sharing of information. There are several ways a supervisor can signal readiness for listening, including:

1. Sitting close to a teacher and facing him or her.
2. Maintaining eye contact with the teacher.
3. Not interrupting when the teacher is talking.

Paraphrasing by such phrases as "Are you saying . . . ," "Do you mean . . . ," "Your point is . . . ." Restating what the teacher says before you add words of your own shows the teacher that you care and want to respond with an accurate idea of his or her message.

Perception checking deals more with the affective than cognitive aspect of a message received from a teacher. Using phrases such as "You appear to be...," "It sounds to me like you...," demonstrates that you are aware of the feelings of the speaker.

Behavior description involves the supervisor describing exactly what the person did, not what you think or inferred were her or his intentions. For instance, using an observational system, the supervisor may say "You lectured for five minutes," or "You asked twenty questions during the 15-minute teaching period."

After hearing exactly the behaviors he or she has used, the teacher can make inferences, plan steps for change, and seek specific help from the supervisor.

Avoiding arguments involves strategies for rerouting arguments into more constructive channels:

1. Listen to what the other person has to say, instead of planning your own reply or trying impatiently to interrupt.
2. Try to agree with at least some of the other person's points, and emphasize your agreement.
3. State the other person's position accurately in the course of discussion.

---

[15] Ronald Hyman, *School Administrators Handbook of Teacher Supervision and Evaluation Methods* (Englewood Cliffs, N.J.: Prentice-Hall, 1975), pp. 177–83.

4. Avoid flat statements of disagreement, and concentrate instead on probing questions.
5. Back up your viewpoint with reason and facts, not with emotion.

By being aware of the problems of communication and utilizing the skills such as those discussed above, the supervisor can facilitate effective communication.

Table 7.3
Eight Irritating Habits of Supervisors

1. Supervisor says something and then denies it at the next meeting.
2. Passes the buck on problems.
3. Says, "We'll have to think about it."
4. Doesn't give me a chance to talk.
5. Belittles my suggestions.
6. Interrupts me when I talk.
7. Argues with everything I say.
8. Rephrases and puts words in my mouth.

SOURCE: Joseph J. Walker, "Georgia Teachers List Irritating Supervisory Habits," *Phi Delta Kappan* 57 (January 1976): 350. Used with permission.

WORKING WITH GROUPS

There are a number of techniques a supervisor may use to increase teacher or parent involvement and participation in discussions. The same techniques may be used by teachers to get students involved in a class discussion.

Large Group Techniques

In any large group setting, discussions between the leader and members of the audience generally are infrequent. When discussions do occur, typically only several members of the audience consistently participate while others play only a passive role. This section describes techniques a supervisor may use to strengthen the large group approach.

The large group technique may be used for giving directions, raising problems, summarizing student ideas, and for further discussion. To facilitate discussion items, the supervisory leader can organize the group into any one of the following arrangements:[16]

---

[16] J. D. Wiggins and Dori English, *Affective Education: A Manual for Growth* (Dover: Delaware Department of Public Instruction, 1975), pp. 30–35.

1. Mini groups—Breaking the group into smaller discussion or mini groups will increase audience participation. Members of the small groups should be given clear discussion topics and receive training in listening and discussion skills. At the end of a set time, the mini groups can reform into the large group for reporting and summarizing.
2. Buzz groups—Buzz groups are like mini groups except that they are smaller (no more than four or five to a group) and are shorter in their duration. Buzz groups offer an opportunity to get some quick feedback on ideas or issues discussed in the large group. "Brainstorming groups" are buzz groups which are asked to develop suggestions for further discussion by the large group.
3. Case example or situation analysis—Small groups are organized and given a particular case study of a problem or event. Examples might be behavior problems of children, political issues, or school emergency procedures.
4. Dyadic interactions—The supervisor may ask members of the audience to break into pairs to discuss a topic or issue. This technique is particularly useful to draw out shy or timid individuals who would not speak in even a small group.

Arranging a Comfortable Physical Setting

Unless the audience is so large that they must sit in a space larger than a single room, chairs and tables can be arranged to get maximum audience involvement. Seating should be determined by the meeting's objective to increase interaction. The arrangements illlustrated in Figure 7.2 allow each person to see every other person.

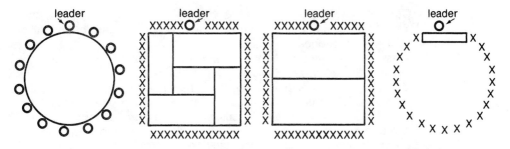

Figure 7.2
Alternate Seating Plans

Facilitating Group Productivity

There are other techniques the supervisor can use in facilitating group productivity. They include:

1. Checking ventilation and lighting and seeing that everyone is comfortable. Who can forget those meetings in the first grade room where teachers had to squeeze into those small desks?

2. Go around the room and let each person introduce himself or herself.
3. Learn the names of group members as soon as you can.
4. Have a recorder ready if necessary and provide writing materials.
5. Start the meeting on time and close at a prearranged time.
6. Avoid speeches by the leader or group member so that no one person monopolizes the discussion.

Small Group Relationships

Effective groups are those in which there is genuine participation by individual members in group discussions and decisions. An effective group climate is one that promotes involvement and self-expression through respect for the feelings and motivations of each member of the group.

There are a number of steps a group can take to facilitate group decision making. They include defining the problem to be solved, selecting ways of solving the problem, assigning specific tasks to members of the group such as gathering data about the problem and suggesting possible solutions, and finally, selecting a plan to solve the problem.

There are generally five methods groups use in arriving at decisions. They include:

1. Leader decision. The leader makes the decision for the group.
2. Leader suggestion. The leader proposes a plan or policy the group may accept, reject, or modify.
3. Compromise. Two or more parties may present proposals or plans. After group discussion, the parties may obtain approval of part, but not all of their original proposal or plan.
4. Voting or majority rule. Group members vote with the preference of the majority prevailing.
5. Consensus. Plans or policies are formulated by the group and there is sufficient communication that all members of the group accept the resulting plan or policy. Consensus implies that a group member may not agree totally with a proposed plan or policy, but supports that plan or policy when the group decision has been made.[17]

There are advantages and disadvantages to each of the decision-making methods discussed. Groups may use one or more of the methods during the course of their existence. For instance, consensus may be used to determine broad policies because it has the advantage of utilizing the ideas of all group members and giving them a sense of belonging. Voting may be used at times to arrive at procedural questions such as

---

[17] Clarence Newell, *Human Behavior in Educational Administration* (Englewood Cliffs, N.J.: Prentice-Hall, 1978), pp. 103–11.

meeting times and dates. A leader decision may come from a principal on where students will board a school bus; because of safety requirements, that decision requires little or no discussion by members of the teaching staff.

Informal Groups

There are many informal groupings of people not found on the organizational chart or formal framework of a school organization. Informal groups are characterized by a feeling of general agreement about certain issues, values, or goals. Leadership of such groups is earned through personality, prestige, or power and tends to shift or change more often than that of formal leadership. Meeting places may vary; often they are outside the school. Informal groups have a highly personalized system of interaction and may or may not agree with the institutional goals of the formal organization.[18]

If supervisors are perceptive, they will be aware of informal groups and use them as a source of information and leadership. Informal groupings often include a mixture of personnel such as the "boiler room gang" or the "lounge crowd" that may include teachers, administrators, noncertified personnel, a custodian or two, and perhaps a few parents.

Informal groups are a part of any organization. The supervisor who recognizes their existence and works with them can make use of their resources to move a formal organization toward its goals. The more congruence of values and goals that the informal and formal group can develop, the more successful the formal organization or group will become.

Principles Governing Group Productivity

1. One of the requirements for the efficient use of staff personnel is that the conditions that make for productive group work must be satisfied in all instances in which the ultimate purposes of the school require that group enterprises be undertaken by staff members.
2. To become productive as a group, the individuals in question must first become a group in a psychological sense by acquiring the feeling of group belongingness that can come only from a central purpose which they all accept.
3. If a group is to be productive, it must have a task of some real consequence to perform.

---

[18] Larry Hughes and Gerald Ubben, *The Elementary Principal's Handbook—A Guide to Effective Action* (Boston: Allyn & Bacon, 1968), pp. 34–35.

4. If a group is to be productive, its members must have a common definition of the undertaking in which they are to engage.

5. If a group is to be productive, its members must feel that something will actually come of what they are expected to do; said differently, its members must not feel that what they are asked to do is simply busywork.

6. If a group is to be productive, the dissatisfaction of its members with the aspect of the status quo to which the group's undertaking relates must outweigh in their minds whatever threats to their comfort they perceive in the performance of this undertaking.

7. If a group is to be productive, its members must not be expected or required to attempt undertakings that are beyond their respective capabilities or which are so easy for the individuals in question to perform that they feel no sense of real accomplishment.

8. If a group is to be maximally productive, decisions as to work planning, assignment, and scheduling must be made whenever possible on a shared basis within the group, and through the method of consensus rather than of majority vote. In instances in which these decisions either have already been made by exterior authority, or in which they must be made by the group leader alone, the basis for the decisions made must be clearly explained to all members of the group.

9. If a group is to be maximally productive, each member of the group must clearly understand what he/she is expected to do and why, accept his or her role, and feel responsible to the group for its accomplishment.

10. If a group is to be productive, its members must communicate in a common language.

11. If a group is to be productive, its members must be guided by task-pertinent values which they share in common.

12. If a group is to be productive, it is usually necessary for its members to be in frequent face-to-face association with one another.

13. If a group is to be productive, its members must have a common, though not necessarily discussed, agreement as to their respective statuses within the group.

14. If a group is to be maximally productive, each of its members must gain a feeling of individual importance from his or her personal contributions in performing the work of the group.

15. If a group is to be productive, the distribution of credit for its accomplishments must be seen as equitable by its members.

16. If a group is to be productive, it must keep on the beam and not spend time on inconsequential or irrelevant matters.

17. If a group is to be maximally productive, the way it goes about its

work must be seen by its members as contributing to the fulfillment of their respective tissue and sociopsychological needs, and, by extension, of those of their dependents (if any) as well.

18. If a group is to be maximally productive, the status leader must make the actual leadership group centered, with the leadership role passing freely from member to member.

19. If a group is to be productive, the task it is to perform must be consistent with the purposes of the other groups to which its members belong.

20. If a group is to be productive, the satisfactions its members expect to experience from accomplishing the group's task must outweigh in their minds the satisfactions they gain from their membership in the group *per se*.

Group Evaluation

Group evaluation is necessary to help assure that the work of a group does not deteriorate. When all members of a group feel responsibility for the group and can evaluate its effectiveness without being defensive, then the evaluation will be most useful to the group. There are a number of group processes one might examine in evaluating group effectiveness. Table 7.4 illustrates eight of these processes.

Table 7.4
Group Evaluation Form

GOALS

Poor	1	2	3	4	5	6	7	8	9	10	**Good**

Confused, diverse, conflicting, indifferent, little interest.

Clear to all, shared by all, all care about the goals, feel involved.

PARTICIPATION

Poor	1	2	3	4	5	6	7	8	9	10	**Good**

Few dominate, some passive; some not listened to; several talk at once or interrupt.

All get in, all are really listened to.

Table 7.4—*continued*

FEELINGS

| Poor | 1 | 2 | 3 | 4 | 5 | 6 | 7 | 8 | 9 | 10 | Good |

Unexpected, ignored, or criticized.

Freely expressed, empathic responses.

DIAGNOSIS OF GROUP PROBLEMS

| Poor | 1 | 2 | 3 | 4 | 5 | 6 | 7 | 8 | 9 | 10 | Good |

Jump directly to remedial proposals, treat symptoms rather than basic causes.

When problems arise the situation is carefully diagnosed before action is proposed; remedies attack basic causes.

LEADERSHIP

| Poor | 1 | 2 | 3 | 4 | 5 | 6 | 7 | 8 | 9 | 10 | Good |

Group needs for leadership not met; group depends too much on single person or on a few persons.

As needs for leadership arise, various members meet them ("distributed leadership"); anyone feels free to volunteer as he sees a group need.

DECISIONS

| Poor | 1 | 2 | 3 | 4 | 5 | 6 | 7 | 8 | 9 | 10 | Good |

Needed decisions don't get made; decision made by part of group, others uncommitted.

Consensus sought and tested, deviates appreciated and used to improve decision; decisions when made are fully supported.

TRUST

| Poor | 1 | 2 | 3 | 4 | 5 | 6 | 7 | 8 | 9 | 10 | Good |

Members distrust one another, are polite, careful, closed, guarded; they listen

Members trust one another; they reveal to group what they would be reluctant

Table 7.4—*continued*

TRUST

Poor	1	2	3	4	5	6	7	8	9	10	Good

superficially but inwardly reject what others say; are afraid to criticize or to be criticized.

to expose to others, they respect and use the responses they get; they can freely express negative reactions without fearing reprisal.

CREATIVITY AND GROWTH

Poor	1	2	3	4	5	6	7	8	9	10	Good

Members and group in a rut, operate routinely; persons stereotyped and rigid in their roles; no progress.

Group flexible, seeks new and better ways; individuals changing and growing, creative; individually supported.

Working in Partnership With Parents and Community

A dimension of supervision that is drawing increasing attention is that of fostering positive relations between schools and the parents and community persons who support those schools.

Educational leaders who are working to reverse the flow of public sentiment for lower taxes, less school resources, and limited instructional offerings need the help of parents and lay persons. For the first time, school leaders are asking parents and community leaders to share responsibility with them for the direction and improvement of local school systems.[19]

Those in supervisory positions are being asked to act as liaison persons between the school or school district and parent and community groups. All of the communication skills discussed earlier in this chapter must be used by supervisors to work effectively with these groups. When working with lay groups, the challenge is even greater for supervisors because they must deal with persons with diverse backgrounds and knowledge.

Some of the positive leadership roles a supervisor can play in building a partnership between schools and parents and community are to assist in developing programs such as:

---

[19] Leslie Kindred, Don Bagin, and Donald Gallagher, *The School and Community Relations* (Englewood Cliffs, N.J.: Prentice-Hall, 1976), p. 11.

1. Using the community as a learning laboratory
2. Community schools
3. Parent volunteer programs
4. Community resource persons
5. Townhall meetings on educational issues
6. Improving the teacher image
7. Radio and television shows highlighting educational programs in schools
8. Work-study programs
9. Parent visits and conferences
10. Newsletters to parents
11. School advisory committees
12. Alumni relations
13. "Open house" nights
14. Telephone "hotlines"
15. Parenting and family life programs

SUMMARY

Effective human relations through supervision involves helping students and teachers become more aware of their "selves" so that they can better relate to and communicate with others. Supervisors must possess the same personal skills they are trying to encourage in others. Supervisors must understand dimensions of leadership behavior, know how to overcome resistance to change, be able to assess the climate of a school, develop a climate for changing schools, and plan strategies to solve human relations problems in classrooms.

Interpersonal skills of supervision include being able to work with large and small groups, assist individual teachers with problems, and improve communication skills of students, teachers, and parents.

There are a number of techniques a supervisor may use in facilitating group productivity. Skills of working with groups must include those necessary to build a partnership between teachers and parents and between school and community.

Helping improve interpersonal and intergroup relations is a fundamental role of supervisors in today's schools.

Suggested Learning Activities

1. You have been asked by the superintendent to develop a plan for teacher evaluation in your district. Teachers are resisting such a plan. What steps would you take to overcome their resistance?

2. With a group of teachers, practice the listening skills outlined in this chapter. Divide the group into pairs and role play each listening skill.

3. Develop a presentation on group decision making that will discuss the five methods groups use in arriving at decisions.

4. Develop an instrument for evaluating the effectiveness of an interdisciplinary team in your school.

5. There has been a great deal of emotional discussion about a new sex education program to be taught in the schools. In terms of community involvement, what are some of the steps you as a supervisory leader can take to make the situation more positive?

Books to Review

Association for Supervision and Curriculum Development. *Perceiving, Behaving, Becoming.* Washington, D.C.: Association for Supervision and Curriculum Development, 1961.

Carkhuff, Robert R. *Helping and Human Relations,* vols. I & II. New York: Holt, Rinehart & Winston, 1969.

Combs, Arthur; Avila, Donald; and Purkey, William. *Helping Relationships: Basic Concepts for the Helping Professions.* Boston: Allyn & Bacon, 1972.

Combs, Arthur, and Snygg, Donald. *Individual Behavior: A Perceptual Approach to Behavior.* New York: Harper & Bros., 1959.

Grambs, Jean. *Intergroup Education—Methods and Materials.* Englewood Cliffs, N.J.: Prentice-Hall, 1968.

Harris, Ben. *Supervisory Behavior in Education,* 2nd ed. Englewood Cliffs, N.J.: Prentice-Hall, 1975.

Johnson, David, and Johnson, Frank. *Joining Together—Group Theory and Group Skills.* Englewood Cliffs, N. J.: Prentice-Hall, 1975.

Kindred, Leslie; Bagin, Don; and Gallagher, Donald. *The School and Community Relations.* Englewood Cliffs, N.J.: Prentice-Hall, 1976.

Newell, Clarence. *Human Behavior in Educational Administration.* Englewood Cliffs, N.J.: Prentice-Hall, 1978.

Swick, Kevin, and Duff, R. *The Parent-Bond—Relating, Responding, Rewarding.* Dubuque, Iowa: Kendall/Hunt, 1978.

8

Leading Curriculum Development Through Supervision

INTRODUCTION

In the past, the role of the supervisor in leading curriculum development consisted primarily of helping develop and implement new courses of study. Curriculum development for the modern supervisor involves much more. It is a process involving coordination of all facets of a school program where there is not only content change, but also social change in patterns of personal and group relations among teachers and community. Curriculum development today involves the personalities of students, teachers, parents, and the structure of the school system.

What are the leadership roles required of modern supervisors in leading curriculum development? We have identified the following:

1. Coordinating curriculum planning and development.
2. Helping identify and apply curriculum theory.
3. Designing and applying curriculum research.
4. Identifying resources and support systems for curriculum development.
5. Helping develop a systematic approach to curriculum development.
6. Maintaining balance in the curriculum.
7. Determining curriculum priorities.
8. Determining curriculum needs in a pluralistic society.

There are, of course, other leadership roles affecting curriculum development that modern supervisors must assume. Review the other chapters in Part Two dealing with other leadership roles in supervision.

COORDINATING CURRICULUM PLANNING AND DEVELOPMENT

In developing any educational program there must be curriculum planning. A major role of the supervisor in coordinating curriculum planning is to bring together all persons involved in the planning process, including teachers, students, administrators, parents, resource persons, and citizens. The supervisor must be a coordinator, change agent, and communicator. As discussed in Chapter 7, he or she must foster effective human relations among those charged with curriculum planning and development. The supervisor must have the skills to recognize and help others recognize the interpersonal and instructional problems that arise because of lack of communication and coordination.

Before curriculum planning begins, there must be a needs assessment. Needs assessment is a process of defining the desired end or product of a given sequence of curriculum development.[1] Needs assessment is a tool that allows supervisors and other curriculum planners to determine the steps necessary for curriculum development, and provides for assessment of curriculum in terms of what it was shaped to accomplish.

Modern supervisors need to be able to assist curriculum workers in carrying out the following steps of a needs assessment:

1. *Planning to Plan.* There is much planning that must precede a needs assessment. Some schools and school districts take six months to a year to complete the full cycle of a needs assessment. The supervisor must help decide who should become involved, help identify resources, and assist planners in determining which needs are most critical. All of these tasks are time consuming.

---

[1] Fenwick English and Roger Kaufman, *Needs Assessment: A Focus for Curriculum Development* (Washington, D.C.: Association for Supervison and Curriculum Development, 1975), p. 3.

2. *Determining Goals*. There are several ways of determining goals. One way is to have curriculum planners list goals on the basis of "felt needs." This is followed by an assessment of what is currently the state of the curriculum. The supervisor can help members of the group prepare a simple discrepancy list. For instance, if some members of the planning group feel an enrichment program is needed, it is followed by an assessment of what enrichment experiences are presently being offered in the school. If it is established that there are only a few enrichment experiences being offered, then a goal of establishing enrichment programs may be derived. The last step is called validating goals.

3. *Goal Prioritization*. Prioritizing goals is usually accomplished through the utilization of questionnaires or surveys. Respondents are asked to rank order goals. Ranking the goals helps school boards to budget funds to attain the most important goals of the system.

4. *Goal Translation*. After goals have been ranked, they must be translated into measurable terms. This involves construction of behavioral objectives or performance standards. Performance objectives allow the translation of lofty goals into measurable outcomes.

5. *Reassessment of Goals*. As time passes, a school or school district might want to reassess goals and reorder certain goals. For instance, one school district had listed bilingual education as a low priority until there was a sudden influx of Spanish-speaking students into the district. The establishment of a bilingual program then became the number one goal of the district.

Needs assessment should be an ongoing process. Figure 8.1 presents a schema for developing a continuous system of needs assessment.

After a plan has been developed and goals established and ranked, a budget must be prepared for implementation of the plan. Strategies have to be developed to close the gaps that have been identified between what exists and what is desired. Finally, a timetable must be established and responsible agents identified for carrying out the strategies. Curriculum must be developed and finally implemented. The last step in the curriculum development process is evaluation to see if goals are reached. The supervisor should help planners assess data to indicate unexpected results (goal-free evaluation). The supervisor must provide leadership in carrying out each of the steps listed above.

The Teacher and Curriculum Development

That the teacher is the prime decision maker in the development of teaching-learning situations for students is a viewpoint that all supervisors must emphasize and re-emphasize. Finding appropriate answers to instructional questions and problems regarding the improvement of

Figure 8.1
Schema for Developing a Continuous System of Needs Assessment

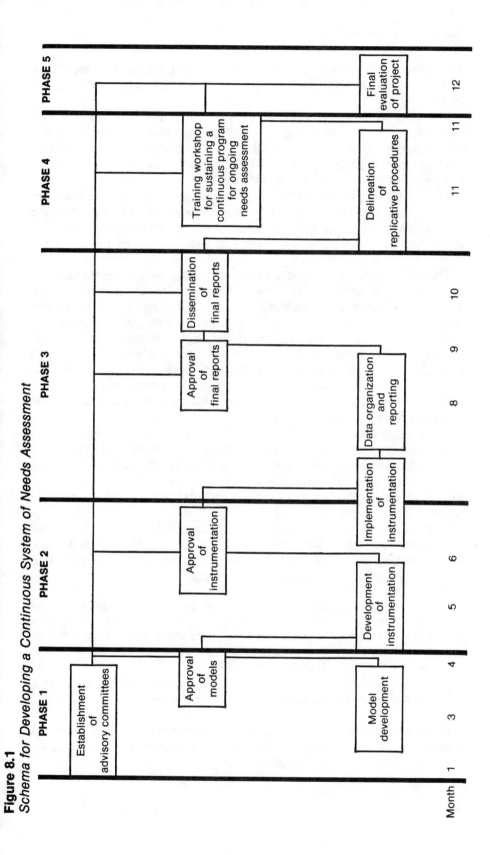

instruction is the purpose of curriculum planning. Supervisors must take an active role in assisting teachers in curriculum planning at the school level.

Teachers in the past had a limited role in determining how the curriculum should be designed. Today the situation is different. Teachers have a very important part in revising and improving the curriculum, and are beginning to participate as full-fledged partners with other educators and lay people in curriculum development.

There are many reasons why teachers should participate in curriculum development. Perhaps the most important reason is that teachers bring curriculum to life. The most detailed plan has no meaning until it is translated by the teacher into learning experiences of pupils in the classroom.

The growing power of teacher unions has resulted in teachers today demanding and attaining more participation in curriculum development. The trend towards accountability makes it only reasonable for teachers unions to demand a greater role in determining the goals and objectives that teachers are being held responsible for implementing in the classroom. Collective bargaining has resulted in a reversal of school board positions that curriculum matters were not negotiable. The Chicago Teachers' Union, for instance, recently negotiated provisions in their contract that provide for extensive teacher participation in curriculum committees.

Long before unions were calling for involvement of teachers in curriculum development, others were citing the contributions of teachers in curriculum improvement. John Dewey in 1929 said, "The contributions of teachers [are] an unworked mine." Caswell and Campbell in their 1935 text, *Curriculum Development*, called for total teacher participation in curriculum planning.

In an address before the 24th Annual Education Conference sponsored by the American Council on Education and Educational Records Bureau, Samuel B. Gould, then chancellor of the University of California, pointed out the significance of teachers in curriculum improvement.

> The teacher's influence should cause the curriculum to be a vast reservoir of unanswered and unanswerable questions. By his approach to teaching, he can see to it that all answers and all solutions are only partial, leaving open doors through which the student must go, driven by curiosity or patient conscientiousness or pride or ambition.
>
> The greatest attitudes of education are the teacher, the student, and the curriculum, and the greatest of these is the teacher.

Guidelines should be followed to insure that teacher involvement is meaningful. The following are specific suggestions for teacher involvement in curriculum development.

1. Don't involve teachers in curriculum development by administrative decree. Unless teachers want to participate willingly, and see a need for curriculum improvement, their involvement will at best be halfhearted.
2. If we start with the needs and concerns of learners in curriculum improvement, teachers are in a position to be familiar with those needs and concerns. Have teachers directly involved in gathering data about students and in identifying particular needs of students as they see them.
3. Use some group dynamic techniques in getting teachers to interact with each other and with other members of a planning group. Make the first meeting of teachers a success in a sense that teachers go home enthusiastic about the process of curriculum development. Teachers talk to other teachers, and if they see the importance of curriculum work, the word will soon get around that something beneficial is underway.
4. Provide released time for teachers during the school day for curriculum development.
5. Once a new program has been implemented, ask teachers to evaluate the success of the program. Too often we ask outsiders to evaluate a program rather than go directly to the teachers involved in implementing the program.

Student Involvement in Curriculum Development

Student involvement in curriculum development has long been overlooked. What better resources are there for planning educational programs than the recipients of learning experiences provided in educational programs? Students, as members of curriculum committees, can provide immediate feedback to fellow committee members about the relevancy of content or the processes involved in a new instructional program. Schools should not have to wait until a new program is implemented before students have a chance to react to it.

Token student involvement in curriculum development is worse than no involvement. Practice of democratic procedures will allow student members of a curriculum committee to be heard as well as seen. Lack of experience in group interaction with adults might result in students not contributing in the group planning, but a skilled leader and understanding adults can soon break down that barrier. Adults, by interacting with students in planning new programs, will get a better look at student needs and interests. Even more important, students participating in the development of their own programs will feel ownership in those programs and will come to feel that schools are really *their* schools.

Involvement of Lay People In Curriculum Improvement

Another group that has been overlooked in curriculum development are lay members of the community. The advantages of involving citizens in curriculum development include (1) lay people often have technical knowledge and creative ideas that can be included in new programs; (2) schools belong to the people and the people should have a direct voice in determining the goals of schools; and (3) involvement of citizens brings understanding and support from these same persons.

Curriculum committees organized in school districts should include not only school personnel, but parents and other community persons. Too often citizens' committees are organized to study various programs or to advise on issues such as discipline codes. Many citizens' committees grow out of dissatisfaction with programs in a school district. PTA study groups and local school committees sometime evolve from pressure groups exerting their influence in a school district. That sort of involvement of lay people does little to improve communication lines between school personnel and members of the community.

Nonprofessionals should be involved from the beginning in any curriculum improvement plan. They may become involved as participants in workshops with teachers and help design new programs.

Members of professional and business groups are often valuable participants in curriculum improvement. Work-study programs have brought professional and business persons into a direct partnership with educators.

Comprehensive Curriculum Development

A curriculum plan at the school level, as at the district level, has to be comprehensive. It has to take into consideration all aspects of a school, including courses of study, extra class activities, school services such as guidance, health, and special services for exceptional children, organizational procedures and policies for providing the instructional program, and the interpersonal relationships among students and teachers. Most school plans are not comprehensive. They focus on roles or procedures found in handbooks or policy manuals, or on courses of study found in curriculum guides.

Curriculum development has lagged in schools because of past factors (e.g., rapid growth of enrollment and teacher turnover). Curriculum development consisted in many schools of adopting commercial packaged programs. The blending of those programs with teacher-designed and traditional textbook programs resulted in a hodgepodge of courses with little continuity within or across grade levels.

Today's decline in enrollment and stabilizing of staffs in schools and school districts has afforded teachers a new opportunity to review and update curricula. Supervisors are being asked to work with curriculum committees at the school and district level to develop articulated school programs. As indicated earlier, supervisors must assume a coordinating, rather than a dictating, role in working with curriculum planning groups. When teachers assume leadership roles in curriculum planning and development, they feel an ownership of the curriculum. The coordinating supervisor will find that teachers who make decisions about the curriculum they plan and develop will often share feelings of closeness to one another and that "something has been accomplished."

DESIGNING AND APPLYING CURRICULUM RESEARCH

The supervisor must be competent in the area of educational research so that he or she can help teachers and other curriculum workers find specific answers to problems and conditions in educational settings.

Research problems grow out of the instructional problems that teachers have in the classroom. Teachers seeking answers to these problems must be encouraged to read about the research relating to the problems and even develop research designs to come up with their own answers. Supervisors can help teachers design and apply curriculum research to study teaching-learning situations and develop new materials, techniques, and strategies to overcome existing problems.

Recently many new curricular and instructional programs and practices have been implemented in schools. Yet, there is little agreement on the effectiveness of these programs; they are commonly adopted with little sound evidence to support their use.

There are several steps supervisors can take to help teachers plan programs for the evaluation of curriculum and instruction. They include:

1. Getting teachers to state in behavioral terms the desired outcomes of curricular and instructional programs.
2. Having teachers describe in operational terms the planned classroom transactions for a given instructional program. They must state appropriate independent and dependent variables and state the specific relationships to be evaluated.
3. Help teachers select the most practical and valid design for investigating the specific relationship. Supervisors can help teachers overcome their shyness about experimental research and objective evaluation if they provide teachers with sound, practical methods and techniques of evaluation.
4. Have teachers identify cause-and-effect relationships and describe them in realistic terms. For example, state precisely the level of student behavior that must be met so that a given process factor can be determined acceptable.
5. Help teachers specify the inferences that can be made from the results of a specific study. Teachers must avoid statements of conclusions that are not warranted by the data from reported studies.

Table 8.1
*How Many of These Questions Were Answered
Before You Made Your Last Curriculum Decision?*

Should you build your *own* curriculum, or adopt one that's already well developed?

Are learner behaviors specified in terms of instructional objectives?

How do you define *goals* and *objectives*?

Which is the more economical—your current curriculum or one of the new instructional systems?

Will replacement and equipment costs make adoption prohibitive?

Do the new instructional materials really fit your students' *needs*?

Do the teaching methods include *discovery* or inquiry?

Are the salesman's *claims* completely accurate?

Can the new materials be used with "disadvantaged" children?

What about process versus content?

What about personnel, time, and space?

Will special kinds of multimedia *hardware* be needed?

Should teachers use only a textbook?

Will the new elementary curriculum "match" your secondary program?

Will the new curriculum be flexible enough for your teachers' individual styles?

How do the alternative models compare in terms of cost?

Do local budget restrictions eliminate any consideration of certain curricula?

What advertising claims can be refuted after using one of these units?

How much evaluation time can your staff save by using an information unit?

Is the prospective new program really based on well-researched learning theories?

Are methods for individualizing provided?

What about individual differences, levels of abilities, readability, and so on.

How was content selected and how is it organized?

What are the anticipated cognitive, affective, or psychomotor outcomes?

What kind of staff training will be necessary?

Table 8.2 illustrates questions teachers might pose in studying curriculum change.

Table 8.2
Questions Useful in Studying Curriculum Change

Background of the Curriculum Change

Where did the impetus for change come from?
Who spearheaded the effort?
When did it get underway?
What specific events or activities were involved?

Process of the Curriculum Change

Who was involved?
How many participated?
Who coordinated the efforts?
How long a period of time was involved?
What kinds of activities did participants engage in?
What was the cost?

Nature of the Curriculum Change

What are the objectives of the new curriculum?
What was changed?
Who decided what changes should be made?
What criteria were employed in deciding to make the changes?
What kind of learning theory underlies the changes?

Results of the Change

How widespread is change today?
What is the present direction of the change today?
How is the change being evaluated?
What plans are presently available regarding the future of the change?

What Research Has Been Done on the Change (Study of studies: includes abstracts)

How much research has been done?
Where was the research done?
Who did the research?
How available and how trustworthy are the data?
What does the research show?
What problems have been identified in the research thus far?
What conclusions are apparent from the research done?

ASSESSING EDUCATIONAL RESEARCH

Supervisors can assist teachers in assessing the merits of educational research by distinguishing between high quality studies and those marred by procedural errors. Good research possesses a number of characteristics that can be revealed by supervisors. The following guidelines can be used to help teachers evaluate research.

1. The problem should be clearly stated, be limited, and have contemporary significance. In the proposal the purpose, objectives, hypotheses, and specific questions should be presented concisely. Important terms should be defined.
2. Previous and related studies should be reported, indicating their relationship to the present study.
3. The variables (controlled or manipulated) should be identified.
4. A description of procedures to be used should be clear enough to be replicated. Details such as the duration of the study and the treatments utilized should be spelled out in depth.
5. The groups being studied should be defined in terms of significant characteristics.
6. The report should note the school setting, describing among other things organization, scale of operations, and any special influences.
7. The evaluation instruments should be applicable to the purpose of the study. Evidence of validity (is this test the correct one?) and reliability (does the test measure what it's supposed to?) should be given for all evaluation instruments.
8. Scoring of measures should be done by the most appropriate method, whether it be means, medians, percentages, quartiles, rank, and so on.
9. Results of findings should be clearly stated in the report in a prominent location.
10. Limitations on findings—there are almost always limitations—should be clearly stated.

Supervisors can also assist teachers in understanding the "process" of educational research. All research is an interchange between a conceptualization and operational procedure. The following schemata by Karlene Roberts (Figure 8.2) outlines the research process.

IDENTIFYING RESOURCES AND SUPPORT SYSTEMS FOR CURRICULUM DEVELOPMENT

The supervisor must be able to identify appropriate resources and support systems that will help achieve the objectives of the curriculum. Instructional materials play a central role in the instructional process. Finding new materials and other resources for curriculum planners to review and use takes much effort on the part of the supervisor.

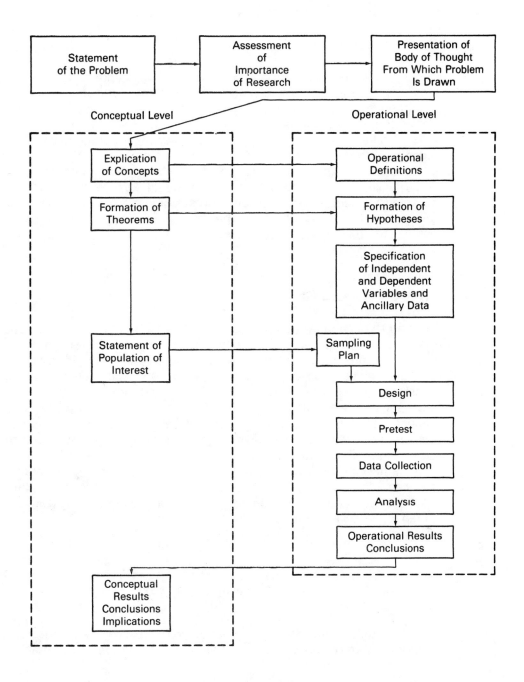

Figure 8.2
Decision Points in Research

SOURCE. Karlene H. Roberts, "Understanding Research: Some Thoughts on Evaluating Completed Educational Projects," An occasional paper from ERIC at Stanford, 26 (ED 032 759).

Organizing Resources for Planning

There are numerous support systems for curriculum development, including teachers, schools, school districts, universities, state departments of education, regional agencies, national networks, professional associations, and commercial publishers and businesses.

With so many persons and groups available for supporting curriculum planning and development, there must be a plan for organizing those persons and groups to accomplish the goals for curriculum change.[2] Once the support persons and systems are identified, the supervisor must be able to schedule those persons and systems in a way that planning groups will not be overwhelmed. The coordinating role of the supervisor comes into full play in getting cooperation rather than competition from support systems.

Superiority of Local Resources

Turning to outside groups or agencies to assist in curriculum development may be valuable because they are more representative of a larger world than an inside resource. However, the most lasting curriculum change comes from using local resources. Local resources are constantly accessible to students, teachers, and parents, and they are more supportive of the developmental growth of persons in a local school district. The supervisor can help identify a broad spectrum of local resources that will probably add more relevance and reality to curriculum development than outside resources and support systems.[3] In Appendix C the authors have identified a rich source of newsletters, information services, directories, research and development centers, consultant organizations, and other resources available for supervisors and teachers to tap when developing curriculum.

HELPING DEVISE A SYSTEMATIC APPROACH TO CURRICULUM DEVELOPMENT AND IMPLEMENTATION

Curriculum development is not a haphazard process.[4] For supervisors, it involves coordinating curriculum planning, helping identify and apply

---

[2] Jon Wiles and Joseph Bondi, *Curriculum Development: A Guide to Practice* (Columbus, Ohio: Charles E. Merrill, 1979), p. 264.

[3] Frank P. Morley, "Outside Curriculum Resources," *Educational Leadership* 34 (October 1976): 31–34.

[4] Lucille Jordon, "Systematizing Curricular Planning and Implementation: What a Supervisor Can Do," *Educational Leadership* 34 (October 1978): 41–45.

curriculum theory, assisting in design and application of curriculum research, and identifying resources and support systems for curriculum development. The supervisor has to be skilled in interpersonal relations when working with individual teachers and planning groups. He or she must also be skilled in designing a curriculum development model that pulls together the various elements of a proposed school improvement plan. Stone's Model for Objective Progress in Curriculum Development (Table 8.3) illustrates one such model for communicating how change will proceed.

Table 8.3
A Model for Objective Progress in Curriculum Development

Substantive-Content (Program)	**Objective Study Area (Evaluation-Research)**
STAGE I—DEVELOPMENT	
1. *Creative Generation* The Birth of the New Idea.	1. *Receptive Openness and Genuine Interaction* Tolerance for Deviation
2. *Intellectual-Theoretical Conceptualization* Functional integration of ideas into an intelligible program worthy of trial.	2. *Application of Systematic, Theoretical and Logical Criteria* Critical questions raised and answered tentatively. Explicit statements required as to A. Basic educational objectives B. Main program dimensions C. Rationale for program D. Possible evaluation techniques—Potential techniques to be used in Step 3—Quality control evaluation.
3. *Practical Implementation* Engineering conceptual program into operational form—A potential experimental program emerges.	3. *Quality Control Evaluation* Continuing study of the engineering process and its effects. A. How well is program functioning from moment to moment as a social process?

Table 8.3—*continued*

Substantive-Content (Program)	Objective Study Area (Evaluation-Research)
	B. To what degree are identifiable objectives being attained in short run?
	C. Modifications required in conceptual design of program—How does operating program compare with conceptual program?
	D. Reconciliation of conceptual design with engineered reality.
	E. Preliminary estimate of degree to which terminal objectives are attained.
4. *Definitive Description of Operating Program*	4. Explicit re-application of criteria questions in Step 2 above.

STAGE II—FIELD RESEARCH

1. *Identification, Description, and Implementation of Sensible Alternative Programs* Summarizing and systematizing existant alternatives.	1. A. *Abbreviated Application of Points 2, 3, and 4 in Stage I* Alternative programs must also be describable and operational and share important common objectives with experimental program.
	B. *Formulation of Testable Hypotheses* Relationship independent variables (programs and/or component parts), and dependent variables (learning outcomes and objectives).
2. *Stable Implementation of Experimental and Alternative Programs* Conducting programs for purpose of scientific study	2. *Formulation and Implementation of Experimental Design* & Establishment of maximum scientific controls to test 3. hypotheses.
3. *Maintenance of Experimental and Alternative Programs* Fidelity to engineered concepts and scientific needs.	

Table 8.3—*continued*

Substantive-Content (Program)	Objective Study Area (Evaluation-Research)

4. *Interpretative Program Implications*
Meaning for subsequent curriculum development.

4. *Acceptance or Rejection of Hypotheses* Conclusions of empirical data analysis.

STAGE III—DISSEMINATION

1. *Communication, Display, Demonstration, Guidance, and Persuasion*

A. Expository-descriptive account of program and related research evaluation data.
B. Audiovisual depiction of program highlights.
C. Behavioral demonstration (active communication) of program highlights.
D. Involvement of subjects in exploration of new program, considering both its advantages and disadvantages.
E. Obtaining affective commitment to *trial usage* of program in local school.

1. *Evaluation of Dissemination-Persuasion Process and Product*
Analysis of transmittal procedures and results.

Fidelity with which the experimentally validated program and all related components are represented to, and understood by, interested educators.
A. Clarity of materials description.
B. Role definitions for teachers and students.
C. Specification of educational objectives.
D. Presentation of research-evaluation findings regarding program.
E. Inclusion of evaluation guidelines for application to local implementation.

2. Extent to which transmitted program is, and can be, adopted and retained in its prescribed form, within a local situation.
A. Purge dissemination procedures of any program features that are parochial and not generalizable to all situations.

3. Unanticipated problems created by gaps in the dissemination procedures.

Table 8.3—*continued*

Substantive-Content (Program)	**Objective Study Area (Evaluation-Research)**
2. *Introduction and Maintenance of Program in New, Local* & *Situation* Incorporation of innovation 3. into local school curriculum. A. Future curriculum planning and policy.	2. *Abbreviated Quality Control Evaluation* Samplings of points applied to determine the appropriateness of the operational program being disseminated to the local school situation. A. Data revealing necessary "local" adjustments peculiar to a particular situation. 1. Conducted within local school, and primarily of local interest and help. 3. Comparative analysis of outcomes where possible: field research type data, unique to a local school, is always desirable. A. Confirm that relationships generally established in Stage II do prevail in local situations.

SOURCE: Dr. Douglas E. Stone, Research Coordinator, University of South Florida College of Education. Used with permission.

MAINTAINING BALANCE IN THE CURRICULUM

A crucial leadership role for supervisors in curriculum development is that of helping maintain balance in the curriculum. Supervisors can do much to provide a balanced program by seeing that all major areas of human competence are comprehended within the curriculum.[5] Perhaps, the major coordinating role of supervisors in maintaining balance is to help curriculum planners focus on what is valued for the growth of individual learners and apply those values in selecting content, in

[5] Ronald Doll, *Curriculum Improvement—Decision Making and Process*, 4th ed. (Boston: Allyn & Bacon, 1978), p. 139.

providing for scope, sequence, and continuity in the curriculum, in providing resources for teaching and learning, and in grouping pupils for instruction.[6]

Maintaining balance in the curriculum really provides for the maximum development of the individual student within the curriculum. A school program that is truly balanced will provide for the personal development of the individual (mental, physical, social, and emotional development), basic skills (not only skills in communication and numbers, but opportunities for problem solving and interpersonal skills), and, finally, basic knowledge (content, courses of study, and other learning leading toward social competence).

Determining Curriculum Priorities

Many early federal programs in education were based on pressing social concerns. Following Sputnik, for example, National Science Foundation programs were created to fulfill the need for persons trained in math and science. In an attempt to integrate the public schools, the federal government has created numerous assistance programs. Similar program development occurs at the state and local levels as curriculum priorities are established.

How should such needs and priorities be established? Is the past an accurate predictor of future needs? Who could have predicted, during the baby boom of the fifties and sixties, that the seventies would see school closings due to low enrollments brought on by a declining birthrate? Can curriculum workers and supervisors use information from the present or projections of the future in a meaningful way to establish curriculum priorities?

Another important question in determining curriculum priorities is: How are local perceptions of need to be balanced against the judgment of those recognized as knowledgeable about educational solutions? Do local districts, for instance, have any option but to follow legislated edicts that require consumer education or a return to "the basics" as an educational priority?

Concern about what schools should be doing is on the minds of many. What is needed is a better process for determining priorities rather than more suggestions as to what should be offered or emphasized in schools.

Determining Curriculum Needs in a Pluralistic Society

The United States is characterized by a culturally pluralistic society. Many of the educational organizations and agencies in the U.S. have adopted policies of pluralism in curriculum matters.

---

[6] Association for Supervision and Curriculum Development, *Balance in the Curriculum*, 1961 Yearbook (Washington, D.C.: Association for Supervision and Curriculum Development, 1961).

With increasing complexity and interdependence in economic, political, and social affairs, differences and similarities among cultural groups become more pronounced. Although a single national culture is not acceptable, there is still a problem of compatability between concerns for national unity and provisions for the demands of diversity. How pluralism is characterized and assessed is one of the questions facing curriculum planners. The question still unanswered is, should there only be value-free curricula in the public schools? If value-oriented curricula is the answer, then how can we gain consensus on what values should be appropriate and what adoption strategies would be consistent with local autonomy? The value issue is a complex one. For instance, most individuals value the freedom to read, but there are strong concerns over what should be the content of certain books. Determining curriculum needs in our society will continue to be a challenge as long as our society remains so diverse.

BASIC PRINCIPLES IN CURRICULUM DEVELOPMENT

Smith, Stanley, and Shores identified four principles explaining why the teacher is the key to effective curriculum development:

1. The curriculum will improve only when the professional competence of teachers improves.
2. The competence of teachers will be improved only when teachers become personally involved in curriculum revision.
3. Teachers will be involved when they share in the shaping of goals, in selecting, defining, and solving the problems to be encountered, and in judging their results.
4. As people encounter each other face to face, they will be able to understand one another better and reach a consensus on basic goals, principles, and plans.[7]

Diagnosis is an essential part of curriculum development. Diagnosis in curriculum development or revision means determining the facts that need to be considered in making curriculum decisions. The first step in a diagnostic study of curriculum problems is the identification of problems that are of concern to the classroom teacher. If, as supervisors, we assume that the functioning curriculum is in the hands of teachers who must translate objectives and plans into an operating curriculum, then we must start with problems that come from them. Whether it is getting help on how to deal with slow learners, managing time and materials more efficiently to teach basic skills, or learning how to handle social problems

---

[7] B. O. Smith, William Stanley, and J. Harlan Shores, *Curriculum Developing: Theory and Practice*, rev. ed. (New York: Harcourt Brace Jovanovich, 1957), p. 429.

of students, the classroom teacher wants curriculum development to provide them with the content or approaches to deal with these problems.

The supervisor is the facilitator of curriculum development. He or she can provide meeting times, assist in the selection of committee members, provide resource information, and coordinate new programs with other programs in a school or school district.

Leadership abilities of supervisors in facilitating curriculum development should include skills in involving personnel in the activation of planning and in monitoring goal achievement.

The success of any new program depends on the attitude of the working group that produces the new program. If the group works well together and everyone feels they are contributing to the development of the new program, then the implementation will be much smoother. Supervisors are the persons who can be the catalysts for getting positive group interaction.

Monitoring goal achievement of either the planning or implementation phase of a new program is another role of the supervisor. The monitoring of group planning process is a role that demands the skills of a social engineer. Knowing the personality traits, as well as curriculum strengths, of group members helps the supervisor harness all the talents of curriculum planning group members.

Criteria for Selecting Instructional Programs

1. The first consideration in the selection of instructional programs has to be the purposes for which the instructional program is being planned. Whether it is the objectives stated for a particular lesson in a classroom or the general educational goals for a school or district, planning occurs on the basis of the purposes defined. As stated early in this text, the authors believe a good instructional program must adequately reflect the aims of the school or agency from which they come. At the school level, the faculty, students, and parents need to define comprehensive educational goals, and all curriculum opportunities offered at the school should be planned with reference to one or more of those goals.
2. A good instructional program must provide for continuity of learning experiences. Students should progress through a particular program on the basis of their achievement, not on the basis of how much time they have spent in the program. Instructional programs in a school that are planned over several years lend themselves to better vertical progress. Continuity of learning experiences within a program dictates that a relationship between disciplines be established. Core or interdisciplinary programs allow students to see purpose and meaning in their total instructional program.
3. All principles of learning need to be drawn upon in selecting an

instructional program. Programs that rely solely on operant conditioning as a psychological base for teaching neglect the important theories of Combs, Piaget, and others. All those in education understand the difficulty of putting psychological principles into practice. A careful analysis of new programs can reveal the psychological bases of those programs.

4. Selected programs should make maximum provision for the development of each learner. Any program selected should include a wide range of opportunities for individuals of varying abilities, interests, and needs. Each child is characterized by his or her own pattern of development. Youngsters are curious, explorative, and interested in many things. An instructional program must promote individual development in students rather than making them conform to a hypothetical standard.

5. An instructional program must provide for clear focus. Whether a program is organized around separate subjects such as history or science, or around related subjects such as social studies, it is important that the one selecting the program know which dimensions to pursue, which relationships of facts and ideas should stand out, and which should be submerged. The problem for those who are reviewing programs is to decide which element of the program is the center of organization. Instructional programs may be organized around life problems, content topics, interests, or experiences. In selecting instructional programs, however, the organizing focus must also be examined to see which topics are emphasized, which details are relevant, and which relationships are significant.

6. A good instructional program should be well planned and must include a built-in process for evaluation. Steps need to be defined that would include a periodic assessment of the success of the program and a continuous process for reviewing and updating the program.

SUMMARY

Curriculum planning must be a cooperative effort. In the past, curriculum planning was often limited to a small work group of administrators, supervisors, or subject matter experts. Too often curriculum development was the result of administrative decree. Modern curriculum planning has to involve all segments of a school system or agency. The teacher, who ultimately must provide learning situations, will be the key element in the success of any curriculum plan; the learner is the focal point of the total endeavor. Lay people must also be involved, (e.g., parents, school board members, and interested members of the community). Consultants are often involved. They may come from universities, state departments of education, other school districts and agencies, and from the business community.

A model of human behavior for curriculum development is presented in Figure 8.3 to help persons directly involved in curriculum planning and development examine the behavior of students in schools.

The supervisor has a major responsibility for coordinating the efforts of all groups and persons involved in curriculum planning.

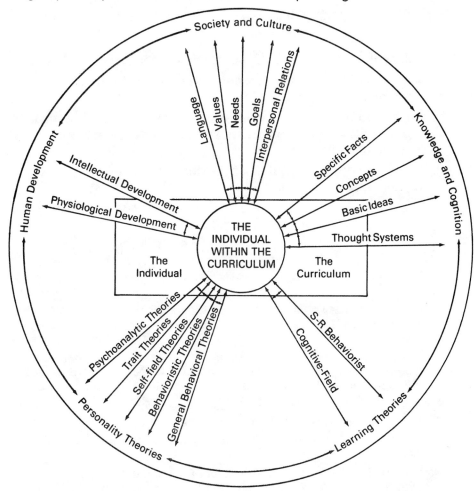

Figure 8.3
A Model of Human Behavior for Curriculum Development

Curriculum development arises out of a particular need found in a school or school system. It cannot begin with everything at once, but must begin with a specific situation that requires attention because it is of concern to students, parents, community, or to professional personnel. The learner is the focal point of all curriculum development, but it is the teacher who must recognize the need for curriculum change to benefit the learner.

The effective supervisor of the future will be able to assist curriculum planners to develop cooperative, systematic curriculum development procedures that will lead to a balanced curriculum for the learners served.

Suggested Learning Activities

1. Outline the steps you would include in a needs assessment plan.
2. Prepare a research design to examine the effectiveness of a basic skills program in your school.
3. You have been asked to chair a committee to outline curriculum priorities for your school district. Where and from whom would you seek information?
4. Prepare a presentation on "Balance in the Curriculum" to be presented to your local school board.
5. Develop criteria for selecting resources and support systems for curriculum development at your school.

Books to Review

Christensen, Donald, et al. *Curriculum Leaders: Improving Their Influence*. Washington, D.C.: Association for Supervision and Curriculum Development, 1976.

English, Fenwick, and Kaufman, Roger. *Needs Assessment: A Focus on Curriculum Development*. Washington, D.C.: Association for Supervision and Curriculum Development, 1975.

Eye, Glen; Netzer, Lanore; and Krey, Robert. *Supervision of Instruction*, 2nd ed. New York: Harper & Row, 1971.

Firth, Gerald, and Kimpston, Richard. *The Curriculum Continuum in Perspective*. Itasca, Ill.: F.E. Peacock, 1973.

Hass, Glen: Bondi, Joseph; and Wiles, Jon. *Curriculum Planning: A New Approach*. Boston: Allyn and Bacon, 1974.

Lewis, Art, and Miel, Alice. *Supervision for Improved Instruction: New Challenges, New Responses*. Belmont, Calif: Wadsworth Publishing, 1972.

Oliver, Albert. *Curriculum Improvement—A Guide to Problems, Principles and Process*, 2nd ed. New York: Harper & Row, 1977.

Saylor, Galen, and Alexander, William. *Curriculum Planning for Modern Schools*. New York: Holt, Rinehart & Winston, 1966.

Saylor, Galen, and Alexander, William. *Planning Curriculum for Schools*. New York: Holt, Rinehart & Winston, 1974.

Skeel, Dorothy, and Hagen, Owen. *The Process of Curriculum Change*. Pacific Palisades, Calif.: Goodyear Publishing, 1971.

Smith, B.; Stanley, William; and Shores, J. Harlan. *Fundamentals of Curriculum Development*, rev. ed. New York: World Book, 1957.

Tanner, Daniel, and Tanner, Laurel. *Curriculum Development—Theory and Practice*. New York: MacMillan, 1975.

Wiles, Jon, and Bondi, Joseph. *Curriculum Development: A Guide to Practice*. Columbus, Ohio: Charles E. Merrill Publishing, 1979.

part three

Improving Supervisory Performance

9

Research Orientations for the Supervisor

INTRODUCTION

While supervisors in elementary, middle, and secondary schools have many concerns and tasks, their primary role is to provide instructional leadership in improving instruction. Basic approaches to leading instructional improvement will be dealt with in Chapter 12. This chapter will examine the role of educational research in guiding supervisory behavior. We believe that educational research, particularly research focused on teacher effectiveness, can assist the supervisor in both evaluating teachers and providing strong leadership for instructional improvement.

Supervisors who look to educational research for absolutes will be disappointed. The current state of our knowledge about the act of teaching is primitive, and we are a long way from being able to provide prescriptions for effective teaching. Yet inquiry into teacher effectiveness has yielded valuable information during the 1970s, and the continued refinement of research technique may provide such prescription in the not-too-distant future. To be both objective and effective in their role, supervisors must keep abreast of research developments.

SUPERVISORS AS EVALUATORS

A role often inherited by instructional supervisors is the evaluation of classroom teachers. Such a role is difficult for many supervisors because, on the one hand, they know too much about teaching and, on the other hand, they know very little about teaching. In extreme cases, most supervisors can distinguish quality teaching from undesirable teaching performances. Beyond gross assessment, however, common sense can sometimes blind the observer. As American humorist Artemus Ward once said, "It ain't the things we don't know that gets us into trouble. It's the things we know that ain't so." Common sense would tell us, for instance, that the world is flat—anyone can see that just by looking. . . .

In evaluating classroom teaching the "stakes" are high. Supervisory evaluations can lead to promotion, merit pay, tenure, or sometimes to dismissal. Supervisors are constantly in the posture of defining "good teaching," and those definitions sometimes have legal implications. Definitions of good teaching are varied as Scriven observes:

> It is clear that good teaching cannot be defined simply in terms of achieving the goals of the teacher or the student since these may be—and often are— trivial or indefensible. Good teaching must make a significant contribution to meeting the educational needs of the student and society and must be reasonably effective by comparison with the teaching alternatives available—e.g., must not make a smaller contribution than could be made by another teacher or by using other teaching strategies (reading a text).[1]

Supervisors use a variety of appraisal techniques in providing judgments about teaching. Most common among those techniques are classroom observations, student ratings, self-rating, peer ratings, classroom environment measures (management, organization), contracts for student gains, and performance tests. Still, in many districts, the purpose of evaluating teachers is unclear and the criteria for such evaluation are largely undefined.

Evaluation of instruction does not always have to mean a judging role for the supervisor. Among the functions of supervision are:

---

[1] Michael Scriven, "The Evaluation of Teachers and Teaching," in *The Appraisal of Teaching: Concepts and Process*, ed. Gary Borich (Reading, Mass.: Addison-Wesley Publishing, 1977), p. 186.

1. Assisting the teacher in self-improvement.
2. Providing information to assist teachers.
3. Providing information for consumers of teaching (students).
4. Building a data base for decision making about teaching.
5. Building a data base for managerial decisions about instructional programs.
6. Establishing research models that will answer questions about instructional concerns.

Anderson has developed a "force field" analysis of the conflict over teacher evaluation that clearly shows the restraining and contributing attitudes at play in the evaluation process (Figure 9.1).

Developing criteria for the evaluation of teaching is a difficult process because there is no clear definition of good teaching. As Frederick McDonald of the Educational Testing Service has written:

> The practical object of research on teaching is to describe teaching effectiveness. This requires that we state a desired effect—a desired change in children—and the actions which produce it. We must also describe social conditions under which these teaching actions occur, and how these actions and their effects vary as social conditions of teaching change. This concept of teaching effectiveness implies that there may be many kinds of teaching effectiveness.[2]

As research closes in on empirically verified descriptions of teaching actions, conditions, and effects, we will come closer to being able to accurately define "good" teaching. For this reason alone, supervisors must become students of teaching research and make such knowledge the foundation of an instructional evaluation program. The body of knowledge addressing teacher effectiveness is expanding at an astounding rate at the time of this writing.

THE RESEARCH PERSPECTIVE

Most research in education directed toward the assessment of teaching effectiveness has been conducted since 1950.[3] During the last decade there have been tremendous advances in both designs for investigating teacher effectiveness and methodology for conducting such research. The focus of education research on teaching has been refined and the role of the researcher clarified. Stake and Denny describe the role of the researcher in improving instruction in this way:

---

[2] Frederick J. McDonald, "Report on Phase II of the Beginning Teacher Evaluation Study," *Journal of Teacher Education* 27 (Spring 1976): 39.

[3] For an excellent overview of this research see R. W. Travers, *Introduction to Educational Research* (Chicago: Rand-McNally, 1978), Chapter 8.

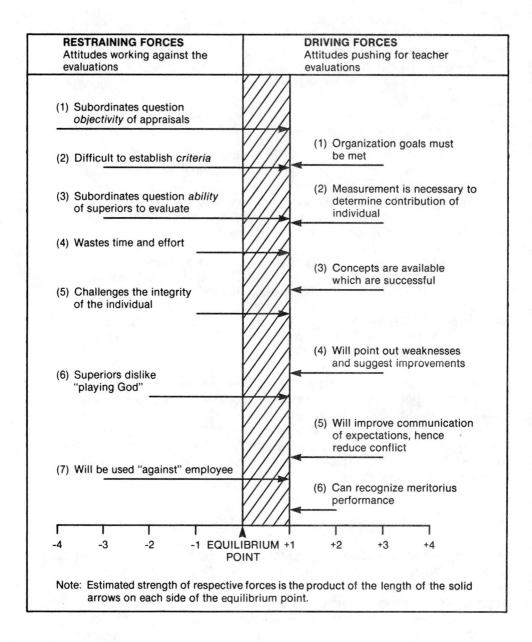

Figure 9.1

Force Field Analysis of the Conflict Over Teacher Evaluation

SOURCE: From L. W. Anderson, "More About Teacher Evaluation," *OCLEA* (Toronto: Ontario Council for Leadership in Educational Administration, September 1975), p. 3. Used with permission.

> The researcher is concerned foremost with the discovery and building of principles—lawful relationships with a high degree of generalizability over several instances of a class of problems. He seeks to develop rules (explanatory statements) about processes which govern common educational activities. He seeks to understand the basic forces that interact wherever there is teaching and learning.[4]

In short, teaching effectiveness research is concerned with the relationship between the characteristics of the teachers, teaching acts, and their effects on the educational outcomes of classroom teaching.

Trying to establish an empirical relationship between the independent variable of teacher behavior and student achievement as a dependent variable—a recent research thrust—is difficult to say the least. Not only is teaching an incredibly complex act, but the very definition of effectiveness is itself dependent on the definition of student achievement. Some of the major problem areas in establishing this relationship are:

1. The impact of the context on teacher behavior.
2. The impact of student background.
3. The individual differences among students in a classroom.
4. The relationship of subject matter to teacher effectiveness.
5. The problem of establishing a cognitive match (pairing between teacher and student).
6. The causal impact of student behavior on teacher behavior.

Clearly, effectiveness in teaching is dependent upon a great number of variables that are interpersonal, social, and institutional. Among the important classes of teacher variables are teacher characteristics, knowledge, skills of instruction, perceptions, confidence levels, and language usage. Student variables include student characteristics, knowledge, perceptions, confidence levels, language usage, and so on.

Borich provides a summary of presage (prior to teaching) variables that have been related to effective teaching (Table 9.1).

Another indicator of the complexity of the research task in identifying the effective teacher is provided by a list of teaching behaviors generated during the California Beginning Teacher Evaluation Study.

61 DIMENSIONS FOR COMPARING KNOWN SAMPLE CLASSROOMS

(T, C, or S denote the variable of the teacher, student or classroom as the focus of observation.)

1. *abruptness (T):* unanticipated "switching" by teacher, e.g., from instruction to classroom management, to behavior management, to instruction, to behavior management.

---

[4] Robert Stake and Terry Denny, "Needed Concepts and Techniques for Utilizing More Fully the Potential of Evaluation," in *Educational Evaluation: New Roles, New Means,* 68th Yearbook of the National Society for the Study of Education (Chicago: University of Illinois Press, 1969), p. 372.

Table 9.1

Presage Variables for Effective Teaching

Personality

Permissiveness
Dogmatism
Authoritarianism
Achievement-motivation
Introversion-extroversion
Abstractness-concreteness
Directness-indirectness
Locus of control
Anxiety
  1. general
  2. teaching

Attitude

Motivation to teach
Attitude toward children
Attitude toward teaching
Attitude toward authority
Vocational interest
Attitude toward self
  (self-concept)
Attitude toward subject taught

Experience

Years of teaching experience
Experience in subject taught
Experience in grade level
  taught
Workshops attended
Graduate courses taken
Degrees held
Professional papers written

Aptitude/Achievement

National Teachers Exam
Graduate Record Exam
Scholastic Aptitude Test
  1. verbal
  2. quantitative
Special ability tests, e.g., reasoning ability, logical ability,
  verbal fluency
Grade-point average
  1. overall
  2. in major subject
Professional recommendations
Student evaluations of teaching effectiveness
Student teaching evaluations

SOURCE: Gary D. Borich, *The Appraisal of Teaching: Concepts and Process* (Reading, Mass.: Addison-Wesley, 1977), p. 15.

2. *accepting (T):* teacher reacts constructively (overt, verbal, non-verbal) to students' feelings and attitudes.
3. *adult involvement (C):* adults other than the teacher are allowed to instruct.
4. *attending (T):* teacher actively listens to what student is saying, reading, reciting.
5. *awareness of developmental levels (T):* teacher is aware of a student's emotional, social educational needs and therefore assigns tasks appropriate for these.
6. *being liked(T):* teacher seeks approval from students in an ingratiating manner, often at expense of instruction.
7. *belittling (T):* teacher berates child in front of others.
8. *competing (T):* competition, outdoing others is emphasized by the teacher.

9. *complimenting (control) (T):* teacher's action reinforces student(s) whose behavior is in the right direction.
10. *consistency of message (control) (T):* teacher gives a direction or a threat and follows through with it.
11. *conviviality (C):* warmth, family-like quality to classroom interaction; good feelings between teacher-students, students-students.
12. *cooperation (S):* students cooperate with other students, teacher; willingness on part of students to help each other.
13. *defending (T):* teacher defends a student from verbal or physical assault by another.
14. *defiance (S):* a student's open resistance to teacher direction; refuses to comply.
15. *democracy (T):* teacher provides opportunities to involve students in decision making re: class standards, instruction, procedures, etc.
16. *distrust (T):* teacher expresses doubt for validity of student's work or behavior.
17. *drilling (T):* teacher emphasizes regularization, rote memory, retrieval of facts on part of student learning.
18. *encouraging (T):* teacher admonishes student effort in order to motivate.
19. *engagement (S):* students express eagerness to participate, appear actively, productively involved in learning activities.
20. *equity (T):* teacher appears to divide time, attention equally among all students.
21. *ethnicity (T):* teacher expresses positive, informative comments about racial, class, ethnic contributions; encourages class discussion about cultural contributions.
22. *excluding (T):* teacher banishes student from class activity—to corner, cloakroom, out of room, etc.
23. *expectation (T):* teacher attributes scholastic problems or predicts success for student on basis of past information or student's "background."
24. *filling time (T):* teacher fills "empty" time periods with "busy work."
25. *flexibility (T):* teacher adjusts instruction easily to accommodate change in plans, time schedule, absenteeism, or change of students' behavior.
26. *gendering (T):* teacher assigns roles on basis of male or female (boy-girl) and reinforces these.
27. *harrassing (T): teacher taunts, pesters, nags, hazes, "puts down," or physically hits a student.*
28. *ignoring (T):* teacher appears to deliberately "not hear" or "not see" so as to treat a student as being invisible.
29. *illogical statements (T):* teacher makes a statement whose consequences would be ridiculous if carried out.
30. *individualizing (T):* teacher assigns to each student learning tasks designed to match his/her individual abilities and interests.
31. *job satisfaction (T):* * teacher seems to enjoy teaching.
32. *knowledge of subject (T):* teacher seems confident in teaching a given subject, and demonstrates a grasp of it.
33. *manipulation (S):* student is able to get on demand a desired response from the teacher.
34. *mobility (S):* students move freely and purposefully around the room;

teacher allows students to work at places other than at their assigned seats.

35. *mobility (T):* teacher moves spontaneously about the room.
36. *modeling/imitation (S):* students copy teacher's behavior, and are encouraged to do so by teacher.
37. *monitoring learning (T):* teacher checks in on student's progress regularly and adjusts instruction accordingly.
38. *moralizing (T):* teacher emphasizes goodness vs. badness, verbally expresses ideal behavior model.
39. *oneness (T):* teacher treats whole group as "one" often in order to maintain peer control.
40. *openness (T):* teacher verbally acknowledges to students feelings of anger or frustration, admits mistakes, expresses need for self-improvement.
41. *open questioning (T):* teacher asks questions which call for interpretive responses and are open-ended.
42. *optimism (T):* teacher expresses positive, pleasant, optimistic attitudes and feelings.
43. *pacing (T):* teacher appears to perceive learning rate of students and adjusts teaching pace accordingly.
44. *peer teaching (S):* students help other students instructionally and are encouraged to do so, whether "olders" with "youngers" or students of same age group.
45. *personalizing (T):* teacher calls on students by name.
46. *policing (T):* undue emphasis on quietness, orderliness, good behavior, and teacher spends disproportionate time with monitoring student behavior and controlling for discipline.
47. *politeness (T):* teacher requests rather than commands, uses "please" and "thank you," encourages same in student-student interaction.
48. *praising (T):* teacher verbally rewards student.
49. *promoting self-sufficiency (T):* teacher encourages students to take responsibility for their own classwork.
50. *recognition-seeking (T):* teacher calls attention to self for no apparent instructional purpose.
51. *rushing (T):* teacher does not give students adequate response time, or answers for them; is tied to a pre-set time limit, and hurries students to finish work.
52. *sarcasm (T):* teacher responds in a demeaning manner, uses destructive/cutting remarks.
53. *shaming (T):* teacher instills guilt in students for their behavior in order to establish control.
54. *signaling (control) (T):* teacher uses body language, nonverbal signals to change students' behavior.
55. *spontaneity (T):* teacher capitalizes instructionally on unexpected incidents that arise during class time.
56. *stereotyping (T):* teacher labels and judges students by socioeconomic, ethnic, or racial characteristics.
57. *structuring (T):* teacher prepares students for lesson by reviewing, outlining, explaining objectives, summarizing.

58. *teacher-made materials (T):* teacher provides instructional materials other than textbooks, and arranges for their use by students.
59. *time fixedness (T):* teacher emphasizes promptness, begins and ends activities by clock rather than by student interest.
60. *waiting (T):* after asking a question, teacher waits in silence for student responses or waits in silence after student response before reacting.
61. *warmth (T):* teacher seeks contact with students, talks with them, shows affection toward them.

SOURCE: From William J. Tikunoff, David C. Berliner, and Ray C. Rist, *An Ethnographic Study of the Forty Classrooms of the Beginning Teacher Evaluation Study Known Sample,* Technical Report 75-10-5 (San Francisco: Far West Laboratory for Educational Research and Development, 1975), pp. 71–72. Used with permission.

Finally, Coker lists a set of generic competencies thought to be important in a 1974 study conducted in Georgia (Table 9.2).

Table 9.2
Generic Competencies List for Teachers

G- 1 *Gathers and uses information relating to individual differences among students.*

    1A-T) Maintains & uses formal/informal up-to-date records on individual students.

    1B-T) Consults appropriate authorities to select & administer appropriate standardized tests.

    1C-T) Recognizes limitations and seeks additional professional help.

G- 2 *Organizes pupils, resources, and materials for effective instruction.*

    2A-T) Selects goals & objectives appropriate to pupil need.

    2B-T) Matches student with appropriate material.

    2C-T) Gathers multi-level materials.

    2D-T) Teacher involves student in organizing and planning.

G- 3 *Demonstrates ability to communicate effectively with students.*

    3A-T) Gives clear, explicit directions.

    3B-T) Pauses, elicits, and responds to student questions.

    3C-T) Uses a variety of methods, verbal and nonverbal.

G- 4 *Assists students in using variety of relevant communication techniques.*

    4A-T) Demonstrates proper listening skills.

    4B-T) Respects individual's right to speak.

    4C-T) Utilizes non-verbal communication skills.

Table 9.2—*continued*

G- 5 *Assists students in dealing with their misconceptions and confusions.*

    5A-T) Utilizes student feedback, verbal and non-verbal to modify teaching behavior.

    5B-T) Demonstrates flexibility in classroom management practices.

    5C-T) When student is not on task, teacher makes contact.

    5D-T) Provides feedback to pupil on his behavior.

    5E-T) Teacher helps pupil correct cognitive misperceptions.

G- 6 *Responds appropriately to coping behavior of students.*

    6A-T) Maintains self-control in classroom situation and with students.

    6B-T) Recognizes and treats individual student behavior.

    6C-T) Accepts necessity of dealing with individual students.

G- 7 *Uses a variety of methods & materials to stimulate and promote pupil learning.*

    7A-T) Uses more than one instructional activity simultaneously.

G- 8 *Promotes self-awareness and positive self-concepts in students.*

    8A-T) Teacher provides opportunity for student to meet success daily.

    8B-T) Evidence of a personal one-to-one relationship with students.

    8C-T) Evidence of praise and/or rewards in operation.

    8D-T) Supportive classroom management.

G- 9 *Reacts with sensitivity to the needs and feelings of others.*

    9A-T) Accepts and incorporates student ideas.

    9B-T) Listens to students and provides feedback.

    9C-T) Evidence of opportunity for one-to-one counseling.

G-10 *Engages in personal and professional growth.*

    10A-T) Reads widely and critically.

    10B-T) Membership and active participation in appropriate professional organization.

SOURCE: Homer Coker, from a paper read at a conference of the American Association of Colleges of Teacher Education, Chicago, February 22, 1978. Used with permission. Not all of the above competencies have been found to contribute to teacher effectiveness.

As researchers continue to grapple with the complex network of variables found in the normal classroom, some guidelines concerning effective teaching are becoming visible. Such findings represent a broad outline of emerging principles that may soon guide practice in supervision.

CURRENT RESEARCH FINDINGS

While the roots of organized inquiry into teacher effectiveness can be traced to the early 1940s, serious study did not begin until the mid-1950s. Barak Rosenshine, a pioneer in the area of process-product studies, summarized the infant stage of current research:

> The number of studies has been small. Fewer than 25 studies have been conducted on any specific variable such as teacher praise or teacher questions, and these studies are spread across all grade levels, subject areas, and student backgrounds.
> The number of investigators in this field is also small. There are no more than twelve researchers or groups of researchers currently studying the relationship between classroom instruction and student achievement. . . .
> Although recent studies represent methodological and conceptual expansion of previous work, research on observed teaching behavior is new, sparse, and not always consistent in results. What we have learned to date is offered more as hypotheses for future study than as validated variables for the training and evaluation of teachers. Although practitioners can easily amass a large number of questions on teaching methods for which they would like clear answers, at the rate we are going it will be years before many of these questions are even studied.[5]

Early studies that raised important questions about the connection between teacher behavior and student achievement were rarely focused at the classroom level. A landmark study, called the "30 Schools Study" or "Eight-Year Study" was conducted in the 1930s under the auspices of the Progressive Education Association. In this study some 2,000 students from experimental schools entered 179 different colleges and were compared to other college students who attended traditional high school programs. Students from the experimental schools earned higher grades in college in all subjects except foreign language, raising the question of what type of teaching and curriculum best prepares students for later academic achievement.[6]

A similiar study of graduates of the Ohio State University Laboratory School, entitled "Guinea Pigs 20 Years After," documented striking success in school and upon graduation in spite of a pattern of

---

[5] Barak Rosenshine, "Recent Research On Teaching Behaviors and Student Achievement," *Journal of Teacher Education* 27, (Spring 1976): 61

[6] Wilford M. Aiken, *The Story of the Eight Year Study* (New York: Harper & Bros., 1942).

nontraditional instruction.[7] Other such studies began to suggest that the style of teaching had less to do with academic success than other factors such as socioeconomic level of the parents.

A major study by Dr. James Coleman, known as the Coleman Report, analyzed the schooling of 600,000 economicially and culturally deprived children. The report concluded that the primary determinants of student achievement were a sense of self-worth (high self concept) and the socioeconomic status of the parents. The role of the teacher in determining academic success was given little credibility.

Finally, an early study by Rosenthal and Jacobson, entitled "Pygmalion in the Classroom," documented the concept of teacher-induced student performance through a "self-fulfilling prophecy."[8] While the Rosenthal study has been challenged because of the statistical procedures used, the whole idea of a relation between teacher expectation and method of instruction used by teachers raised interesting research questions and stimulated thinking about the analysis of teaching.

By the conclusion of the 1960s considerable debate raged concerning the best method of promoting academic achievement. Such interest led to increased activity in teacher effectiveness research. At that point in time, the only comprehensive study of the literature on teacher effectiveness was one conducted in 1954 by Morsh and Wilder. They had concluded:

> No single specific observable teacher act has yet been found whose frequency or percent of occurrence is invariably and significantly correlated with student achievement.[9]

By 1971, a new review of the teacher effectiveness literature had been conducted by Rosenshine and Furst; their findings became the focus for a decade's inquiry into teaching and learning. Looking at what they considered to be relevant studies to that date, Rosenshine and Furst identified eleven teacher variables that had shown promising relationships to student gains in cognitive achievement. Five of the variables, the researchers contended, had strong support from major correlational studies. Six variables had less support, but were thought to be promising and, therefore, warranted further inquiry.

---

[7] For a discussion of this and other related studies see Wayne Jennings and Joe Nathan, "Starting/Disturbing Research on School Program Effectiveness," *Phi Delta Kappan* 58 (March 1977): 568-70.

[8] Robert Rosenthal and Lenore Jacobson, *Pygmalion in the Classroom: Teacher Expectation and Pupil's Intellectual Development* (New York: Holt, Rinehart & Winston, 1968).

[9] J. E. Morsh and E. W. Wilder, "Identifying the Effective Instructor: A Review of Quantitative Studies 1900-1952," *USAF Research Bulletin* AFPTRC-TR-54-44 (San Antonio, Tex.: United States Air Force, 1952).

The eleven teacher variables that were found to be strongly supported by existing research are listed and defined below. The number in parentheses after each item indicated how many correlational studies were found to support the particular variable.[10]

1. *Clarity* (7)—The cognitive clarity of the teacher's presentation.
2. *Variability* (8)—The teacher's use of variety during the lesson such as using different instructional materials, tests, or varying the level of cognitive discourse.
3. *Enthusiasm* (6)—Degree of stimulation, originality, or vigor presented by the teacher in the classroom.
4. *Task-oriented Behavior* (7)—Degree to which the teacher is businesslike or achievement-oriented in presentation.
5. *Student Opportunity to Learn Criterion Materials* (4)— Relationship between the material covered in class and the criterion pupil performance. Rosenshine and Furst also identified six variables of secondary importance that suggest significant teacher behaviors in instruction.
6. *Use of Student Ideas and General Indirectness* (8)— Acknowledging, modifying, applying, comparing, and summarizing student statements.
7. *Criticism* (17)—A strong negative relationship between teacher criticism and student achievement. Criticism includes hostility, strong disapproval, or need to justify authority.
8. *Use of Structuring Comments (Advanced Organizers)* (4)— Teacher provides "cognitive scaffolding" for completed or planned lesson.
9. *Types of Questions Asked* (7)—Questions categorized into low cognitive and high cognitive. Questions appropriate to task and group.
10. *Probing* (3)—Teacher responses that encourage the student to elaborate on his or her question.
11. *Level of Difficulty of Instruction* (4)—Student perception of the level of difficulty.

The effect of the Rosenshine and Furst summary on educational research was varied. The summary suggested an absoluteness, a certainty that some variables might be identified that could be shown to contribute to teacher effectiveness. This positivism spawned a number of large and complex studies on teacher behavior. The Rosenshine summary also focused research attention on the teacher, as opposed to other promising variables such as the student, the environment, or the curriculum experienced by the student. The past decade has largely been

---

[10] Adapted from Barak Rosenshine and Norma Furst, "Research On Teacher Performance Criteria," in *Research in Teacher Education: A Symposium*, ed. B. O. Smith, Englewood Cliffs, N.J.: Prentice-Hall, 1969), pp. 43–51.

an attempt to verify the "promising variables" proposed by these two researchers.

A number of major studies are worthy of mention as examples of process-product research on teacher effectiveness conducted in the 1970s: The Texas Teacher Effectiveness Project, the California Beginning Teacher Evaluation Study, Robert Soar's Follow Through Study, David Aspy's Study of the Effects of Self-Concept on Student Achievement, and Donald Medley's recent survey of other empirical studies on teacher effectiveness. While numerous other studies might be described here, the studies mentioned will suffice to illustrate the problems associated with varifying the Rosenshine and Furst proposal for identifying effective teachers.

One major study, the Texas Teacher Effectiveness Project, was an attempt to determine whether specific teacher behaviors contribute to student achievement as measured by performance on the Metropolitan Achievement Tests. In this study researchers discovered the complexity of interaction among critical variables. Brophy and Evertson report:

> The majority of significant relationships with learning gain (Metropolitan Achievement Tests) scores were negative. In short, we found out more about what not to do than we did about what to do. . . .The upshot of all this is that teaching involves orchestration of a large number of different behaviors which the teacher must have mastered to at least a certain minimal level and can adapt to different situations, as opposed to application of a few basic teaching skills that are "all-important." These behaviors were many and complex rather than few and simple. There are no magical "keys" to successful teaching.[11]

The Texas study did find that to increase achievement scores, a teacher should use strong classroom management, positive rather than negative reinforcement, possess high expectations for students, and maintain an optimal level of learning difficulty. Using materials that are too hard, holding low expectation for pupils, and not responding to the substance of student questions were all shown to detract from student achievement gains.

Perhaps more important for teacher education research was the finding of the Texas study that related teacher behavior to socioeconomic status (SES) of the learner. It was found that the general attitude of warmth and encouragement was characteristic of successful teachers in low SES schools, whereas "successful" teachers in high SES schools were not especially warm or encouraging. Such a finding suggests that teaching behaviors that are important to student achievement gains are, to some extent, situationally specific.

---

[11] Jere E. Brophy and Carolyn M. Evertson, "Teacher Behavior and Student Learning in Second and Third Grades," in *The Appraisal of Teaching: Concepts and Process*, ed. Gary Borich (Reading, Mass.: Addison-Wesley Publishing, 1977), pp. 79–89.

This finding (i.e., that some teaching behaviors are more effective in encouraging student gains in certain environments) was supported by a study conducted by Robert Soar in 1973. Using Project Follow Through classrooms as a subject, Soar found that positive affect is more functional, and negative affect more dysfunctional, for low SES students than for high SES students. Soar also found that teacher-initiated "structuring behavior" was functional for low socioeconomic status pupils, but dysfunctional for high SES students. Commenting on the importance of socioeconomic status for teaching effectiveness, Soar observed:

> These findings suggest that an intermediate amount of different kinds of teacher behaviors are best for a particular goal and for a particular group of pupils, but they don't begin to answer the question of the classroom teacher—how much of a certain behavior is best for which goal for which pupil? What we have so far is an organizing principle which can be used by the teacher and the researcher in thinking about effective teaching; we do not have specific answers for the teacher's question. This will require a more detailed research methodology than we have used, but it seems to be a very logical next step.[12]

Soar's "organizing principle" (i.e., certain teacher behaviors are functional for certain types of students) received support from a major review of empirical studies on teacher effectiveness conducted by Medley. Reporting on 289 studies in a 1977 monograph, Medley identified behaviors of teachers that seem effective or ineffective with pupils of low socioeconomic status in the primary grades (Table 9.3).

Another summary by Gage also pointed to desirable teacher behaviors supported by research studies. Clustering studies on teacher effectiveness, Gage makes the following suggestions for teachers:

> Teachers should have a system of rules that allow pupils to attend to their personal and procedural needs without having to check with the teacher.

> Teachers should move around the room a lot, monitoring pupils' . . . work and communicating to their pupils an awareness of their behavior, while also attending to their academic needs.

> When pupils work independently, teachers should ensure that the assignments are interesting and worthwhile, yet still easy enough to be completed by each—working without teacher direction.

> Teachers should keep to a minimum such activities as (orally) giving directions and organizing the class for instruction. Teachers can do this by writing the daily schedule on the board, ensuring that pupils know where to go and what to do, and so on.

---

[12] R. S. Soar, *Follow Through Classroom Process Measurement* (Gainesville: Florida Educational Research and Development Council, University of Florida, 1971), p. 10.

Table 9.3—*continued*

Behaviors Found to be Characteristic of Effective and Ineffective Teachers of Pupils of Low Socioeconomic Status in the Primary Grades

Effective Teachers	Ineffective Teachers
1. *Maintenance of Learning Environment*	
Less deviant, disruptive pupil behavior	More deviant, disruptive pupil behavior
Fewer teacher rebukes	More teacher rebukes, more
Less criticism	criticism
Less time spent on classroom management	More time spent on classroom management
More praise, positive motivation	Less praise, positive interaction
2. *Use of Pupil Time*	
More time spent in task-related "academic" activities	Less class time spent in task-related, "academic" activities
More time working with large groups or whole class	Less time working with large groups or whole class
Less time working with small groups	More time working with small groups
Small groups of pupils work independently less of the time	Small groups of pupils work independently more of the time
Less independent seatwork	More independent seatwork
3. *Quality of Instruction*	
More "low-level" questions	Fewer "low-level" questions
Fewer "high-level" questions	More "high-level" questions
Less likely to amplify, discuss, or use pupil answers	More likely to amplify, discuss or use pupil answers
Fewer pupil-initiated questions and comments	More pupil-initiated questions and comments
Less feedback on pupil questions	More feedback on pupil questions
More attentive to pupils when they are working independently	Less attentive to pupils when they are working independently

SOURCE: From D. Medley, "Teacher Competence and Teacher Effectiveness," monograph (Washington, D.C.: American Association of Colleges of Teacher Education, 1977), p. 15.

In selecting pupils to respond to questions, teachers should call on a child by name before asking the question as a means of ensuring that all pupils are given an equal number of opportunities to answer questions.

With less academically oriented pupils, teachers should always aim at getting the child to give some kind of response to a question. Rephrasing, giving cues, or asking a new question can be useful techniques for bringing forth some answer from a previously silent pupil or one who says "I don't know" or answers incorrectly.

During . . . group instruction, teachers should give a maximal amount of brief feedback and provide fast-paced activities of the "drill" type.

Teachers should criticize, but infrequently, and primarily the academically oriented pupils and those of higher socioeconomic status.

Teachers should optimize "academic learning time"—time during which pupils are actively and productively engaged in their academic learning tasks.

When time is taken for exploration, creativity, self-direction, and games, it should not infringe upon "academic learning time," if achievement is desired.

Characteristics of teacher behavior such as clarity, enthusiasm, and vividness correlate with pupil achievement.[13]

A recent study by Brooks and Wilson underlines the need to view teacher behaviors in terms of their application toward selected pupils. They observe:

Knowing how to act is important to instructional effectiveness, but knowing in what interpersonal context to exhibit a particular behavior is a higher level of prescription for teachers.[14]

Another major study on teacher effectiveness conducted in the 1970s was the California Beginning Teacher Evaluation Study (BTES), which looked at elementary reading and mathematics achievement in forty-three California schools. This study was unique in its use of an "ethnographic [descriptive anthropological] approach" to the study of teaching. Using trained anthropologists skilled in observing but unfamiliar with school environments, this study tried to identify and isolate general teaching skills that influence learning. In the final report, the researchers conclude:

The history of research on teaching, for example, has been characterized by the attempt to find general teaching skills which insignificantly influence learning. Did we find any single teaching skill which correlated with learning in both reading and math at both grade levels? No such skills were found. Performances which correlated significantly with outcomes were different by subject matter and by grade level.

This result, if replicated, or if found in comparable studies, is an important one. It indicated that the pattern of effective teaching performances will differ by subject matter and probably grade level. The practical implications

---

[13] N. L. Gage, *The Scientific Basis of the Art of Teaching* (New York: Teachers College Press, 1977). Used with permission.

[14] Douglas Brooks and Barry Wilson, "Teacher Verbal and Nonverbal Behavior Expression Toward Selected Pupils," *Journal of Educational Psychology* 70 (1978): 153.

of such a conclusion are obvious; the goals of training teachers in the primary grades and the intermediate grades will necessarily be different.[15]

While the California Beginning Teacher Evaluation Study did not isolate a specific teaching skill or set of skills that directly correlated with learning, data analysis of observations did unveil a host of dimensions in which effective teachers (those with high student gains) at both levels (grades 2 and 5, reading) are alike. Berliner reports:

> Teachers classified as more effective were found to be more satisfied, accepting, attentive, aware of developmental needs, consistent in controlling classes, democratic, encouraging, tolerant of race and class, flexible, optimistic, equitable in dividing time among students, and knowledgeable of the subject. In addition, more effective teachers provided more structure for the learners, capitalized on unexpected wants, showed more warmth, waited for students to answer questions, promoted students to take responsibility for their work, used more praise, adjusted teaching to the learner's rate, individualized, monitored learning, used less 'busy work,' did not treat the class as a whole, made fewer illogical statements, were less belittling, less harrassing, less ignoring, and less recognition seeking.[16]

A final contribution of the BTES was to suggest a clear linkage between the cognitive styles of teachers and students. Such commonality in "ways of thinking" could mean that students might learn best under teachers with particular cognitive patterns. Stone explains:

> Cognitive style is an individual difference variable defined as a consistent mode of information processing. The field-dependence-independence dimension of cognitive style is a continuum, with the field-dependent end characterized by a more global, undifferentiated approach and the field-independent end by a more analytical, differentiated approach to perceptual processing.
>
> This cognitive style dimension has been shown to relate to both how teachers teach and how students learn. Field-dependent teachers tend to prefer teaching situations which allow for interaction with the students, whereas, field-independent teachers prefer more impersonal situations and tend to stress the cognitive aspects of teaching.
>
> The field-dependence-independence dimension of cognitive style also relates to how children learn. Due to their greater social sensitivity, field-dependent children tend to be more adept at learning and remembering materials that have social content, and to be more affected by criticism than field-independent children. On the other hand, field-independent children

---

[15] Frederick McDonald and Patricia Elias, "The Effects of Teacher Performance on Pupil Learning," in *BTES Phase II*, vol. I (Princeton, N.J.: Educational Testing Service, 1975), pp. 368–69.

[16] David C. Berliner, "Impediments to the Study of Teacher Effectiveness Research," *Journal of Teacher Education* 27 (Spring 1976): 5-6.

are able to impose their own structure on ambiguous or unstructured learning tasks.[17]

A final study worth noting is not as well known as the previously cited studies, but definitely of potential importance to supervisors who make judgments about teacher effectiveness. In a Florida study, Aspy found that the self-concept of teachers related positively to the cognitive growth of students. This positive relationship was found for four subtests of the Stanford Achievement Test. Aspy observes:

> This study supports the general hypothesis that there is a positive relationship between the levels of teacher self concept and the cognitive growth of the students. In particular, it points up the need for assessing teachers on other than intellective indices.[18]

While Aspy's study suffers in design from an extremely small number of teachers observed, the findings suggest the need for further inquiry into effective influences on teacher effectiveness.

The conclusion one must draw in reviewing research on teacher effectiveness during the past ten years is that the eleven variables identified as promising by Rosenshine and Furst will not be easily validated. As Kennedy and Bush have observed,

> it is difficult to argue with the spirit of Rosenshine's recent contention that the greatest current need is to conduct more research which is designed to link teacher variables with student outcomes. However, studies which attempt to explore further the relationships between student growth and the 11 or so correlates advanced by Rosenshine will be greatly hampered and their value possibly reduced, until serious attention is given to the problem of defining these abstract constructs in terms of low-inference behaviors.[19]

It should be obvious to the reader that research on teacher effectiveness is in an embryonic stage of development. In fact, the past ten years of inquiry have served only to reveal the complexity of pupil-teacher interaction in a classroom setting and the limitations of our current research methodology.

We seemed to have learned that no single teacher behavior or set of behaviors will universally promote student achievement gains in all subjects. Further, research to date suggests that certain strategies are

---

[17] Meredith K. Stone "Correlates of Teacher and Student Style," in *BTES Phase II 1973-74* (Princeton, N.J.: Educational Testing Service, 1976), p. 13.

[18] David N. Aspy, *The Effect on Teacher Inferred Self Concept Upon Student Achievement 1969* (Gainesville: University of Florida, 1969), p. 1.

[19] John J. Kennedy and Andrew J. Bush, "Overcoming Some Impediments to the Study of Teacher Effectiveness," *Journal of Teacher Education* 27 (Spring 1976): 16.

appropriate for unique groups of pupils, and that the ultimate findings of teacher effectiveness research may call for the matching of teachers and students according to variables as specific as thinking style or personality. The road to prescriptions for classroom teachers by supervisors will be a long one.

Of interest is a recent National Institute of Education (NIE) task force report that reveals the direction the "experts" think teacher effectiveness will take in the 1980s. Writing papers for NIE on future directions for teacher effectiveness research, known researchers identified five principles that will guide inquiry:

1. More descriptive research at the classroom level, paying attention to the ecology or environment of the classroom.
2. More indepth, longitudinal studies using small samples.
3. Greater use of interdisciplinary research including sociologists, anthropologists, economists, and scholars in the area of linguistics.
4. Focusing study on the status quo as opposed to studying the effects of experimental systems in the classroom.
5. Greater involvement of teachers in the research process, using teachers as collaborators in research and not simply as subjects.[20]

In general, an alternative to the "process-product" research of the past decade is emerging. It will be called "descriptive," "qualitative," or "ethnographic" research, and it will be more holistic than previous research.

It should be noted, parenthetically, that the focus of teacher effectiveness research during the past ten years has been exceedingly narrow. It sought only to find teacher characteristics that contribute to student cognitive gains as reported by standardized achievement tests. It is probable that this focus will broaden as more researchers attend to the topic. It is also probable that research in the future will begin to define "systems" of instruction in which certain teacher behaviors, student behaviors, interaction patterns, and environmental conditions are identified with particular types of student growth and learning.

While the complexity of current research does not give a clear direction to the supervisor seeking to assist a classroom teacher in improving instruction, it does indicate general directions for effective teaching. Certainly, no supervisor responsible for evaluating instruction can afford to be ignorant of ongoing teacher effectiveness research.

SUMMARY

As evaluators, supervisors are asked to define and judge good teaching. In the absence of clear definitions of what schools are trying to

---

[20] As reported by Virginia Koehler in "Classroom Process Research: Present and Future," *Journal of Classroom Interaction* 13 (1978): 6–7.

accomplish with students, the definition of good teaching becomes a situational phenomenon. At the lowest level, good teaching may be defined as those teacher behaviors that contribute to student achievement gains as measured by standardized achievement tests.

Educational research can assist the supervisor in developing principles or explanatory statements about effective teaching. Teaching effectiveness research is concerned with the relationships between the characteristics of the teachers and their behavior and their effects on the educational outcomes of classroom teaching.

During the past ten years there has been a concerted effort among researchers to find and verify the existence of a few basic teaching skills that enhance student achievement. The eleven variables identified by Rosenshine and Furst in 1971 have not been certified because low-inference behaviors that define the variables are not yet clear. What *has* been discovered by teacher effectiveness research during the past decade is that teaching and learning are complex constructs with many interacting variables.

It is likely that the future of teacher effectiveness research will seek to define "systems" of variables which, when in a pattern of interaction, lead to certain types of student growth.

Suggested Learning Activities

1. Summarize, in no more than 200 words, the problems associated with establishing teacher effectiveness research.

2. Identify resources that will enable the practicing supervisor to keep up with developing research on teacher effectiveness and student achievement.

3. Outline a plan for communicating research findings relevant to improving instruction to classroom teachers.

Books to Review

Bellack, Arno, and Davitz, Joel. *The Language of Classroom: Meanings Communicated in High School Teaching*, USOE Cooperative Research Project 1947. New York: Columbia University, 1963.

Biddle, Bruce and Ellena, William, eds. *Contemporary Research on Teacher Effectiveness*. New York: Holt, Rinehart & Winston, 1964.

Borich, Gary. *The Appraisal of Teaching: Concepts and Process.* Reading, Mass.: Addison-Wesley Publishing, 1977.

Brophy, Jere, and Evertson, Carolyn. *The Texas Teacher Effectiveness Project.* Austin: Research and Development Center, University of Texas, 1974.

Dunkin, M., and Biddle, Bruce. *The Study of Teaching.* New York: Holt, Rinehart & Winston, 1974.

Flanders, Ned. *Analyzing Teacher Behavior.* Reading, Mass.: Addison-Wesley Publishing, 1970.

Gage, Nathaniel, ed. *Handbook of Research on Teaching.* Chicago: Rand-McNally, 1963.

Good, C. *Introduction To Educational Research,* 2nd ed. New York: Appleton-Century-Croft, 1963.

Kounin, Jacob S. *Discipline and Group Management in Classrooms.* New York: Holt, Rinehart & Winston, 1970.

Neagley, Ross, and Evans, Dean. *Handbook for Effective Supervision of Instruction.* Englewood Cliffs, N.J.: Prentice-Hall, 1970.

Smith, B. O., ed. *Research in Teacher Education: A Symposium.* Englewood Cliffs, N.J.: Prentice-Hall, 1969.

Travers, Robert, ed. *Second Handbook of Research on Teaching.* Chicago: Rand-McNally, 1973.

Travers, Robert. *Introduction to Educational Research.* Chicago: Rand-McNally, 1978.

10

The Supervisor and Improvement of Teaching Behavior

INTRODUCTION

A major leadership role for modern supervisors is helping teachers analyze and improve teaching behavior. Supervisors must be responsible for helping identify competencies needed in teaching, helping analyze the reported proficiencies of teachers in these competencies, and giving teachers assistance in developing the competencies they need.

A major study conducted by Fred Pigge at Bowling Green reported on teachers' self-reported need and proficiency in twenty-six competency areas and indicated where the proficiencies were developed.[1] Im-

---

[1] Much of the material in this chapter is taken from Chapter 17, "Analyzing Classrooms and Supervising Instructional Personnel," Jon Wiles and Joseph Bondi, *Curriculum Development: A Guide to Practice* (Columbus, Ohio: Charles E. Merrill Publishing, 1979), pp. 306-27.

plications from this study are important because they indicate that teachers obtain the competencies they need not in pre-service teacher training institutions, but in training programs in the field.[2] As stressed earlier in this text, we believe supervisors must provide leadership in designing and directing meaningful in-service programs to help teachers achieve professional growth.

Table 10.1 identifies teachers' self-reported need in twenty-six competency areas and indicates where the proficiencies were developed.

IMPROVING TEACHER EFFECTIVENESS

Until recently, educational practitioners have had little help from educational researchers in helping identify and improve teacher behavior. Other than a general checklist of teacher competencies, a supervisor was armed with little else to judge the effectiveness of a particular teacher. Since about 1960, however, systems and instruments have been developed to help us look at classroom instruction in a more systematic way. Observational systems that measure classroom interaction probably show the most promise as learning devices for both pre- and in-service teachers.[3] An observational system is defined here as any systematic technique for identifying, examining, classifying, and/or quantifying specific teaching activities. Of the observational systems available, Flander's System of Interaction Analysis of verbal behavior is probably the most widely known and used.[4]

Interaction Analysis

During the past ten years, a number of innovations have been developed and implemented in teacher education programs in an attempt to improve the ultimate effectiveness of the teachers who come out of these programs. The concept of systematic observation is certainly one of the more widely publicized of these recent innovations. By its very nature and basic construct, an observational system represents an effective means

---

[2] Fred Pigge, "Teacher Competencies: Need, Proficiency, and Where the Proficiency Was Developed," *Journal of Teacher Education* 29 (July–August 1978): 70–76. There were over 2,600 teachers and principals involved in this study.

[3] Joseph C. Bondi, Jr., "The Effects of Interaction Analysis Feedback on the Verbal Behavior of Student Teachers," *Educational Leadership* 26 (May 1969): 794–99.

[4] Ned A. Flanders, *Teacher Influence—Pupil Attitudes and Achievement.* (Washington D.C.: Research Monograph 12, H.E.W., 1965).

Table 10.1

Teachers' Self-Reported Need and Proficiency in 26 Competency Areas and an Indication of Where the Proficiencies Were Developed

	MEDIAN RANKS PERTAINING TO:				WHERE NEEDED PROFICIENCY DEVELOPED			
	Need for Competency		Proficiency in Applying Skill		Teacher Education Institution		Work Experience	
	Mdn	Rank	Mdn	Rank	Percent	Rank	Percent	Rank
1. Ability to maintain order in a classroom and to assist students in the development of self-discipline.	4.84	1	3.52	3	8	26	71	1
2. Ability to motivate student achievement via modeling, reinforcement, provision of success experiences, and appeal to student interests.	4.75	2	3.26	9	28	15	50	5
3. Ability to apply appropriate evaluative techniques for the systematic evaluation of pupil progress.	4.61	3.5	3.43	5	47	7	38	12.5
4. Ability to individualize instruction to meet the varying needs of students, via techniques such as mastery learning, alternative assignments, individual contracting, and group work.	4.61	3.5	3.13	12	21	19.5	47	7
5. Ability to utilize audiovisual equipment and materials in teaching.	4.51	5	3.64	1	42	8	38	12.5
6. Ability to provide instruction leading to the different cognitive goals of acquisition, comprehension, and application of knowledge.	4.45	6	3.18	11	34	10	45	8.5
7. Ability to encourage and facilitate the development of social skills and enhanced self-concept.	4.37	7	3.10	13	19	21.5	53	4
8. Ability to prepare teacher-made tests.	4.30	8	3.62	2	54	3.5	30	17
9. Ability to utilize observational techniques effectively in classroom.	4.28	9	3.28	8	31	13.5	48	6

Table 10.1—continued

10. Ability to utilize an understanding of the formal chain of control, decision making, communication, and authority within each school unit and their effects upon the daily operation of the classroom.	4.22	10	3.30	7	18	23.5	60	2
11. Ability to interpret and report student performance on teacher-made tests.	4.10	11	3.35	6	53	5	29	19
12. Ability to understand the role of teacher organizations with the formal and informal competition for control of education and one's own personal role in joining or not joining such organizations.	4.08	12	3.04	14	18	23.5	56	3
13. Ability to continue the development and clarification of one's own philosophy of education.	4.03	13	3.21	10	32	11.5	40	10.5
14. Ability to construct behavior/performance objectives in subject matter field.	3.99	14	3.46	4	63	1	15	23
15. Ability to apply the major principles of school law to areas such as due process, contracts, certification, teacher liability, and corporal punishment.	3.97	15	2.66	20.5	32	11.5	36	14.5
16. Ability to use value clarification techniques at any age level.	3.87	16	2.80	16	22	18	29	19
17. Ability to distinguish between bonafide educational innovation and temporary, fleeting fads.	3.82	17	2.99	15	19	21.5	45	8.5
18. Ability to utilize the sources of pressure for change in education, understand currently suggested innovations, and perceive potential consequences of alternatives.	3.77	18	2.72	18	21	19.5	40	10.5
19. Ability to apply the basic principles of how schools are financed, sources of income and major areas of expenditure, and how these factors directly affect classroom operation.	3.65	19	2.68	19	31	13.5	36	14.5
20. Ability to understand the implications of the legal control of education by the state legislature, state department, and state board of education.	3.64	20	2.40	22	25	17	34	16
21. Ability to understand the effects of federal legislation and programs in education through financial support and Supreme Court decisions.	3.52	21	2.29	26	27	16	29	19
22. Ability to utilize reading organization skills to divide a class into reading groups.	3.45	22	2.36	24	17	25	24	21

Table 10.1—continued

23. Ability to interpret and report student performance on standardized tests.	3.15	23	2.78	17	55	2	14	24.5
24. Ability to compare and contrast various philosophical viewpoints.	3.03	24	2.66	20.5	52	6	14	24.5
25. Knowledge of the interaction between the cultural matrices and educational systems.	3.02	25	2.38	23	39	9	19	22
26. Ability to choose from a broad knowledge of history of education the ideas that have shaped our culture.	2.62	26	2.32	25	54	3.5	4	26

a) *Rank order correlation between need and proficiency ranks = .83.*
b) *Rank order correlation between ranks of needs and ranks of competencies developed at the teacher education institution = -.20.*
c) *Rank order correlation between ranks of needs and ranks of competencies developed through work experience = .74.*

SOURCE: Fred Pigge, "Teacher Competencies: Need, Proficiency, and Where the Proficiency Was Developed," *Journal of Teacher Education* 29 (July–August 1978):70–76. Used with permission.

for providing objective empirical data describing specific teacher and student variables that are found to interact in a given teaching-learning situation. Data of this kind have been found to be quite helpful in assisting teachers to analyze and improve their individual teaching effectiveness.

Currently, several manageable observational systems are available for teacher use. Each is specifically designed to assess a different and particular dimension of the classroom situation. Originally developed by Flanders, interaction analysis is designed to assess the verbal dimension of teacher-pupil interaction in the classroom.

Flanders developed a category system that takes into account the verbal interaction between teachers and pupils in the classroom. The system enables one to determine whether the teacher controls students in such a way as to increase or decrease freedom or action. Through the use of observers or audio or videotape equipment, a teacher can review the results of a teaching lesson. Every three seconds an observer writes down the category number of the interaction he or she has just observed; the numbers are recorded in sequence in a column. Whether the observer is using a live classroom or tape recording for observations, it is best that he or she spend ten to fifteen minutes getting oriented to the situation before categorizing. The observer stops classifying whenever the classroom activity is inappropriate as, for instance, when there is silent reading or when various groups are working in the classroom, or when children are working in their workbooks.

A modification of the Flanders system of ten categories is a system developed by Hough and used by Bondi and Ober in research studies.[5] This system provides three more categories of behavior than the Flanders system. In the thirteen category system, teacher statements are classified as either indirect or direct. This classification gives central attention to the amount of freedom a teacher gives to the student. In a given situation, the teacher can choose to be indirect, maximizing freedom of a student to respond, or direct, minimizing the freedom of a student to respond. Teacher response is classified under the first nine categories.

Student talk is classified under three categories and a fourth category provides for silence or confusion where neither a student or the teacher can be heard. All categories are mutually exclusive, yet include all verbal interaction occurring in the classroom. Table 10.2 describes the categories in the thirteen category modification of the Flanders System of Interaction Analysis. Table 10.3 describes the Reciprocal Category System. This system, developed by Richard Ober, is an elaboration of the ten and thirteen category systems of interaction analysis.

---

[5] Joseph Bondi and Richard Ober, "The Effects of Interaction Analysis Feedback on the Verbal Behavior of Student Teachers" (Paper presented at the annual meeting of the American Educational Research Association, Los Angeles, February 1969).

Table 10.2

Description of Categories for a Thirteen-Category Modification of the Flanders System of Interaction Analysis

Category Number	Description of Verbal Behavior

TEACHER — **INDIRECT**

1   ACCEPTS FEELING: Accepts and clarifies the feeling tone of students in a friendly manner. Student feelings may be of a positive or negative nature. Prediting and recalling student feelings are also included.

2   PRAISES OR ENCOURAGES: Praises or encourages student action, behavior, recitation, comments, ideas, etc. Jokes that release tension not at the expense of another individual. Teacher nodding head or saying "uh-huh" or "go on" are included.

3   ACCEPTS OR USES IDEAS OF STUDENT: Clarifying, building on, developing, and accepting the action, behavior, and ideas of the student.

4   ASKS QUESTIONS: Asking a question about the content (subject matter) or procedure with the intent that the student should answer.

5   ANSWERS STUDENT QUESTIONS (STUDENT-INITIATED TEACHER TALK): Giving direct answers to student questions regarding content or procedures.

TALK — **DIRECT**

6   LECTURE (TEACHER-INITIATED TEACHER TALK): Giving facts, information, or opinions about content or procedure. Teacher expressing his or her own ideas. Asking rhetorical questions (not intended to be answered).

7   GIVES DIRECTIONS: Directions, commands, or orders to which the student is expected to comply.

8   CORRECTIVE FEEDBACK: Telling a student that his answer is wrong when the correctness of his answer can be established by other than opinions (i.e., empirical validation, definition, or custom).

9   CRITICIZES STUDENT(S) OR JUSTIFIES AUTHORITY: Statements intended to change student behavior from a nonacceptable to an acceptable pattern; scolding someone; stating why the teacher is doing what he is doing so as to gain or maintain control; rejecting or criticizing a student's opinion or judgment.

10   TEACHER-INITIATED STUDENT TALK: Talk by students in response to requests or narrow teacher questions. The teacher initiates the contact or solicits student's statements.

Table 10.2—*continued*

		11	STUDENT QUESTIONS: Student questions concerning content or procedure that are directed to the teacher.
S T U D E N T	T A L K	12	STUDENT-INITIATED STUDENT TALK: Talk by students in response to broad teacher questions which require judgment or opinion. Voluntary declarative statements offered by the student, but not called for by the teacher.
		13	SILENCE OR CONFUSION: Pauses, short periods of silence, and periods of confusion in which communication cannot be understood by an observer.

Indirect-Direct Ratio $= \dfrac{\text{categories } 1, 2, 3, 4, 5}{\text{categories } 6, 7, 8, 9}$

Revised Indirect-Direct Ratio $= \dfrac{\text{categories } 1, 2, 3}{\text{categories } 7, 8, 9}$

Student-Teacher Ratio $= \dfrac{\text{categories } 10, 11, 12}{\text{categories } 1, 2, 3, 4, 5, 6, 7, 8, 9}$

SOURCE: John B. Hough, "A Thirteen Category Modification of Flanders' System of Interaction Analysis," mimeograph (Columbus: The Ohio State University, 1965).

TEACHERS' VERBAL PATTERNS IN THE CLASSROOM

Utilizing the Flanders system and its other modifications, teachers and supervisors can begin to isolate the essential elements of effective teaching by analyzing and categorizing the verbal behavioral patterns of teachers and students.

Four classroom patterns that particularly affect pupil learning are thrown into sharp relief when verbal patterns are identified and revealed by these techniques. The first pattern can be labeled "the excessive teacher-talk pattern." This occurs when teachers talk two-thirds or more of the time in the classroom. Obviously, if teachers are talking that much, there is very little time for students to get in the act. In classrooms where teachers talk this much, pity the curriculum approaches that emphasize extensive student participation in learning. Yet such a percentage of teacher-talk is found in many classrooms today. Teachers can become aware of and able to control the amount of time they spend talking in the classroom through the use of feedback from interaction analysis.[6] This finding alone makes interaction analysis an effective teaching and supervisory tool.

A second verbal pattern is recitation. Arno Bellack, a pioneer in

Table 10.3
Summary of Categories for the Ober Reciprocal Category System

Category Number Assigned to Party 1*	Description of Verbal Behavior	Category Number Assigned to Party 2+
1	"WARMS" (INFORMALIZES) THE CLIMATE: Tends to open up and/or eliminate the tension of the situation; praises or encourages the action, behavior, comments, ideas, and/or contributions of another; jokes that release tension not at the expense of others; accepts and clarifies the feeling tone of another in a friendly manner (feelings may be positive or negative; predicting or recalling the feelings of another are included).	11
2	ACCEPTS: Accepts the action, behavior, comments, ideas, and/or contributions of another; *positive reinforcement* of these.	12
3	AMPLIFIES THE CONTRIBUTIONS OF ANOTHER: Asks for clarification of, builds on, and/or develops the action, behavior, comments, ideas and/or contributions of another.	13
4	ELICITS: Asks a question or requests information about the content subject, or procedure being considered with the intent that another should answer (respond).	14
5	RESPONDS: Gives direct answer or response to questions or requests for information that are initiated by another; includes answers to ones own questions.	15
6	INITIATES: Presents facts, information, and/or opinion concerning the content, subject, or procedures being considered that are self-initiated; expresses ones own ideas; lectures (includes rhetorical questions—not intended to be answered).	16
7	DIRECTS: Gives directions, instructions, order, and/or assignments to which another is expected to comply.	17
8	CORRECTS: Tells another that his answer or behavior is inappropriate or incorrect.	18

Table 10.3—*continued*

9   "COOLS" (FORMALIZES) THE CLIMATE: Makes statements   19
intended to modify the behavior of another from an inappropriate to an appropriate pattern; may tend to create a certain
amount of tension (i.e., bawling out someone, exercising
authority in order to gain or maintain control of the situation,
rejecting or criticizing the opinion or judgement of another).

10   SILENCE OR CONFUSION: Pauses, short periods of silence,   10
and periods of confusion in which communication cannot be
understood by the observer.

* Category numbers assigned to Teacher Talk when used in classroom
situation.
+ Category numbers assigned to Student Talk when used in classroom
situation.

SOURCE: From Richard L. Ober, "The Reciprocal Category System—A System for
Assessing Classroom Verbal Interaction" (Tampa: University of South Florida, 1971),
Used with permission.

describing verbal behavior of teachers and pupils, has noted that despite
differences in ability or background, teachers acted very much like one
another.[7] They talked between two-thirds and three-quarters of the time.
The majority of their activity was asking and reacting to questions that
called for factual answers from students. Bellack and his colleagues
presented an elaborate description of the verbal behavior of teachers and
students during a study of fifteen New York City area high school social
studies classrooms.[8] They summarized the results of their analysis in a
set of descriptive "rules of the language game of teaching." Among their
observations were the following:

1. The teacher-pupil ratio of activity in lines of typescript is 3 to 1. Therefore,
teachers are considerably more active in amount of verbal activity.
2. The pedagogical roles of the classroom are clearly delineated for pupils
and teachers. Teachers are responsible for structuring the lesson and

---

[6] Joseph C. Bondi, Jr., "Feedback in the Form of Printed Interaction Analysis
Matrices as a Technique for Training Student Teachers" (Paper read at the
annual meeting of the American Educational Research Association, Los
Angeles, February 1969).
[7] Arno A. Bellack et al., *The Language of the Classroom* (New York: Teachers
College Press, 1966).
[8] Ibid, p. 84.

soliciting responses. The primary task of the pupil is to respond to the teacher's solicitations.

3. In most cases, structuring accounts for about ten lines spoken; soliciting, responding, and reacting each account for twenty to thirty percent of the lines.

4. The basic verbal interchange in the classroom is the solicitation-response. Classes differ in the rate at which verbal interchanges take place.

5. By far, the largest proportion of the discourse involved empirical (factual) meanings. Most of the units studied were devoted to stating facts and explaining principles while much less of the discourse involved defining terms or expressing or justifying opinions. The core of the teaching sequence found in the classrooms studied was a teacher question, a pupil response, and more often than not, a teacher's reaction to that response.[9]

William Hoetker studied junior high English classes in 1967 and his findings were much the same as Bellack's.[10]

Hoetker compared his findings to Bellack's in a report in the *American Educational Research Journal*. Those comparisons are found in Table 10.4.

The findings of Bellack and Hoetker hardly seem earthshaking to those who have observed teaching over the years. As a pedagogical method, the question-answer sequence was fully recognized fifty years ago when teacher education consisted of considerable training in the skill of asking questions. Unfortunately, it is still with us, despite the fact that successive generations of otherwise quite disparate educational leaders have condemned the rapid-fire question-answer pattern of instruction. This leads us to question the efficiency, or, in this case, the inefficiency of teacher training institutions in molding the classroom behavior of teachers. If recitation is indeed a poor pedagogical method, why have teacher educators not been able to deter teachers from using it? Is recitation of textbook facts still to be the representative method of teaching pupils in American schools?

A classroom where recitation predominates suggests not only that a teacher is doing most of the work, but is giving little attention to individual needs of students. Moreover, the educational assets of role recitation are only verbal memory and superficial judgement.[11]

A third verbal pattern of teachers that affects student learning is teacher acceptance of student ideas. There is ample evidence that teachers who accept the ideas and feelings of students enhance learning

---

[9] Ibid., pp. 84–6.

[10] William J. Hoetker, "An Analysis of the Subject Matter Related Verbal Behavior in Nine Junior High English Classes" (Ed.D. diss., Washington University, 1967).

[11] Joseph C. Bondi, Jr., "Verbal Patterns of Teachers in the Classroom," *The National Elementary Principal* 50 (April 1971): 60–61.

Table 10.4
*Comparisions Between Selected Mean Measures
of Classroom Verbal Behavior in Bellack (1966) and Hoetker (1967)*

Measure	Bellack	Hoetker
A. Percentage of teacher talk, moves	61.7	65.7
B. Percentage of teacher talk, lines of typescript	72.1	74.5
C. Distribution of teacher moves, as percentage of all moves		
STRUCTURING	4.8	3.6
SOLICITING	28.8	32.3
RESPONDING	3.5	1.8
REACTING	24.3	27.0
D. Distribution of pupil moves, as percentage of all moves		
STRUCTURING	0.4	0.3
SOLICITING	4.4	2.0
RESPONDING	25.0	30.4
REACTING	5.7	1.1
E. Distribution of teacher moves, as percentage of total lines of typescript		
STRUCTURING	14.5	22.4
SOLICITING	20.3	20.6
RESPONDING	5.0	4.3
REACTING	24.8	31.4
F. Distribution of pupil moves, as percentage of total lines of typescript		
STRUCTURING	3.0	3.4
SOLICITING	2.5	1.2
RESPONDING	15.6	13.1
REACTING	5.1	0.6
G. Percentage of teacher questions calling for memory processes	80.8*	87.9

SOURCE: James Hoetker and William Ahlbrand, "The Persistence of the Recitation," *American Educational Research Journal* 6 (March 1969): 147. Copyright 1969, American Educational Research Association, Washington, D.C. Used with permission.

in the classroom. A number of observational systems have been used to identify teacher acceptance. In a large-scale study, Flanders isolated junior high school teachers whose students learned the most and the least in social studies and mathematics. He found teachers of higher achieving classes used five to six times as much acceptance and encouragement of student ideas than teachers in lower achieving classes. Teachers in higher achieving classes were also less directive and critical of student behavior.[12] Findings similar to Flanders were found by Amidon and Giammatteo when they compared thirty superior teachers with 150 randomly selected teachers in elementary schools.[13]

The fourth teacher pattern that affects pupil learning reveals a teacher's flexibility or inflexibility. Arno Bellack, dramatically points up the power of the teacher. The teacher structures the game, asks the questions, evaluates the responses, and speaks "The Truth" while students have no part in structuring the game, respond to questions, keep their own questions to a minimum, and depend upon the teacher to decide whether or not they have spoken the truth.[14]

Hughes, in a study of classroom behavior, found the most frequent teaching acts were controlling ones.[15] In her study teachers considered "good teachers" were those well organized and generally attentive. Control meant goal setting and directing children to the precise thing to which they gave attention. Not only is content identified for pupils, but they are held to a specific answer and process of working. The teacher wants one answer. As long as the question or statement that structures the class requires but one answer, the teacher is in absolute control.

Implications for Training

Can teachers recognize these patterns and change them? Will supervisors be able to assist teachers in changing patterns of teaching that inhibit student learning? The answer is *yes*—but more must be done in pre-service and in-service teacher training programs to help teachers identify and change verbal behavior. Educators in teacher training institutions must not just provide instruction when students read about verbal behavior, but help students to learn to "read" behavior itself. When teachers learn to read behavior, they will be able to identify and modify

---

[12] Flanders, *Teacher Influence—Pupil Attitudes and Achievement*, p. 97.

[13] E. Amidon and M. Giammatteo, "The Verbal Behavior of Superior Teachers," *Elementary School Journal* 65. (February 1965): 283–85.

[14] Bellack, *The Language of the Classroom*, p. 13.

[15] Marie Hughes, "What is Teaching? One Viewpoint," *Educational Leadership* 19 (January 1962): 37.

the behavioral patterns that facilitate or inhibit pupil learning in the classroom.

If we are to sensitize people to the importance of verbal patterns, we must provide training in the use of a variety of language patterns. Training requires practice in the acquisition of new behaviors. There is ample evidence that children learn more effective social, cognitive, and affective behavior if adults learn to modify and expand their verbal behavior as they interact with children; a means for providing this practice should be sought. Materials and systems for training teachers to widen their verbal behavior are available and should be put to use in universities and school districts.

Classroom Questions

In the Flanders or Modified Flanders System of Interaction Analysis, only one category of behavior deals with questions. That category concerns a teacher asking questions about content or procedure in order to elicit a student response. For a teacher to encourage greater understanding of her or his questions, other types of feedback instruments must be used.

Questioning is probably the most ancient pedagogical method. The Socratic dialectics and Plato's dialogues have been used throughout history as models for teachers. As pointed out when we discussed recitation, unfortunately most of the questions asked by teachers require little thinking on the part of students. A number of reports in recent years have confirmed the high frequency of teacher questions that require little more than the recall of memorized material.[16]

Perhaps these reports of the low level of teachers' questioning are the result of a tradition of asking set questions requiring memorized answers. In improving classroom instruction, we must examine ways teachers' questioning ability can be developed. One of the most frequently used guides to the cognitive level of teachers' questions has been Bloom's *Taxonomy of Educational Objectives.*[17] A report of studies conducted by Farley and Clegg indicated that training in the knowledge and use of Bloom's taxonomy helps teachers increase their use of questions at higher cognitive levels.[18] Table 10.5 illustrates the use of Bloom's taxonomy in classifying teacher questions.

---

[16] Ambrose A. Clegg, Jr. et al., "Teacher Strategies of Questioning for Eliciting Selected Cognitive Student Responses," (Report of the Tri-University Project, University of Washington, 1970), p. 1.

[17] Benjamin S. Bloom, ed., *Taxonomy of Educational Objectives: Handbook I— Cognitive Domain* (New York: David McKay, 1956).

[18] George Farley and Ambrose Clegg, Jr., "Increasing the Cognitive Level of Classroom Questions in Social Studies" (Paper read at the annual meeting of the American Educational Research Association, Los Angeles, February, 1969).

Table 10.5
Classifying Classroom Questions

Category	Key Word	Typical Question Words
1. KNOWLEDGE (Any question, regardless of complexity, that can be answered through simple recall of previously learned material.) e.g., "What reasons did Columbus give for wanting to sail west to find a new world?"	Remember	1. Name 2. List; Tell 3. Define 4. Who? Wher? What? 5. Yes or No questions: e.g., "Did . . . ?" "Was . . . ?" "Is . . . ?" 6. How many? How much? 7. Recall or identify terminology. 8. What did the book say . . . ?
2. COMPREHENSION Questions that can be answered by merely restating or reorganizing material in a rather literal manner to show that the student understands the essential meaning.) e.g. , "Give the ideas in your own words."	Understand	1. Give an example . . . 2. What is the most important idea? 3. What will probably happen? 4. What caused this? 5. Compare. (What things are the same?) 6. Contrast. (What things are different?) 7. Why did you say that? 8. Give the idea in your own words.
3. APPLICATION (Questions that involve problem solving in new situations with minimal identification or prompting of the appropriate rules, principles, or concepts.) e.g., "How big an air conditioner?"	Solve the problem	1. Solve 2. How could you find an answer to . . . ? 3. Apply the generalization to . . .
4. ANALYSIS Questions that require the student to break an idea into its component parts for logical analysis: assumptions, facts, opinions, logical conclusions, etc.) e.g., "Are the conclusions supported by facts or opinion?"	Logical Order	1. What reason does he give for his conclusions? 2. What method is he using to convince you? 3. What does the author seem to believe? 4. What words indicate bias or emotion? 5. Does the evidence given support the conclusion?
5. SYNTHESIS (Questions that require the student to combine his	Create	1. Create a plan . . . 2. Develop a model . . . 3. Combine those parts . . .

Table 10.5—*continued*

Category	Key Word	Typical Question Words
ideas into a statement, plan, product, etc., that is new for him.) e.g., "Can you develop a program that includes the best parts of each of those ideas?"		
6. EVALUATION (Questions that require the student to make a judgement about something using some criteria or standard for making his judgment.)	Judge	1. Evaluate that idea in terms of . . . 2. For what reasons do you favor . . . 3. Which policy do you think would result in the greatest good for the greatest number? [22]

SOURCE. Rosemarie McCartin, "Raising the Level of Teacher Questions by Systematic Reinforcement" (Paper read at the annual meeting of the American Educational Research Association, Los Angeles, February, 1969).

Another guide to cognitive level of teachers' questions has been Norris Sanders's taxonomy of questions.[19] Sanders has classified questions into seven categories:

Memory Questions—These are questions that ask students to recall or recognize ideas previously presented to them.

Translation Questions—These occur when students are presented with an idea and asked to restate the same idea in a different way.

Interpretation Questions—Students are asked to compare certain ideas or use ideas studied previously to solve problems that are new to them.

Application Questions—Application questions are similar to interpretation questions in that a student has to use an idea learned previously to solve a new problem. However, in application a student has to use an idea when not told to do so, but when the problem demands it. This involves transfer of training to a new situation.

Analysis Questions—Analysis questions ask students to solve problems through logical processes such as induction, deduction, cause, and effect.

[19] Adapted from Norris Sanders, "Synopsis of Taxonomy of Questions," mimeo, n.p., n.d. See also Sanders's excellent text, *Classroom Questions, What Kinds* (New York: Harper & Row, 1966).

Synthesis Questions—Students put ideas together to create something. This could be a physical object, a communication, or even a set of abstract relations.

Evaluation Questions—Students must make a value judgment based on certain considerations such as usefulness, effectiveness, and so on.

Inquiry or discovery methods of teaching have focused attention on questioning techniques. Richard Suchman[20] has reported on a system of inquiry training to help teachers ask the appropriate "why" questions to get students to hypothesize about the relationship of events to explain phenomena. Suchman's studies suggest that children can learn to develop a questioning style that will lead them to form testable hypotheses and procedures for verifying hypotheses.

Another approach to questioning has been developed in Taba's system of cognitive processes or tasks.[21] Taba developed a set of eliciting questions for use with each of the cognitive tasks of concept formation, development of generalizations, and application of principles to new situations. The teacher questions were formulated to elicit certain essential behaviors from students that are necessary to accomplish cognitive tasks. Teachers in pre-service or in-service programs might apply this approach to gain experience in a particular learning process before analyzing it as a teaching process.

The Gallagher-Aschner system of analyzing and controlling classroom questioning behavior has been widely used in pre- and in-service teacher training programs.

This system is derived from intensive analyses of human mental abilities done by J. P. Guilford and his associates. Although there are many subcategories in the system, the use of just four of the major categories of classifying levels of questions can give a teacher strong clues as to the level of thinking demanded of students by that teacher.

Table 10.6 lists four of the major categories of the Gallagher-Aschner system with examples of types of questions used in each.

In their work with their system, Gallagher and Aschner found that a majority of teacher behavior falls in the first level, cognitive memory, but that even a slight increase in divergent questions leads to a major increase in divergent ideas produced by students. Sanders's work indicated that for teachers not acquainted with a system of looking at questioning, very few questions asked by those teachers fell above category one. The Florida Taxonomy of Cognitive Behavior, used at the

---

[20] J. Richard Suchman, "Inquiry Training: Building Skills for Autonomous Discovery," *Merrill-Palmer Quarterly of Behavior and Development* 7 (1961): 154–55.

[21] Hilda Taba, *Teaching Strategies and Cognitive Functioning in Elementary School Children.* (Washington, D.C.: HEW, U.S. Office of Education, Cooperative Research Project No. 2404, 1965).

Table 10.6
The Gallagher Aschner System—
A Technique for Analyzing and Controlling
Classroom Questioning Behavior

1. *Cognitive-Memory:* calls for a specific memorized answer or response; anything which can be retrieved from the memory bank.

   1a. What is 2 X 3?
   1b. When did Florida become a state?
   1c. What is a noun?
   1d. At what temperature Centigrade does water boil?

2. *Convergent:* calls for a specific (single) correct answer which may be obtained by the application of a rule or procedure; normally requires the consideration of more than a single quantity of information and/or knowledge.

   2a. What is 30.5 X 62.7?
   2b. How many years was the U.S. under the Prohibition Law?
   2c. Diagram this sentence.
   2d. How many calories are required to melt 160 grams of ice at 0 C?

3. *Divergent:* allows the student a choice between more than one alternative or to create ideas of his own; more than a single answer is appropriate and acceptable.

   3a. What is 10 to three other bases?
   3b. What might have been the effects on the growth of the United States had there not been a Civil War?
   3c. Write a short story about Halloween.
   3d. Design an apparatus that will demonstrate the Law of Conservation of Matter.

4. *Evaluative:* the development and/or establishment of relevant standard of criteria of acceptability involving considerations as usefulness, desirability, social and cultural appropriateness, and moral and ethical propriety, then comparing the issue at hand to these; involves the making of value judgments.

   4a. Is 10 the best base for a number system?
   4b. Was the Civil War defensible?
   4c. Is English the best choice for a universal language?
   4d. Should we continue our space program now that we have landed on the moon?

SOURCE. J J. Gallagher and Mary Jane Aschner, "A Preliminary Report: Analyses of Classroom Interaction," *Merrill-Palmer Quarterly of Behavior and Development* 9 (1963) 183–94

University of Florida and the University of South Florida, parallels the Gallagher-Aschner system. It is based on Bloom's Taxonomy of Educational Objectives and the Sanders system. Use of the Florida taxonomy with teachers has produced findings that indicate extensive teacher use of low levels of questioning.

The need for helping teachers analyze classroom questions and developing appropriate strategies of questioning indicates that systematic training in the use of questions be made available to teachers. A number of systems of analyzing and controlling classroom questioning behavior have been presented in this chapter These and other systems should be used in helping train teachers to stimulate productive thought processes in the classroom.

Nonverbal Communication In the Classroom

The importance of analyzing and controlling verbal behavior of teachers has been well documented. Another dimension of teaching that has drawn the attention of researchers is nonverbal communication, or silent language. Individuals send messages through a variety of conventional and nonconventional means. Facial expressions, body movements, and vocal tones all convey feelings to students. The student may be hearing a teacher verbally praise her work while the teacher's facial expression is communicating disapproval. If a teacher fails to understand the nonverbal message being conveyed to his pupils, he may not be able to comprehend their responses to him. In analyzing a classroom then, it is just as important to examine *how* the teacher behaves and expresses feelings, as *what* the teacher says, does, and feels. Such expressions determine in large measure how pupils perceive those teachers.

In examining the significance of nonverbal communication, it is important to understand that teaching is a highly personal matter. Prospective and in-service teachers need to face themselves, as well as acquire pedagogical skills. Teachers need to become more aware of the connection between the messages they communicate and the consequences that follow. Teachers also need to capitalize on the nonverbal cues expressed by students as keys to their clarity and understanding. While nonverbal interaction in the classroom is less amenable to systematic objective inquiry than verbal interaction, the meanings pupils give to a teacher's nonverbal message have significance for learning and teaching.

Through continued study of nonverbal behavior, teachers can sharpen, alter, and modify the nonverbal messages they transmit to students. The advantage of adding nonverbal analysis in a study of teaching is that teachers can look at their behavior in two ways—what their behavior means to pupils, and how their behavior is being interpreted by their pupils.

Classroom Management

Another aspect of teaching, and one that is of increasing importance in today's classrooms, is that of classroom management. The changing family structure and increased conflict found in all elements of our society have led to concern about a general breakdown of school discipline and the need for better classroom management. There are a number of techniques to help a teacher maintain an effective learning environment in the classroom.

Kounin has developed a system for analyzing classroom management that deals with transitions from one unit to another. The following are examples:

> **Group alerting**: The teacher notifies pupils of an imminent change in activity, watches to see that pupils are finishing the previous activity, and initiates the new one only when all of the class members are ready. In contrast, *thrusting* is represented when the teacher "bursts" in on pupil activity with no warning and no awareness, apparently, of anything but his own internal needs.
>
> **Stimulus boundedness** is represented by behavior in which the teacher is apparently trapped by some stimulus as a moth by a flame. For example, a piece of paper on the floor leads to interruption of the on-going activities of the classroom while the teacher berates the class members for the presence of the paper on the floor or tries to find out how it got there.
>
> **Overlappingness** is the teacher's ability to carry on two operations at once. For example, while the teacher is working with a reading group, a pupil comes to ask a question about arithmetic. The teacher handles the situation in a way which keeps the reading group at work while he simultaneously helps the child with his arithmetic.
>
> A **dangle** occurs when the teacher calls for the end of one activity, initiates another one, then returns to the previous activity. For example, "Now pupils, put away your arithmetic books and papers and get out your spelling books; we're going to have spelling." After the pupils have put away their arithmetic materials and gotten out their spelling materials the teacher asks, "Oh, by the way, did everybody get problem four right?"
>
> If the teacher never gets back to the new activity which he initiated (for example, if he had never returned to the spelling in the previous example) this would be a **truncation**.
>
> **With-itness** is the teacher's demonstration of his awareness of deviant behavior. It is scored both for timing and for target accuracy. Timing involves stopping the deviant behavior before it contages, and target accuracy involves identifying the responsible pupil. If, for example, an occurrence of whispering in the back of the room spread to several other children, and at this point the teacher criticizes one of the later class members who joined in, this would be scored negatively both for timing and for target accuracy.[22]

---

[22] From notes of presentation by Dr. Robert Soar at conference, "The Planning and Analysis of Classroom Instruction," The University of Florida, November, 1975, pp. 7–8. For a detailed report of Kounin's work, see Jacob S. Kounin, *Discipline and Group Management in Classrooms*. (New York: Holt, Rinehart and Winston, 1970).

The Kounin examples illustrate the ways teachers can maintain the group and not hinder learning in the classroom. In analyzing classrooms, we must not ignore the techniques of group management teachers must utilize daily. Teachers must be provided feedback of their own behavior if they are to improve instruction.

Young teachers enter the classroom filled with such pedagogical terms as social control, group dynamics, behavior patterns, and democratic procedures. These terms mean little to the worried teacher who must get Johnny to sit down and keep quiet—at least long enough for the teacher to get the day started.

What is good discipline? Certainly not a classroom in which no one speaks but the teacher. A classroom where students respond willingly and quickly to routine requests of the teacher is a well-controlled class. A teacher who can maintain good working conditions and control noise when necessary, without pressure, makes it possible for children to learn.

The 1979 Gallup Poll of public attitudes toward public schools indicated, as it had in eight of the last nine years, that discipline was the major problem facing public schools in the nation. Parents still blamed themselves for the problems of discipline, motivation, and drug and alcohol addiction that normally have their origin in the home.

In spite of the breakdown of the family and parental acceptance of blame for many student problems, teachers must still cope with the day-by-day discipline problems in the classroom. The literature is filled with the dos and don'ts of good teaching. School districts provide numerous materials about discipline for teachers to read and have procedures for helping teachers with discipline problems in the classroom. Suggesting any practical approach in dealing with classroom discipline will appear to be an oversimplification. Everything the teacher does or does not do in the classroom improves or destroys discipline. Diagnosing the problem(s) in a classroom in which a teacher has trouble maintaining good discipline and providing the teacher with help are two major tasks of supervisors and administrators in today's schools.

In the first section of this chapter, a number of different instruments and systems were identified that look at classroom instruction and provide teachers with feedback about teaching performance. The use of evaluation instruments involves appropriate procedures and techniques. The following guideline should be used by professional personnel in using evaluation instruments:

1. Evaluation instruments should be as objective as possible.
2. Evaluation instruments should be relatively simple, understandable, and convenient to use.
3. Evaluation criteria should focus on performance.
4. All personnel should be familiar with the instruments used and procedures followed in evaluating effectiveness.

5. Personnel should be encouraged to make self-evaluations prior to formal evaluations by others.

TEACHER BEHAVIOR AND STUDENT LEARNING

In reviewing studies of teacher behavior, the supervisor will find that many of his or her intuitive notions about good instruction are confirmed in current research. For instance, teachers do make a difference in how much students learn. In spite of students' home conditions and prior instruction, the actions of teachers influence what and how much students learn.[23]

Teaching is a complex operation. No one behavior or behaviors can be universally effective. One method of teaching or one set of teaching behaviors does not automatically guarantee student learning. A key to successful teaching is flexibility. The teacher needs to use a repertoire of teaching behavior patterns and know what patterns to use. There must be a great deal of room for professional judgement on the part of teachers. In using instruments to look at teaching behavior, the supervisor must not just consider a few behaviors in isolation; all aspects of the instructional setting must be considered.

Supervisors must help teachers deal with individual learner difference in cognitive styles. As we learn more about cognitive processes and modes of problem solving, we must help teachers design instructional programs that accommodate the unique abilities of the individual student.[24]

TEACHER BEHAVIOR IN TEAM SETTINGS

The importance of identifying and improving teacher behavior is not limited to the individual teacher in a classroom. A growing number of teachers today are functioning in team settings. For many, little training is provided prior to joining a team. Generally, there is no apparatus designed for the continuing evaluation of a team once it is organized.

It is important that those who have spent most of their teaching lives by

---

[23] Marjorie Powell, "Research on Teaching," *The Educational Forum* 43 (November 1978): 27–37

[24] John Thornell, "Research on Cognitive Styles: Implications for Teaching and Learning," *Educational Leadership* 33 (April 1976): 502–4.

themselves in classrooms have the opportunity to look at their own operation within a group and have the opportunity to evaluate their interaction with others within a team. There is also a need to evaluate the interaction techniques of a team as a unit.

Table 10.7 presents a summary of team building diagnosis that looks at personal and team characteristics in terms of climate, goals of the teav, and expectations of all persons in the team.

By encouraging the use of simple instruments such as the one found in Table 10.7, supervisors can work with team teachers to improve individual behavior, which in turn improves group behavior.

THE SUPERVISOR'S ROLE IN SUPERVISING INSTRUCTIONAL PERSONNEL

The field of instructional supervision has changed dramatically in the past ten years. There are new demands for supervisors to improve teaching and learning. Supervisors are faced with an upsurge of governmental regulations, mandates, assessments, competency tests, and other accountability measures from state and national governments, which attempt to control the quality of instruction. Other pressures are coming from needed attention to culturally diverse youth; mature, tenured, and unionized faculties that are scornful of persons in supervisory roles; and public apathy toward providing increased financing for public schools.

Supervisors are unsure as to their role in supervising instructional personnel, especially when that role includes teacher evaluation. Modern, sophisticated faculties are often distrustful of supervisors. Improving instruction is often times secondary to reacting to teacher complaints about sizes of classes, extra duties, and so forth.

These and other problems are not likely to go away in the future. Supervisors must provide leadership for improving the quality of instruction. They must provide leadership for joint planning and vigorous participation by all those engaged in in-service and curriculum development programs.

SUMMARY

There have been a number of instruments and systems developed in recent years that supervisors can use in helping teachers analyze and improve teaching behavior. Observational systems that examine verbal,

Table 10.7
Summary of Team Building Diagnosis

TEAM _____   DATE _____

Team Building Component	Item	Team Member's Rating							Sum	Average	Need to Improve
1. Climate of the Team	1. Treated as human										
	2. Closeness										
	3. Cooperation/teamwork										
	4. Aid to personal growth										
	5. Trust of others										
	6. Support toward others										
	7. Satisfaction										
	8. Psychological closeness										
	9. Sense of accomplishment										
	10. Honesty										
	11. Share information										
	12. Free to discuss										
2. Goals of the Team	13. Goal orientation										
	14. Integrative approach										
	15. Problem solving										
	16. Integration of group activities and individual needs										

Table 10.7—*continued*

	17. Personal needs and group activities						
	18. Sense of responsibility						
	19. Sense of being manipulated						
	20. Level of manipulation						
	21. Written specific goals						
	22. Achievement review						
	23. Goal revision						
	24. Problem solving						
3. *Contract of the team (expectations of all persons on the team)*	25. Written expectations						
	25a. Meeting time						
	25b. Meeting place						
	25c. Agenda-building						
	25d. Participation						
	25e. Records						
	25 f. Feedback						
	25g. Performance review						
	26. Expectations of leader by others						
	27. Expectations of other team leaders by leader						

nonverbal, and other dimensions of teaching are providing supervisors and teachers with more systematic ways of looking at the teaching-learning process. They provide teachers with the feedback necessary to improve learning opportunities in the classroom.

The Pigge study and others have indicated that teachers feel they get the greatest assistance in developing needed teaching proficiencies in the field, rather than in pre-service teacher training. Supervisors in the field must respond to this need.

Supervisory practices are changing in today's schools. The role of the supervisor has changed in recent years because of the "back to the basics movement," minimum competency testing of students and teachers, and other accountability measures. New demands are exerted on supervisors to improve teaching and student achievement.

By focusing on teacher behavior in supervision as a means of improving instruction, we do not imply that teacher behavior should be the only focus of supervision. Helping teachers to not only gain the technical skills necessary for teaching, but also develop values for themselves and their students must not be ignored in the supervisory process.

Suggested Learning Activities

1. Prepare a list of teaching competencies you think are important. Try to identify instruments or systems available that would provide feedback on whether these competencies are being demonstrated in the classroom.

2. Prepare a survey similar to the one used in the Pigge study to be given to teachers in your school district.

3. After instruction in the Reciprocal Category System, audio- or videotape a fifteen-minute teaching lesson. Determine the percent of use for each category listed in the system.

4. Develop with team members a questionnaire that would examine the climate of a teaching teav.

5. Review Traver's *The Second Handbook of Research on Teaching*. Especially read Chapter 5, "The Use of Direct Observation to Study Teaching," pp. 122–83.

6. Prepare a presentation for a school board on "Methods of Analyzing and Improving Teaching Behavior."

Books to Review

Bellon, Jerry J., et al. *Classroom Supervision and Instructional Improvement: A Synergetic Process*. Dubuque, Iowa: Kendall/Hunt, 1976.

Henning, Dorothy Grant. *Mastering Classroom Communication—What Interaction Analysis Tells the Teacher*. Pacific Palisades, Calif.: Goodyear Publishing, 1975.

Hunkins, Francis P. *Questioning Strategies and Techniques*. Boston: Allyn & Bacon, 1972.

Kounin, Jacob S. *Discipline and Group Management in Classrooms*. New York: Holt, Rinehart & Winston, 1970.

Leeper, Robert R., ed. *Supervision: Emerging Profession*. Washington, D.C.: Association for Supervision and Curriculum Development, 1969.

Ober, Richard L.; Bentley, Ernest; and Miller, Edith. *Systematic Observation of Teaching*. Englewood Cliffs, N.J.: Prentice-Hall, 1971.

Sanders, Norris M. *Classroom Questions: What Kinds?* New York: Harper & Row, 1966.

Schlechty, Phillip. *Teaching and Social Behavior*. Boston: Allyn & Bacon, 1976.

Sergiovanni, Thomas J., ed. *Professional Supervision for Professional Teachers*. Washington, D.C.: Association for Supervision and Curriculum Development, 1975.

Travers, Robert M. W., ed. *Second Handbook of Research on Teaching*. Chicago: Rand McNally, 1973.

11

Supervision and Modern Day Accountability

INTRODUCTION

In the vocabulary of the educator, the word *accountability* is a relatively new entry with a wide range of definitions. Because those definitions are often imprecise, applying the concept of accountability to schools is difficult.[1] Definitions of accountability from business and industry use (cost effectiveness, resource allocation, and systems input and output) are generally inappropriate for educators to apply to schools. Educational leaders have chosen to define educational accountability in terms such as behavioral objectives, performance contracting, manage-

---

[1] Richard DeNovellis and Arthur Lewis, *Schools Become Accountable—a PACT Approach*. (Washington, D.C.: Association for Supervision and Curriculum Development, 1974), p. ix.

ment by objectives, program planning and budgeting, competency-based education, performance certification, and many others.

Very simply, accountability in schools is a process of demonstrating that the organization has accomplished what it said it would accomplish. As it relates to supervision, we prefer to define educational accountability as responsible leadership and the effective education of students.

INTERPRETING THE ACCOUNTABILITY MOVEMENT

Some people view educational accountability as a panacea, while others see it as a sinister threat that will undermine all humanistic aspects of education.

The supervisor is caught between a public demand that educators stand accountable for immense expenditures of human and financial resources, and the teachers who feel they are being held accountable for correcting the ills of a deteriorating society. A major role of the supervisor is to help teachers, parents, and the community understand the components and purposes of accountability.

Oftentimes *assessment* is used interchangeably with *measurement*. As a result, both teachers and laypersons have begun to equate assessment with evaluation. Some may conceive of assessment as a euphemism for evaluation because they believe it will be a less offensive term.[2] Thus, we have statewide evaluation projects, clearly designed to evaluate the worth of educational programs that are labeled "assessment projects." If *assessment* is used to mean valueless measurement in one case and systematic evaluation in another, then a confused dialogue results.

Another term that is confusing to teachers and parents alike is *educational research*. Because educational researchers use disciplined inquiry and measurement instruments, they often frighten those groups with which they work. Supervisors can help teachers and the public see the distinctions between evaluation and educational research. The first distinction is in the way researchers and evaluators use the information they secure; researchers want to draw conclusions, while evaluators are interested in decisions. The second distinction is that while researchers are mainly interested in understanding phenomena, evaluators want to understand phenomena in order to guide someone's actions and make better decisions. The distinctions, of course, are fine ones, and there is a gradient of interest in either conclusion or decision. For instance, applied research data certainly are used in reaching decisions.

---

[2] W. James Popham, *Educational Evaluation*. (Englewood Cliffs, N.J.: Prentice-Hall, Inc.), 1975, pp. 10-12.

In addition to defining the language used in accountability, the supervisor can help the public and teachers understand that school accountability is not a new phenomenon. In the 1800s, the community held itself as the accountability agency for schooling. After World War I, the so-called Testing Movement began to make the student accountable for norm-referenced academic performance. During the 1950s and 1960s there was a trend toward making the school the accountable factor. In the 1970s the teacher became the target for accountability. In reality, the school has no identity per se, so when the "school" is held accountable, it really represents the sum of all the efforts of the professional staff.

The 1978 Gallup Poll on education revealed for the first time that parents were accepting responsibility for what was going wrong with their children, but they still expected schools to do something about it. A Gallup study completed in late 1978 revealed the existence of a vast resource of volunteer citizen energy that could be used in practical ways to alleviate many of the problems found in schools. More than two out of three adult citizens (69 percent) said they would work on community projects, with schools being the first priority.

We believe supervisors can be the key educational leaders in bringing schools and community together again. They can help parents and community persons see that in the 1980s *society* must become the real basis for accountability. Only a strong partnership between schools and the supporting society can bring about the educational improvement desired by teachers, parents, and all other groups.

LEARNING FROM THE PAST

Even in the best of times, public schools are highly vulnerable to criticism because of their visibility. School boards are criticized if children are punished. If misbehavior goes unpunished, parents criticize the schools as being lax on discipline. Over the years schools have alternately been criticized as too academic, needing to go back to the basics, too vocationally oriented, or not teaching students "marketable skills."

Criticism of schools seems to come in waves, and generally the wave of the late seventies closely resembled that of the fifties. "Back to the basics" after Sputnik I meant back to more science, mathematics, and foreign languages. In the seventies, "back to the basics" meant reading, writing, and mathematics. Agreeing on what is basic has been one of the problems we have not resolved.[3]

The recent basics movement has resulted from a genuine concern of

---

[3] Paul Wooding, "School Criticism in the 1950's and 1970's," *Phi Delta Kappan* 59 (April 1978): 515–17.

parents and community persons that many students could not read, write, or use numbers to hold down jobs. The testing movement that evolved from that concern has resulted in more information about deficiencies in student learning, but has not provided the solutions. Improving student learning will have to involve not only the school, but also the home—over which the school has no control.

In recent times, critics in the community have expressed alarm that 50 or 60 percent of children in their schools were falling below the national norm, yet few are aware that norm as used by testmakers, means "average" and that half of the children in the nation must always be below the norm.

One source of misunderstanding between the public and educators has resulted from unclear statements by educators regarding the schools status and progress. Parents were exposed to educational jargon that left them bewildered and disgusted about their schools. At the same time, the public expected too much of schools, and, in some cases, the schools promised too much.

Supervisors can provide leadership that can help schools and communities learn from the past, set realistic expectations of each other, and work in tandem to improve educational opportunities for students.

THE ACCOUNTABILITY MOVEMENT AND TEACHER EVALUATION

The accountability movement of the 1970s renewed an interest in teacher evaluation. Teacher evaluation is a complex process that usually involves three sources of data: (1) pupil scores on standardized tests, (2) notes made following classroom visits by a supervisor or principal, and (3) completion of a judgmental checklist of behaviors not related to pupil outcomes.[4]

Standardized tests measure content and competencies that are not the exclusive domain of the school. Few tests identify teacher practices, or the strengths or weaknesses of a program.

Visits by supervisors or principals acting in the infrequent role of supervisor-evaluator do little to improve teaching competence. Too often, the visits are infrequent and made without prior knowledge of the instructional objectives. The clinical supervision model discussed (Chapter 10) provides a systematic process for classroom observations by a principal or supervisor.

---

[4] Pamela Eckard and James McElhinney, "Teacher Evaluation and Educational Accountability," *Educational Leadership* 30, (May 1977): 613–18.

The third source of data, checklists or rating scales, frequently reflects information based on subjective observations rather than objective evidence.

A major trend in teacher evaluation in the accountability movement is the shift away from subjective factors to the criterion of pupil progress.[5] Tools such as criterion-referenced tests, performance or behavioral objectives, and mastery learning are now used to look at student learning and its relationship to teaching performance.

The present emphasis on teacher evaluation has come out of a decade of teacher unrest and lack of satisfaction by legislators and school board members with the system in which all teachers are assumed to be equally competent to teach just because they have licenses or credentials.

School board members who see 80 percent of their budget going to teacher salaries are facing angry citizens who demand cuts in school budgets. Inflation and declining enrollment has forced new pressures on legislators and the school board. When looking for major areas of the budget to cut, boards of education can only look to personnel. Teacher unions which demanded higher salaries and benefits in periods of growth now find themselves pressured to weed out poor teachers.

Since state legislatures appropriate a growing amount of funds for schools, they, too, have demanded greater accountability in student achievement and teacher performance. Legislatures that demanded competency testing for students have also insisted on competency testing for teachers. Although it is unlikely that veteran teachers will be tested, new teachers entering the profession will be faced with new requirements such as literacy tests, one-year internships, and tests on teaching competencies or skills.

Supervisors who moved from line staff roles to supporting staff roles in the 1970s are, in the 1980s, finding themselves in an administrative-supervisory position in which they must evaluate teacher performance.

Teacher organizations are insisting on the right to have input into the criteria and processes by which they and their programs are evaluated, and to identify the learner behaviors that will be accepted as evidence of quality in teaching and learning. Teacher organizations are also questioning the competencies of supervisor-evaluators to design and conduct adequate evaluations..

Implications for supervisors in teacher evaluation in the accountability movement include not only the possibility of a major shift in job role (staff to line), but the need for extensive training in processes and instrumentation of teacher evaluation also.[6]

---

[5] John McNeil, *Toward Accountable Teachers: Their Appraisal and Improvement.* (New York: Holt, Rinehart & Winston, 1970), pp. v–vi.

[6] Eckard and McElhinney, "Teacher Evaluation," pp. 613–18.

THE ACCOUNTABILITY MOVEMENT AND MINIMUM COMPETENCY TESTING

Competency-based education became a major reform movement in American education in the late 1970s. With support for the movement coming more from the lay community than professional educators, legislatures passed laws establishing minimum competency requirements for promotion and graduation. Most of the competencies required on examinations deal with reading, writing, arithmetic, and other academic skills. Many states require competencies to reflect "survival skills" such as filling out applications for jobs or balancing a checkbook. Lay persons expressed concern about students leaving school unable to read, write, or compute. Major studies showed that many adults tested for jobs did not have minimum skills to cope in a modern, technological society.

As a result of these concerns and findings, politicians rushed to pass legislation requiring that prespecified competencies be demonstrated before promotion or graduation occurred. The "back to the basics movement" reflected public interest in more and better teaching of reading, writing, and arithmetic. A logical outgrowth of that movement was to test students to see if they could demonstrate basic skills.

At the same time minimum competencies were being demanded by the public, American educators had undertaken the most ambitious educational undertaking ever conceived by a society. More students are staying in school than at any time in history, and more graduate.

However, as society is sending more of its youth to school for a longer time and demanding more of schools, youths have become alienated from society. The rate of increase of suicides, alcoholism, youth crime, and illegitimate births in the teenage population rose dramatically between 1965 and 1980. The rate of divorce among adults has resulted in one of six children in public schools coming from a one parent home.

The widespread viewing of television and its impact on youth is a major concern today. It is estimated that young people today spend one-third of their waking hours watching television.[7]

Another concern is that students from low income homes, alienated youth, and those with cultural differences are the one who fail competency tests. This has led to the tests being challenged in court.

A final concern is the time limits for initiating testing in states. Some states set three to five years within which to begin testing, while others began testing within a year after the passage of minimum competency legislation. Were pupils given adequate remediation before and after the

---

[7] For a thorough treatment of this subject see *The National Elementary Principal* 56, (January/February 1977).

tests? Why did the present group tested have to "pay for the sins" of past poor teaching and neglect? For those students denied graduation because they failed minimum competency tests, these questions have not been answered.

A related testing movement is referred to as "early out" testing. In Florida, students can elect at age 16 to take the General Education Test and leave high school early. California and other states have adopted similar legislation. Most students, however, have not taken advantage of the opportunity to leave school. A growing number of students at the senior level have elected to take college level examinations to receive early college credits.

Educators have raised a number of important issues related to the competency-based education issue:[8]

1. Students failed proficiency examinations because some of the competencies were not a part of the curriculum. New instructional requirements had to be implemented.
2. There is a proliferation of testing in schools today. Minimum competency tests are being required on top of other state tests and national tests (usually norm-referenced) such as the SAT or CEEB test.
3. The problem of minimum vs. maximum competencies is one faced in states that have minimum competency examinations. Students may be lulled into thinking they have learned all of the skills necessary for life success.
4. The issue of capability vs. competency refers to the difference between capabilities and competencies which confuses educators.[9] The concept of capability refers to the skills of standard school subjects such as mathematics and science. Competency refers to the application of capabilities to adult life situations.
5. Competency testing will result in further imbalance in the curriculum. To find funds for remediation in reading, writing, and arithmetic, many states and school districts have eliminated programs in art, music, health, and physical education. Elective programs have been curtailed in many high schools and students are being required to take more courses in English and mathematics to meet graduation requirements.
6. Research data have revealed that there is little evidence to indicate that grade retention is more beneficial than grade promotion for

---

8 Gordon Cawelti, "Requiring Competencies for Graduation—Some Curricular Issues," *Educational Leadership* 35 (November 1977): 86–91.
9 William Spady and Douglas Mitchell, "Competency Base Education: Organizational Issues and Implications," *Educational Researcher* 6 (February 1977): 9–15.

students experiencing academic difficulties.[10] There is strong evidence that the rate of retention for minority students is two to three times that of nonminority students. In the first year of testing in Florida, 64 percent of nonminority students passed the minimum competency test for graduation while only 35 percent of minority students passed the test.

7. A final issue relates to the identification of "life" or "survival" skills. For instance, knowing how to balance a checkbook may not be important in a computerized checkless society.

Clearly there are benefits in competency testing for graduation; one is to pinpoint deficiencies in learning that can be remediated. Another is to focus resources of a school or school district on a clear set of goals.

There are alternatives to establishing promotion or graduation requirements based on passing minimum competency tests. Supervisors may help develop assessment tests to assess maximal rather than minimal performance. They may use assessment measures to check the degree of congruence between what is assessed and what is taught in the school curricula. An even more exciting potential for supervisory leaders is to help teachers use assessment information to help improve classroom instruction. Using tests to pinpoint weaknesses can help teachers individualize instruction and lead to mastery learning. These leadership tasks can help ensure that testing will be used for information rather than judgment.

Supervisors can use their training and influence to prevent an overproliferation of testing. They can also help ensure the wise use, rather than the misuse, of assessment data. Supervisors can clearly point out the distinction between assessment that describes existing conditions without passing judgment, and evaluation that determines merit or worth inferring value systems.[11]

Because much educational legislation results from pressures from lay persons, supervisors must become a part of the political process. They must appear before legislative committees and inform the public about the pitfalls of minimum competency testing. They must use communication skills to explain in plain terms to school boards what testing can and cannot do to improve the teaching-learning process.

COMPETENCY TESTING IN FLORIDA
—A CASE STUDY

The Florida Educational Accountability Act of 1976 was probably the

---

[10] Gregg Jackson, "The Research Evidence on the Effects of Grade Retention," *Review of Educational Research* 45 (Fall 1975): 627.

[11] A. J. Buhl, "Assessing the Assessment Movement," *School and Community* 64 (February 1978): 17–19.

most ambitious effort ever undertaken by a state to evaluate the effectiveness of instructional programs and help students attain minimum competencies in reading, writing, and mathematics. It mandated competency testing in grades 3, 5, 8, and 11. (See Tables 11.1 and 11.2 for sample reporting forms.) It also mandated that a functional literacy test be passed by all high school students before they can be granted a regular high school diploma.

The statewide assessment tests were based on minimum performance standards prepared by a task force of teachers, district curriculum specialists, and lay persons, and was published by the State Department of Education.

The Educational Accountability Act identified ten functions as elements of the State System of Accountability:

1. Educational Planning
2. Management Information Systems
3. Educational Research and Development
4. Educational Evaluation Procedures
5. Student Assessment Testing Programs
6. Public Reporting Procedures
7. District and School Advisory Committees
8. Secondary Level Examination Program
9. Pupil Progression
10. Cost Accounting and Reporting

Each of these functions required school district personnel and the commissioner of education to develop numerous reporting systems, as well as planning, budgeting, and auditing procedures. Each of the sixty-seven school districts was required to develop a pupil progression plan based on evaluation of each pupil's achievement in relation to district performance standards for each grade level.

Subsequent legislation required each district to provide extensive remediation for those students not achieving the skills tested on the assessment tests.

Results of the first round of testing in 1977 revealed that 64 percent passed the mathematics portion of the test, while 92 percent passed the communications part. Students had to pass both parts of the examination to pass the whole test. The second round of testing in 1978 revealed a slightly higher number of passing students.

Because the tests were given after little explanation to the public and little preparation for students and teachers, a storm of protests resulted. In addition, a majority of those failing the test were minority students. Court suits resulted.

In 1978, Ralph Tyler led a NEA Study panel that concluded that the strategy chosen by Florida for accountability and the way it was

NAME	Stewart Wilson	BIRTHDATE	4-17
STUDENT I.D.		DIST. DATA	

STATE STUDENT ASSESSMENT TEST, PART I

			SKILL ACHIEVED	CORRECT ANSWERS NEEDED	STUDENT ANSWERED CORRECTLY	ITEM ACHIEVEMENT INFORMATION
Reading						
A	1.	Identify synonyms and antonyms.	yes	7/10	7	+ + +J+ +IB+ +
A	3.	Identify literal definitions of words.	yes	4/5	4	+ + +H+
B	5.	Use context to determine word meaning.	yes	4/5	5	+ + + + +
C	7.	Choose prefix or suffix so word fits sentence context.	yes	4/5	5	+ + + + +
E	9.	Determine main idea stated in a paragraph.	yes	3/4	4	+ + + +
E	10.	Infer main idea of a paragraph.	no	3/4	2	BI+ +
F	12.	Find specific information in a selection.	yes	4/5	4	G+ + + +
H	17.	Identify the conclusion supported by a paragraph.	no	3/4	2	+ +CH
H	19.	Identify outcomes based on inferences.	no	3/4	2	HB+ +
I	20.	Identify facts and opinions.	no	3/4	2	GA+ +
I	21.	Identify an unstated opinion.	no	3/4	1	+AHA
J	23.	Identify conclusions based on insufficient evidence.	yes	4/5	4	+ + + +H
L	26.	Identify source to obtain information on a topic.	yes	4/5	4	+I+ + +
M	27.	Identify dictionary definitions of word used in context.	yes	4/5	5	+ + + + +
Writing						
B	2.	Identify appropriate headings for groups of objects.	yes	4/5	5	+ + + + +
G	22.	Identify correct spelling of common words.	yes	7/10	10	+ + + + + + + + + +
G	23.	Identify correct spelling of "consumer" words.	no	4/5	3	AH+ + +
H	29.	Use apostrophe for possessive nouns not ending in "s"	no	4/5	3	+ +F+I
H	30.	Identify proper punctuation before conjunctions.	no	3/4	2	GA+ +
I	31.	Capitalize proper nouns.	yes	4/5	4	G+ + + +

STANDARDS NOT ACHIEVED **(Reading):** H,I
(Writing): H

TOTALS
78 items correct of 103
12 skills achieved of 20
11 stands. ach. of 14

STATE STUDENT ASSESSMENT TEST, Part II

11.	Infer the main idea of selection.	yes	5/6	5
12.	Find specific information in a selection.	yes	4/5	4
16.	Infer the cause or effect of an action.	yes	4/5	4
20.	Identify facts and opinions.	no	4/5	3
21.	Identify an unstated opinion.	no	4/5	3
26.	Identify source to obtain information on a topic.	yes	4/5	5
28.	Use index cross-references to find information.	yes	5/6	6
29.	Use highway and city maps.	yes	5/6	6
32.	Include necessary information in letters.	yes	4/5	5
33.	Complete a check and its stub.	yes	5/6	5
34.	Complete accurately common application forms.	yes	5/6	5

TOTALS
51 items correct of 60
9 skills achieved of 11

STUDENT DID PASS THE SSAT, PART II COMMUNICATION SKILLS TEST

NAME	Stewart Wilson	BIRTHDATE	4-17
STUDENT I.D.		DIST. DATA	

STATE STUDENT ASSESSMENT TEST, PART I		SKILL ACHIEVED	CORRECT ANSWERS NEEDED	STUDENT ANSWERED CORRECTLY	ITEM ACHIEVEMENT INFORMATION
C	1. Round number with no more than three decimal places.	yes	4/5	5	+ + + + +
C	2. Round a mixed number to the nearest whole number.	yes	4/5	5	+ + + + +
D	3. Put three numbers in order (through millions).	yes	4/5	5	+ + + + +
E	4. Identify an improper fraction equal to a mixed number.	yes	4/5	5	+ + + + +
E	5. Identify a mixed number equal to an improper fraction.	yes	4/5	5	+ + + + +
E	6. Identify decimals and percents equal to common fractions.	yes	4/5	5	+ + + + +
H	7. Multiply two 3-digit numbers.	yes	4/5	4	C + + + +
I	8. Divide a 5-digit number by a 2-digit number.	yes	4/5	5	+ + + + +
J	9. Add two mixed numbers.	yes	4/5	4	H + + + +
J	10. Subtract a whole number and a mixed number.	yes	4/5	5	+ + + + +
J	11. Subtract two mixed numbers.	yes	4/5	5	+ + + + +
K	12. Multiply a whole number and a mixed number.	no	4/5	3	+ + +**BG**
M	13. Multiply two decimal numbers.	yes	4/5	5	+ + + + +
M	14. Divide decimal numbers.	yes	4/5	5	+ + + + +
N	15. Multiply a whole number and a whole number percent.	no	3/4	2	+ +**HC**
N	16. Multiply a decimal number and a percent.	no	4/5	3	+ + +**OH**
T	29. Solve word problems involving averages.	yes	3/4	3	**B** + + +
U	31. Solve word problems involving proper fractions.	yes	3/4	3	+ + +**G**

STANDARDS NOT ACHIEVED: **K,N**

TOTALS
77 items correct of 87
15 skills achieved of 18
9 stands. ach. of 11

STATE STUDENT ASSESSMENT TEST, Part II

17. Determine the time between two events.		NT	4/5	0
24. Determine equivalent amounts of money.		NT	3/4	0
30. Solve problems involving whole numbers.		NT	4/5	0
32. Solve problems involving decimal numbers & percents.		NT	4/5	0
33. Solve problems involving comparison shopping.		NT	4/5	0
34. Solve problems involving a rate of interest.		NT	3/4	0
35. Solve purchase problems involving sales tax.		NT	4/5	0
36. Solve purchase problems involving discounts.		NT	3/4	0
37. Solve problems involving measurement.		NT	3/4	0
38. Solve problems involving the area of a rectangle.		NT	4/5	0
39. Solve problems involving capacity.		NT	3/4	0
40. Solve problems involving weight.		NT	4/5	0
41. Find information in graphs and tables.		NT	4/5	0

TOTALS
0 items correct of 60
0 skills achieved of 13

STUDENT DID NOT PASS THE SSAT, PART II MATHEMATICS TEST

implemented were seriously faulty.[12] Florida educators defended the program as being both necessary and valuable.

TEACHER POWER AND ACCOUNTABILITY

The growing power of teacher unions has resulted in not only teachers demanding the right for more input into the criteria by which they are evaluated, but in a questioning of the competencies and skills of those charged with evaluating teachers. Grievance procedures negotiated through contract and guaranteed by legislation and court decisions have required that supervisors use precise, objective means of evaluation. Teachers have not challenged the right of supervisors to evaluate them, but the ways in which they have been evaluated. Table 11.3 illustrates evaluation procedures negotiated by teacher groups in Florida.

The Teacher Education Center movement, with teachers controlling majority voting rights, has led teachers to demand a greater role in developing curricula, setting goals for school programs, determining criteria for admission to the profession, and evaluating teaching performance.

Teachers and supervisors have moved from adversary roles to a collegial relationship, which will demand greater patience, greater responsiveness, and greater leadership from both groups.

SUPERVISORY LEADERSHIP
—BEYOND ACCOUNTABILITY

The accountability movement moved supervision toward a neoscientific management stance concerned with control and efficiency. Rather than the control being exercised through personal face-to-face supervision, scientific management has substituted impersonal technical control mechanisms, such as tests, to see that teaching tasks are performed adequately.[13] "Cost benefit analysis," "program planning and budgeting," "management by objectives" are all terms used in applying business and industry practices to public schools.

Along with neoscientific supervisory techniques came an increasing attempt by federal and state governments to exert more control over

---

[12] Ralph W. Tyler et. al., *The Florida Accountability Program: An Evaluation of Its Educational Soundness and Implementation* (Washington, D.C.: National Education Association, 1978).

[13] Ernest House, "Beyond Accountability," in *Professional Supervision for Professional Teachers* (Washington, D.C.: Association for Supervision and Curriculum Development, 1975), pp. 65–77.

Table 11.3
Teacher Evaluation

I. Procedures for Teacher Evaluation

A. Professional personnel representing different areas of specialization and levels of teaching should develop specific criteria to be used in evaluating professional effectiveness.
B. Evaluation instruments should be as objective as possible.
C. Evaluation instruments should be relatively simple, understandable, and convenient to use.
D. Evaluation criteria should focus on performance, and minimize emphasis upon nebulous personal and personality factors.
E. Evaluation instruments should include spaces for:
    1. Identification of evaluator(s).
    2. Sources of information used in reaching judgments, including number of observations of professional performance.
    3. Signature of the person evaluated, with space for comments.
    4. Recommendations for improvements.
F. All personnel should be familiar with the instruments used and procedures followed in evaluating effectiveness.
G. Personnel should be encouraged to make self-evaluations prior to formal evaluations by others.

II. Questions for Determining the Effectiveness
    of an Evaluation System

A. Does the evaluation system focus on the entire range of factors that affect the quality of teaching and learning, not only on the teacher (i.e., working conditions, program provisions, and other members of the school personnel)? Is a systems approach used in planning the entire evaluation program?
B. Is the purpose of the evaluation system to improve the quality of teaching and learning? Is it conducted in relation to goals and objectives of the school district? Is it to be used only for continuing contract? Staff assignments? Merit pay?
C. Is it cooperatively developed by representatives from all of the groups to be evaluated? Has the local teacher association selected the teacher representatives and approved the final product?
D. Is it carried out as a cooperative activity designed to establish rapport and communication between evaluator and evaluatee?
E. Does it help the evaluatee identify the scope of his or her duties and prerogatives and to clarify the relationship of his or her personal and professional objectives to those of the school district? Do all employees affected have a relevant job description that is meaningful to them?
F. Does it include self-assessment designed to motivate the evaluatee to improve? Is it diagnostic rather than judgmental, defining the dimensions for in-service experiences?

Table 11.3—*continued*

G. Does it establish, in writing, clear "ground rules" and follow-up procedures for both evaluatee and evaluator?
   1. When do evaluations take place?
   2. Who will be evaluators—peers, superiors, self, students, lay people, consultants, county staff?
   3. Quantity, times, places?
   4. Is there an evaluation follow-up? A conference?
H. Does it provide that adequate records be kept of all phases of the process? Is it accompanied by comprehensive, contractual due process provisions?
   1. How will evaluation data be stored? Where, format, uses?
   2. What are employee protections—signed evaluations? Employee receive a copy? Is employee able to request another evaluation? If so, by peers? Does he or she have a choice of alternate evaluators?
I. Does it encourage experimentation, creativity, and flexibility on the part of the evaluatee, rather than conformity to someone else's conception of what constitutes "good performance?"
J. Does it provide for periodic assessment and revision?
   1. Has the evaluation system been submitted to a qualified third party for review?
   2. Does the new evaluation program have a special first-year "trial run" approach which:
      a. Provides for a lot of feedback?
      b. Checks every operational aspect of program?
      c. Allows changes as the system operates rather than waiting?
      d. Provides for a special monitoring committee to suggest in-process changes.
K. Does it provide for training of all concerned before evaluation begins?
L. Is it realistic in terms of time and funds for implementation?
M. Does it provide for evaluator evaluation—Is he evaluated on his consistency with the same employee? With other evaluations of same employee group?
N. If student performance is being used to evaluate teachers, were the criteria and objectives sufficiently tested to guarantee that there is a definite positive correlation between each teaching act evaluated and its concomitant student achievement? Are teachers being evaluated by student performance on a narrow range of cognitive behavioral objectives?

public schools. Accountability laws at the state level demanded that students pass minimum competency tests. Many federal acts provided monies for districts based on setting certain performance standards such as increasing reading level by two stanines.

Declining enrollment and decreased resources led many schools to institute budgetary controls such as Program Planning and Budgeting System (PPBS). The efficiency movement was promoted by federal and state agencies as well as citizens groups.

With teachers and supervisors given little decision power as organizational objectives were systematized, human relations became secondary to organizational efficiency. A number of educators have embraced the neoscientific system of management. One of the leading proponents of this system, Leon Lessinger, believes accountability will result in the redevelopment of the management of our whole educational system.[14]

The application of scientific school management (i.e., that resources can be fully programmed and committed to preset goals) is hindered by the fact that there is much inconsistency in educational goals. Different groups want different things. One group wants a broadened curriculum that includes an emphasis on the arts, while another wants a narrow curriculum focused on the "3 Rs." Needs assessments have attempted to get public consensus, but in practice educators have continued to give the public a mixed bag of educational programs.

Arthur Combs[15] has suggested that teachers cannot be responsible for the behavior of their students any more than any person can be responsible for the behavior of another. Combs does agree that teachers can be held accountable for being concerned and knowledgeable about the welfare of their students, informed about subject matter, responsible for understanding human behavior, especially student behavior, and accountable for the methods used to carry out their purposes and those of society. Teachers must be able to defend what they do in a professional sense, but should not have to guarantee outcomes.

Our view of modern supervision has supervisors helping to loosen the bonds of preset goals, internal programming, and precise management to ensure that children are seen not as products, but as emerging phenomena. Supervisors must also work with other professional educators and the supporting public to build means of evaluating the teaching-learning process that move beyond a criterion function specified in advance.

SUMMARY

The accountability movement has resulted in new pressures—and new challenges—for supervisors.

---

[14] Leon Lessinger, ed., *Accountability in Education*, (Worthington, Ohio: Charles Jones Publishing, 1971).

[15] Arthur Combs, *Educational Accountability: Beyond Behavioral Objectives*. (Washington, D.C.: Association for Supervision and Curriculum Development), 1972.

One of the problems found in educational accountability is that of defining the term. Because a wide range of vague definitions has been assigned to the term, application of the concept of accountability in practice has proven difficult. The use of definitions of accountability borrowed from business and industry often results in a mechanistic, impersonal way of looking at the teaching-learning process. To date, many school districts have chosen a narrow interpretation of accountability, translating their responsibilities into such easily managed concerns as behavioral objectives, competency-based instruction, and performance certification.

The complete interpretation of the accountability movement requires learning from the past. Schools have always been accountable to the public, but it has been only recently that accountability has resulted in a demand to test students for basic competencies in order to issue regular diplomas. Supervisors can assist the public and other educators in fully comprehending the meaning of being accountable by placing the movement in its historical context and by defining the term more clearly. In many districts, problems of accountability are the by-product of faulty goal clarity and communication.

The minimum competency testing movement has led to a renewed interest in teacher performance and evaluation. Unfortunately, many state legislatures are demanding greater teacher accountability in terms of the performance of students on achievement tests. The direct relationship between pupil learning as measured by achievement test scores and the practices of teachers has not yet been established. Because of this pressure on teachers, teacher professional groups are now calling for greater teacher input into the evaluation of teachers. Supervisors, caught in the middle, will be required to develop objective procedures for evaluating teacher performance.

Competency-based education became a major reform movement in the late 1970's, and is likely to remain a force in public school education for the foreseeable future. While the public is concerned about minimum skills needed by students, few citizens fully realize the scale of educational endeavors in this nation. Supervisors can help the public understand accountability by focusing on achievements as well as aspirations. The authors believe that supervisors must become part of the political process in order to effectively communicate the successes of current public school programs.

The authors argue that supervision, as a leadership role, must help schools move beyond the present accountability mentality. They must loosen the bonds of preset goals, internal programming, and precise management to ensure that school children are not viewed as products or system outputs. The effective supervisor must help develop procedures of evaluation that will assure that the public and teachers work together in an atmosphere of freedom and trust while building better schools.

Suggested Learning Activities

1. You have been asked to give a fifteen minute speech to a local service club on the topic of educational accountability. Outline the talk you would give.

2. Develop a list of indicators you as a supervisor would use in evaluating teacher effectiveness. (See chapter nine for review of research on teacher effectiveness.) What assumptions are being made about effective teaching as you develop your list?

3. A pressure group in your community has demanded that your school add extra hours of instruction in English and mathematics and reduce the time spent in art and music in order to be more accountable in basic skills. Respond to that group with a written position paper.

4. Establish a panel to discuss the topic of minimum competency testing. What are some of the concerns such a panel ought to address?

5. Your superintendent has asked you to represent the school system in negotiating a new contract with teachers. You feel your effectiveness as an instructional supervisor will be diminished if teachers see you as an administrative spokesperson. What will you tell the teachers? What might you tell the superintendent?

6. Review previous competency-based education efforts in America during the 1920–1930 period. A good beginning source is Raymond Callahan's *Education and the Cult of Efficiency* (University of Chicago Press, 1962). What are the similarities and differences of that period and now?

7. Develop a plan to increase the understanding of local citizens about the topic of educational accountability. How might the supervisor follow the authors' suggestion to "get into the political process"?

Books to Review

Bellon, Jerry, et al. *Classroom Supervision and Instructional Improvement: A Synergetic Process.* Dubuque, Iowa: Kendall/Hunt Publishing, 1976.

Bloom, Benjamin, ed. *Taxonomy of Educational Objectives: Handbook I-Cognitive Domain.* New York: David McKay Co., Inc., 1956.

Combs, Arthur. *Educational Accountability—Beyond Behavioral Objectives.* Washington, D.C.: Association for Supervision and Curriculum Development, 1972.

DeNovellis, Richard and Lewis, Arthur. *Schools Become Accountable—A PACT Approach*. Washington, D.C.: Association for Supervision and Curriculum Development, 1974.

English, Fenwick, and Kaufman, Roger. *Needs Assessment: A Focus for Curriculum Development*. Washington, D.C.: Association for Supervision and Curriculum Development, 1975.

Hall, Gene, and Jones, Howard. *Competency-Based Education: A Process for the Improvement of Education*. Englewood Cliffs, N.J.: Prentice-Hall, 1976.

Herman, Therese. *Creating Learning Environments*. Boston: Allyn & Bacon, 1977.

Holland, James, et al. *The Analysis of Behavior in Planning Instruction*. Reading, Mass.: Addison-Wesley Publishing Co., 1976.

Krathwohl, David, ed. *Taxonomy of Educational Objectives: Handbook II–Affective Domain*, New York: David McKay Co., Inc., 1964.

Lewis, Arthur, and Miel, Alice. *Supervision for Improved Instruction: New Challenges, New Responses*. Belmont, Calif.: Wadsworth Publishing, 1972.

Lien, Arnold. *Measurement and Evaluation of Learning*, 3rd ed. Dubuque, Io.: William C. Brown Co. Publishers, 1976.

NSSE. *The Curriculum: Retrospect and Prospect*. Seventieth Yearbook of the National Society for the Study of Education. Chicago: University of Chicago Press, 1971.

Popham, W. James. *Educational Evaluation*. Englewood Cliffs, N.J.: Prentice-Hall, 1975.

Sergiovanni, Thomas, ed. *Professional Supervision for Professional Teachers*. Washington, D.C.: Association for Supervision and Curriculum Development, 1975.

Storey, Arthur. *The Measurement of Classroom Learning*. Chicago: Science Research Associates, 1970.

Wiles, David. *Changing Perspectives in Educational Research*. Worthington, Oh.: Charles A. Jones Publishing Co., 1972.

Wiles, Jon, and Bondi, Joseph. *Curriculum Development: A Guide to Practice*. Columbus, Oh.: Charles E. Merrill Publishing Co., 1979.

Worthen, Blaine, and Sanders, James. *Educational Evaluation: Theory and Practice*, Worthington, Oh.: Charles A. Jones Publishing Co., 1973.

part four

Options for Educational Supervision

12

Developing Approaches to School Supervision

To be effective on-the-job, a school supervisor must possess an understanding of the supervisory role and take actions based on such understanding. The collective ideas, experiences, feelings, and perceptions of the supervisor form a core of assumptions about the job that guide behavior. When those assumptions are formally stated as a series of generalizations, there is the beginning of a theory of supervision. It is believed that one difference between the effective and ineffective supervisor in practice is the degree to which such assumptions have been fully examined and arranged into a coherent series of generalizations.

School supervision, as an educational role, does not yet possess formal theories, although some developing approaches to supervision found in schools would suggest that formal theories can be inferred. Such theories of supervision would be based on at least four kinds of assumptions about:

1. the nature of people,
2. the relationship between people and organizations,

3. the uniqueness of schools as an organization, and
4. what schools can become because of people.

Over time, three primary approaches to supervision have evolved in American schools. Each approach makes different assumptions about the four areas listed above, and, while not theories, these approaches do present contrasting ways of conceptualizing supervision. They are three different perspectives of how people interact in school settings and how best to use human resources. For the reader, the value of these emerging approaches is to be found in their strategies for organizing supervisory behaviors.

THREE SUPERVISORY APPROACHES

In this text the three primary approaches to school supervision will be called Type I, Type II, and Type III supervision. Type I supervision sees the supervisor as a designer or manager. Type II supervision sees the supervisor as a linker or coordinator. Type III supervision sees the supervisor as a helper and sometimes as a therapist. The variable that clearly distinguishes the three approaches from one another is the degree to which the human element is incorporated into the plan for supervision. The three approaches may be summarized as follows.

Type I—The Supervisor as Designer-Manager

Supervision from this perspective is an organizational or institutional process. Supervision is defined in schools without reference to any particular person. Planning, organization, and the execution of plans are seen as the most effective way to improve instruction in school settings.

Type II—The Supervisor as Linker/Coordinator

This approach seeks to improve instruction in schools by structuring relationships, both between individuals, and between persons and the organization. A major concern for those favoring this approach to supervision is to capitalize on group power in organizations. By promoting certain interpersonal relationships or restructuring the institution, the full potential of the organization can be released.

Type III—The Supervisor as Helper/Therapist

This approach to supervision is consistently a "person-specific" attempt to accommodate individuals in a school setting. The helper approach focuses squarely on the needs of individuals and attempts to maximize the use of school human resources by assisting people to the full development of their capacities.

In each of these developing approaches, the supervisor enacts a unique role. In Type I, school supervision is seen as an organizing, managing, evaluating function. In Type II, school supervision is a process of coordinating and facilitating the interaction of human and material resources. In Type III, the school supervisor is an analyst, a supporter, a "people developer." The remainder of this chapter is devoted to a description of these three types of supervisory behavior in action. It is important to comprehend the difference in purpose, style, and strategy in each primary approach to school supervision.

THE SUPERVISOR AS DESIGNER/MANAGER

One major approach to school supervision during the past three decades has been to focus on the organizational structures of the school. By designing efficient organizational structures and controlling certain institutional variables, Type I supervisors believe that people can be "organized" for more efficient performance. Such a managerial approach to supervision is characterized by a high degree of administrative control and an organizational structure directed toward predetermined institutional outcomes.

The behaviors exhibited by supervisors who are managers are a reflection of their general concern with organizational structure. Examples of some of the "handles" used by the designer/manager are manipulation of short and long-range planning, program-based budgeting, fiscal investing, and performance evaluation. By working with these organizational tools, Type I supervisors attempt to channel resources toward desired productivity.

The anticipated outcomes of the institutional approach to supervision are significant levels of organizational achievement as measured by productivity, and a predictable capacity to meet target goals. Such an approach to supervision also anticipates high degrees of organizational efficiency and institutional coordination.

The managerial approach often possesses some liabilities. The Type I supervisor runs the risk of myopic leadership because of the emphasis on "execution of plans" as opposed to analysis of options. By the same token, the designer/manager approach can suffer from obsolescence if supervision simply refines activities to greater and greater degrees of efficiency. A final danger with a management strategy is that people experiencing Type I supervision may not feel that their personal needs are being met, or may feel shut out of the decision-making process.

Under such conditions, individuals in a school can contribute a poor day's work while endlessly pursuing institutional objectives.

There are a number of activities and techniques that characterize the designer/managerial approach to supervision. These techniques are indicative of the way a Type I supervisor would approach the job. Among major concerns of the Type I supervisor would be systems management, management by objectives, long-range planning, and daily activities tied to budget.

Systems Management

By definition, a system is a set of components organized to channel action toward the accomplishment of the organization's purposes. The overriding theme of systems management is that organizations are ordered by function and managed by product. In school settings, the use of systems management is a means of dealing with operational problems more effectively—it is a technology for administering programs.

The basic system model has three phases—the input, the process, and the output. The input phase is concerned with goalsetting, needs identification, and strategy development. The process phase includes all activities needed to implement, manage, and monitor programs. The output phase is concerned with the evaluation of the products and the use of evaluative feedback in improving products.[1]

Managing by Objectives

In addition to seeing school settings in terms of an interrelated system of activities, the Type I supervisor would also view supervision by its contribution to predetermined institutional objectives. In so viewing the organization and the role of supervision within the organization, the supervisor is likely to adopt the "management by objectives" technique which is regularly encountered in business and industry environments.

Management by objectives, or simply MBO, is a management tool that seeks to encourage change in an organization by directing activity toward results. As a strategy, MBO decentralizes the accomplishment of goals by allowing individuals in the organization, at all management levels, to plan and be responsible for the achievement of organizational objectives. In the supervision context, the manager-supervisor would work with others to identify goals, set objectives, and monitor the achievement of institutional objectives. The supervisor would oversee this goal-directed process.

---

[1] For a thorough treatment of this subject see Kathryn Feyereisen; A. J. Fiorino; and Alene Nowak. *Supervision and Curriculum Renewal: A Systems Approach.* (New York: Appleton-Century-Croft, 1970).

Providing Long-range Planning

School supervisors who carry out a Type I managerial strategy are generally effective designers and long-range planners. Using three- or five-year projections, they seek to channel resources toward desired goals and establish control over events that might impede the accomplishment of those ends.

A planning technique often used by the designer/manager to coordinate events and implement long-range plans is Program Evaluation Review Technique (PERT). PERT is an attempt to coordinate loosely aligned activities in a way that encourages the maximum use of time and resources. The PERT managerial technique does this by plotting events in a manner that shows the optimum organizational pattern. This optional time pattern is revealed using the Critical Path Method (CPM).

A single illustration of PERT/CPM technology would come from a case in which materials are being ordered to construct a building. Obviously, the contractor on the building site would prefer that the cement for the foundation arrive prior to the roofing materials. Someone must order the materials for delivery in a manner that takes into account the way in which a building is constructed. This same reasoning would hold true for instructional supervision activities.

The planners of such building construction study the many events and analyze them in terms of "completion time" requirements. PERT/CPM is a display of the relationship among events and activities in a complex task, time being the critical variable.

Using circles to indicate events (pouring the foundation) and arrows for activities that accomplish events (ordering the cement), it is possible to visually display a complex organizational program for all persons connected with it.

Figure 12.1
A Simple Linear PERT Series

When a task has multiple events and activities, time of completion becomes a critical concern. Using averaged guesses about the time necessary to complete events, it becomes possible to coordinate events by their time dependence on other events. When a field of events is charted, the greatest time needed for dependent events to be accomplished represents the "critical path" to completion. Stated another way, if the time needed to complete all events that are dependent on other events is calculated, then the shortest possible completion time is the sum of those dependent events.

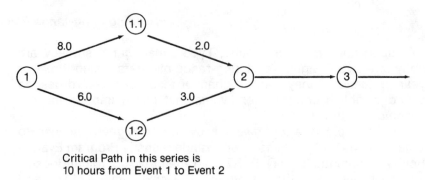

Critical Path in this series is
10 hours from Event 1 to Event 2

Figure 12.2
PERT/CPM Critical Path

PERT/CPM can be used in school environments by Type I supervisors to oversee curriculum renewal, building remodeling, instructional materials purchasing, and a number of other educational concerns.

Program-based Budgeting

Along with a systems perspective of the organization, the use of objectives in organizing activity and long-range planning to schedule and monitor activity, the designer/manager supervisor will normally be concerned with budgeting. In short, budgets represent the fuel for institutional development, and, if the budgets can be coordinated with program goals, then greater efficiency can occur. Two techniques, Program Planning and Budgeting System (PPBS) and Zero-based Budgeting are common fiscal vehicles used by Type I supervisors to coordinate operations.

PPBS is a business technique adopted by educators (also known by PPBES) to coordinate fiscal expenditure with program development. PPBS helps to set policies regarding resource allocation, identify fiscal priorities, facilitate economic coordination in school systems, and tie fiscal spending to curriculum development objectives.

An important role of PPBS is that it encourages multiyear fiscal planning and allocates resources according to anticipated achievements. Thus, planning, budgeting, and evaluation of instructional programs can be tied together in a system that is regularly reviewed from a fiscal perspective.

A parallel technique now in use by some manager-supervisors is a procedure called Zero-based Budgeting (ZBB). This technique, like PPBS, ties budget to programs. Additionally, ZBB causes planners to rank the importance of programs by projecting "levels" of operation, that is, given x amount of money, what can be done? Given x+1 amount of money, what can be done? The zero-based budget technique also has the effect of weeding out old or obsolescent programs that are no longer true organizational priorities.

In summary, it can be said that one developing approach to school supervision is to focus exclusively on the organizational structure of the school or school system and attempt to improve instruction by reallocating institutional resources. The designer/manager approach to supervision looks at the totality of the organization from a systems perspective, manages activities by predetermined objectives, seeks to coordinate activities through long-range planning, and uses control of budgets to make things happen.

Operating out of the central office, the designer/manager is rarely seen at the classroom level, but is often effective in improving general conditions necessary for good teaching. Using institutional variables as levers to structure the application of material resources to programs, the manager supervisors can bring change to the classroom.

THE SUPERVISOR AS A LINKER/COORDINATOR

A second developing pattern of school supervision in the United States is one in which the supervisor acts as a linker, connector, or coordinator of school resources. These Type II supervisors see schools as a collection of people who perform different but related functions so that tasks may be completed. These supervisors feel that one characteristic distinguishing school supervision from other forms of organizational behavior is that supervision seeks to achieve goals through interaction with people. Sergiovanni observes:

> When administrators and others work with things and ideas rather than people as they pursue school goals, they tend to be operating in an administrative rather than a supervisory way. While work on the budget, the master schedule, or the program for the summer workshop and preparation of a memo for the superintendent may all be related to achieving or facilitating school purposes, the principal is often justified in carrying out these activities and responsibilities in a way which does not require his dependency upon others for success.[2]

The major theme of the coordinating approach to supervision is an attempt to create a contextual setting that allows the maximum use of human and material resources. The role of the Type II supervisor is to

---

[2] Thomas Sergiovanni and Robert Starrett, *Emerging Patterns of Supervision: Human Perspectives* (New York, McGraw-Hill, 1971), p. 11.

discover and modify the interlocking programs, roles, norms, and procedures that comprise the school culture. This task is accomplished through the extensive use of group work and organizational analysis.

The linking-coordinating approach to supervision does possess some possible liabilities. Perhaps the most common trouble spot is that the complexity of human and material considerations will overwhelm planning efforts. If the supervisor attempts to monitor too many interpersonal and organizational variables, supervisory efforts may lose direction, or be interpreted as directionless by others in the organization. Contrasted with a highly organized Type I supervisor, the Type II style often lacks crispness in administration and management of programs. Another possible problem is that such an approach may not be satisfying to either those who desire organizational productivity or those who want the supervisor to be humane.

The primary benefit of the linking-coordinating role is that it deals with both the values and norms of people and task-related structures of organizations. Such an orientation makes the Type II approach a long-term investment with the potential of substantial return.

Type II supervisors are likely to employ many of the techniques developed by those educators practicing Organization Development (OD) methodology in schools.[3] Organization Development is an activity that utilizes concepts and research findings from the behavioral sciences for the purpose of facilitating improved functioning in organizations. It is a systematic, problem-solving process undertaken by members of an organization to improve the organization's ability to sustain effective functioning in changing environments. The many concerns of Organization Development methodology are reflected in these priorities:

1. Provision of opportunity for each organization member, as well as for the organization as a whole, to develop to full potential.
2. Provision of opportunity for people to act as human beings rather than as resources in the productive process.
3. Striving to create a work environment in which it is possible to find challenging and exciting work.
4. Provision of opportunity for people in the organization to influence the way in which they engage work.

Terminal goals for a program of Organization Development are:

1. An open problem-solving climate throughout the organization.
2. Decision-making responsibilities located as close to the information source as possible.
3. Authority by role supplanted by authority of knowledge and competence.

---

[3] For a thorough treatment of OD strategies see Richard Schmuck and Matthew Miles, eds., *Organization Development in Schools* (Palo Alto, Calif.: National Press Books, 1971).

4. Increasing degrees of trust among individuals and groups in the organization.
5. Maximized collaborative efforts in daily work.
6. Increased feelings of ownership by organization members.
7. Management according to relevant objectives rather than past practices.
8. Increasing degrees of self-control and self-direction.

The essence of the coordinator approach is to look at processes in the organization and work to build effective organizational relationships. Roles that individuals play, goals of the school, and organizational procedures are all subjects for diagnosis, assessment, and transformation. In the analysis of relationships, subsystems, and work environments, the supervisor attempts to gain commitment for change by involving others in inquiry.

Areas that might be used to further understanding of the contextual fabric of an organization are decision-making patterns, interpersonal relationships, communication patterns, work relationships, and attitudes about collaboration. Type II supervision attempts to deal with the human element in the school collectively as one large interrelated resource.

In contrast to the managerial supervisor, the linker/coordinator avoids formal organization and planning, preferring more temporary arrangements. Under Type II supervision, the power of standing committees, councils, and departments would be replaced by ad hoc study groups and other such bodies. Group efforts of this kind maximize collaborative, two-way communication.

> Group patterns of supervision minimize power visibility as they replace inspection with problem-solving. Further, the supervisory relationship is considered an interchangeable one, with actors assuming client or consultant roles as circumstances warrant and as functional authority changes.[4]

In working with others to analyze the organization, the supervisor structures a data-gathering, diagnostic, action intervention process that allows members of the school to pursue improved relationships. Examples of topic areas that might be explored through this process are:

Use of opinions and ideas
Confidence and trust levels
Attitudes toward goals and objectives
Incentives and rewards
Character of the communication process
Information sharing and usage
Accuracy of information flow
Structure of the organization

---

[4] Sergiovanni and Starrett, *Emerging Patterns*, p. 180.

Decision-making patterns
Use of committees
Allocation of resources
Evaluation processes
Training opportunities for members

The anticipated result of these efforts by the supervisor who links and coordinates is an organization that works more effectively and is more satisfying to those who work within it. By surfacing organizational norms and values, and studying organization functions, it is hoped that all members can come to define their participation in the organization and perceive the school as a place where they can have influence. To the degree that trust can be established and communication is meaningful, linking patterns between human and organizational resources can be maximized.

THE SUPERVISOR AS HELPER/THERAPIST

In contrast to the Type I supervisor's organizational emphasis and the Type II supervisor's concern with relationships, the third major approach to supervision is people-directed. This approach holds that the human dimension in schools should be the one that structures the organization; the job of the supervisor is to support and promote people. The Type III supervisor attempts to improve the instructional program of the school by focusing squarely on the intellectual, social, and emotional enrichment of the individual.

Supervisors who are helpers and therapists acknowledge that the individual in organizations has needs that affect their day-to-day performance. The Type III supervisor is found in the classroom, working with individual teachers on a one-to-one basis. Sometimes the role of supervision is to satisfy increasingly complex needs of individual clients; sometimes supervision is concerned with the rehabilitation of persons who have ceased to be effective or productive in their roles.

Type III supervisors believe that the purpose of supervision remains simple—to improve teaching. Goal statements, administrative arrangements, management systems, fiscal considerations, and evaluation designs are secondary concerns that facilitate the development of school programs. The essence of school supervision is to encourage teachers to be as good as they can be, thereby releasing the potential of the school to educate.

Supervision as seen from this third major approach is ultimately a humane profession. Working with teachers calls for both understanding and compassion. The supervisor must be able to understand the person he or she is working with and tailor a supervisory program that is useful to the teacher being helped. Such an analytic approach to supervision, when practiced and refined, will not be an accidental effort but rather a skilled exercise in helping.

The possible liabilities of the helper/therapist approach to supervision are twofold: (1) This type of supervisor often fails to gain the "big picture" of how individuals interact with each other and the organization, and (2) the Type III supervisor often appears disorganized in the daily routine. Failing to plan ahead and seeing problems one at a time, the Type III supervisor can get bogged down in specifics and fail to attend to general organizational functions.

The advantages of the helper/therapist approach to supervision are multiple. Such an approach builds trust and increases communication upward in the organization. Such an approach assists other organization leaders to gain commitment from persons far removed from the direct supervision capabilities of the line and staff management. Finally, such an approach generally enriches the human resources of the organization by salvaging persons otherwise unuseful or unproductive.

A beginning point for supervisors who perceive themselves as helpers or therapists is to fully understand the professional development profile of most teachers. Stinnert[5] documented that most teachers progress through a regular sequential pattern of growth during their careers. The first year of classroom teaching is normally dominated by various patterns of adjustment, with the new teacher becoming familiar with routines and the environment. The second, third, and sometimes fourth years of classroom teaching are devoted to perfecting delivery techniques and experimenting with instructional styles. Somewhere between the fourth and eighth year of teaching, the individual teacher reaches an instructional plateau, and teaching becomes dominated by routine. At this time, according to Stinnert's findings, teachers must find new challenge in their work or look outside of teaching for personal satisfaction.

An initial step for any Type III supervisor, then, is to recognize that all teachers are unique in their rate of professional development. While predictable stages of development are evident in most cases, each individual teacher has needs, aspirations, and behaviors that are specific to his or her situation. The challenge for supervisors is to be able to see the teacher as an individual and make the school environment one in which the teacher can continue to develop.

Supervisors who approach their role from a helping posture would voice a concern for topics such as individual needs, perceptions, motivation, and the establishment of institutional climates. These topics are reviewed to assist the reader in gaining the feel of Type III supervision.

Human needs

Social science research in the twentieth century has revealed that the

---

[5] T.M. Stinnert, *The Teacher Dropout* (Itasca, Ill.: Peacock Publishers, 1970).

human being is a complex being with extensive needs and interests. People's needs have been found to be varied, and to some extent, ordered. Maslow proposed in the early 1950s that specific needs had a "potency potential" that could monopolize an individual's attention:

> Man is a wanting animal whose desires are never satisfied except relatively. One desire succeeds another. At any time man reflects a complex of desires and satisfactions. Wants, moreover, seem to arrange themselves in some sort of hierarchy or prepotency.[6]

Maslow went on to propose a specific hierarchy of human needs that were satisfied in order of prepotency: physiological needs, safety needs, social needs, ego or status needs, and self-fulfillment needs.

Maslow's "hierarchy" stimulated other models of need satisfaction; Frederick Herzberg's Motivation-Hygiene Schema is one that conceptualizes motivation in the world of work:[7]

16. Achievement
15. Recognition
14. Work itself
13. Responsibility
12. Advancement
11. Possibilities of growth
10. Company policy and administration
9. Supervision-technical
8. Supervision-interpersonal relations
7. Peer-interpersonal relations
6. Subordinates-interpersonal relations
5. Work conditions
4. Status
3. Personal life
2. Security
1. Salary

The helper supervisor, reviewing such literature on human needs, soon begins to recognize the varying level of teacher needs in schools. New teachers, for instance, might have security and belonging needs, while more experienced teachers might be primarily concerned with recognition, status, or personal growth in their jobs.

Individual Perception

Another area of interest to the helper/therapist supervisor is

[6] Abraham H. Maslow, *Motivation and Personality*, 2nd ed. (New York: Harper & Row, 1970), pp. 34–35.

[7] Adapted from Frederick Herzberg, *Work and the Nature of Man* (Cleveland: World Publishing, 1966), p. 124.

phenomenological or perceptual psychology. Perceptual psychology is a personalistic view of behavior that sees the individual engaged in a continuous process of becoming and being. Unlike the traditional external or objective approach of explaining behavior that has dominated other branches of psychology, the perceptual psychologist explains behavior from the internal perspective of the individual.

The basic principle of perceptual psychology is that all behavior, without exception, is a function of the behaver's perceptual field at the instant of behaving. How a person behaves at any moment is always the result of two kinds of perceptions: how the person sees the situation and how he or she sees the self. Motivation, for the perceptual psychologist, is always an expression of the need for self-enhancement or maintenance of the phenomenological self. From such an orientation has come the construct, *self-concept*.

Type III supervisors find individual perception a convenient handle for working with teachers. If all persons act from a posture of individual reality, understanding individual perception assists in understanding individual motivation. Such motivation (behaviors) can be altered by changing the perceptual field of the individual. The perceptual field, according to research, is the product of both experience and vision.[8]

From day to day, the helper/therapist supervisor is found interacting with individual teachers, learning of their needs, structuring experiences and providing information that can alter their perceptions of teaching. Such an approach is both time-consuming and rewarding.

Motivation

In working with individual teachers, a basic objective of Type III supervision is to encourage greater contribution to the school program. Such contribution by teachers is usually dependent upon the aroused motivation of the teacher being assisted.

Atkinson[9] has developed a model that helps describe the arousal of motivation in individuals. According to Atkinson, all individuals possess pools or reservoirs of motivational energy that they carry within. Whether or not this motivational energy is used or activated is dependent upon situational factors or conditions. Such environmental conditions either trigger or retard the release of motivational energy depending upon the individual's needs and perceptions. Seen this way, motives are stable, but aroused motivation is situationally influenced.

Atkinson identified four common types of motivation exhibited by individuals in organizations:

---

[8] For further information see Arthur W. Combs, ed., *Perceiving, Behaving, Becoming*, 1962 Yearbook (Washington, D.C.: Association for Supervision and Curriculum Development, 1962).

[9] J. W. Atkinson, *An Introduction to Motivation* (Princeton, N.J.. D. Van Norstrand, 1964).

Figure 12.3
Sources of Motivation

Using such a conceptualization, supervisors can understand motives and seek to arouse them. Atkinson's model suggests that by controlling the situation, supervisors may even direct the types of motives aroused.

Climates

The idea of controlling motivation through a manipulation of the environment has led Type III supervisors to the study of school climates. Perhaps the most useful work done on the subject was that completed by Litwin and Stringer of Harvard University. Building on the motivation research of Atkinson and others, Litwin and Stringer began to study the environment of organizations and to formulate a "climate theory." They defined *climate* as a concept describing the quality of an organizational environment as subjectively perceived or experienced by the organization's members:

> Climate is made up of expectancies and incentives which interact with a variety of psychological needs to produce aroused motivation and behavior directed toward need satisfaction. Climate is assumed to be influenced by a variety of factors such as the physical situation, nature of the activity, needs of the people, group norms, and behavior and leadership of formal and informal leaders.[10]

Litwin and Stringer identified nine variables through research that are important in establishing a climate. They are:

Structure	The feeling that employees have about the constraints in the group, how many rules, regulations, and procedures there are.

---

[10] G. H. Litwin and R.A. Stringer, *Motivation and Organizational Climate* (Boston: Harvard University, 1968), p. 110.

Responsibility	The feeling of being your own boss, not having to double-check all decisions.
Reward	The feeling of being rewarded for a job well done, emphasizing positive rewards rather than punishments; the perceived fairness of pay and promotion policies.
Risk	The challenge in the job, the emphasis on taking risks as opposed to always "playing it safe".
Warmth	The feeling of general good fellowship that prevails in the work atmosphere; the prevalence of informal social groups.
Support	The perceived helpfulness of the superiors; emphasis on mutual support for above and below.
Standards	The perceived importance of goals and performance expectations.
Conflict	The emphasis placed on getting problems out in the open, of hearing different opinions.
Identity	The feeling of being a member of a working team.

On the basis of organizational studies, Litwin and Stringer concluded that by emphasizing certain variables in an environment, particular types of motivation could be aroused in either individuals or groups of persons. They stated their deductive logic in this manner:

Individuals are attracted to climates which arouse their dominant needs.
Climates are made up of incentives and experiences.
Climates interact with needs to arouse motivation toward need satisfaction.
Climates represent the most powerful lever available to managers in bringing about change in individuals.

For school supervisors favoring the helper/therapist role, climate represents a powerful idea for interacting with individuals. By surrounding an individual with a proper environment, it may be possible to encourage them to display certain types of motivation that contribute to the improvement of school programs.

Type III supervision, then, is a personal approach to improving instruction in schools. It utilizes direct contact between the helper and the individual being assisted. The concerns of the helper/therapist supervisor are the needs of the client. The Type III supervisor studies the needs and perceptions of the teacher and assists the growth of the individual by establishing experiences that will elicit a desired professional response. By working with *people*, the Type III supervisor strengthens the organization and the programs of the school.

THE THREE APPROACHES COMPARED

When compared, the three primary approaches to school supervision present an element of choice to those just entering the field. Not only is the basic focus of each approach unique, but their tools, techniques, strategies, and possible problems are also clearly different. Table 12.1 presents the three approaches to aid comparison.

In studying Table 12.1, do not infer that a supervisor needs only one set of skills to be adequate. In reality, an effective supervisor needs to combine skills from all three supervisory types in order to improve instruction; the three types of supervision should be seen, rather, as priority patterns of behavior. Does the supervisor favor an organizational approach to supervision, a process approach to supervision, or a personal approach to supervision? The pattern selected, in all probability, will reflect basic assumptions held by the supervisor about the nature of people, the relationship between people and organizations, the uniqueness of schools as organizations, and the impact of people on schools. These assumptions will dominate the supervisory approach to improving instruction in schools.

SUMMARY

Assumptions about people, organizations, schools, and people in schools guide supervisory behavior. Supervisors who have examined and arranged such assumptions into coherent patterns are probably more effective in their jobs.

Over time, three primary approaches to supervision have evolved in American schools. These approaches, labeled Type I, Type II, and Type III supervision, differ according to the involvement of the human element in their supervision plan. Type I supervision is dominated by organizational/managerial considerations and uses organizational planning and execution to bring about conditions that would improve classroom instruction. Type II supervision is a coordinating approach that attempts to find optimal patterns to integrate people and resources in schools. By focusing on processes, and by involving others in organizational inquiry, it is hoped that classroom instruction can become more effective. Type III supervision is directly concerned with helping individuals develop and grow professionally. It is believed that as the individual becomes more able to contribute to the school, classroom instruction will improve as a by-product.

The tools, techniques, and strategies employed by all three types of supervision presented in this chapter are important. The type that will be dominant for the reader will probably reflect his or her assumptions about

Table 12.1
Three Primary Approaches to Supervision

	Type I	Type II	Type III
Basic Description	Designer/Manager	Linker/Coordinator	Helper/Therapist
Supervisory Focus	Organizational planning and execution	Integrating people and resources	Assisting individual growth and development
Supervisory Tools	Short and long-range planning, budget control performance evaluation	Assessment of organization processes	Need hierarchies, Motivation theories, Development profiles
Techniques Utilized	Systems management, MBO, PERT/CPM PPBS, ZBB	Organizatio Development (OD) procedures	Structuring perception, manipulating climates, arousing needs, counseling
Strategy Employed	Structure the work flow by control of resources and plans	Diagnosis, assessment, and transformation of organization processes through inquiry/involvement	Upgrading of parts (individuals) contributes to improvement of the whole (school)
Problem Areas	Myopic leadership, Obsolescence, Member alienation	Planning overload; inability to be productive or humane	No "big picture" of organization, an appearance of disorder

High organization emphasis → High individual emphasis

273

people, organizations, schools, and the role of individuals in changing schools to improve instruction.

Suggested Activities

1. Develop a list of characteristics for each of the three primary types of supervision that would help you identify each type of supervisor in a school setting.
2. Over the past two decades, supervision has been influenced by a number of trends such as behavioral objectives, clinical supervision, T-groups, and so on. Make a list of such trends, then see if the three primary approaches we suggest can incorporate these recent influences.

Books to Review

Atkinson, J.W. *An Introduction to Motivation.* Princeton, N.J.: D. Van Nostrand, 1964.

Henry, Nelson B. *Inservice Education for Teachers, Supervisors, and Administrators,* 56th Yearbook of National Society for the Study of Education. Chicago: National Society for the Study of Education, 1957.

Herzberg, Frederick. *Work and the Nature of Man.* Cleveland: World Publishing, 1966.

Hyman, Ronald. *School Administrator's Handbook of Teacher Supervision and Evaluation Methods.* Englewood Cliffs, N.J.: Prentice-Hall, 1975.

Schmuck, Richard, and Miles, Matthew. *Organization Development in Schools.* Palo Alto, Calif.: National Press Books, 1971.

Sergiovanni, Thomas, and Starrett, Robert. *Emerging Patterns of Supervision: Human Perspectives.* 2nd ed. New York: McGraw-Hill, 1979.

13

Future Roles for Supervisors

In the early chapters of this book the authors observed that supervisors face an uncertain future in their school role. The role of the supervisor in schools, in many cases, is undefined. Other forces are rapidly usurping the traditional functions of the school supervisor. We called for a more dynamic and active definition of the role of the supervisor, one in which leadership is exhibited. It appears that in many school districts, supervisors have the latitude to establish a different kind of role for themselves.

If the supervisor in a school setting is to assume a greater leadership role, supervision must begin to bridge existing administrative, curricular, and teaching concerns in some meaningful way. It is no longer appropriate for supervisors to define their role in a residual fashion, or duplicate the efforts of others. The supervisor can establish a role and build such bridges by using specialized knowledge to influence others. Increased influence in a school district will also come by placing professional emphasis on those supervisory activities that will act to release the potential of a school. This chapter will explore these new roles.

HUMAN POTENTIAL

It is a fact that we know little about the potential of the human organism. We do know that an individual's capacities are regularly expanded and tested, and most research indicates that people develop very little of their innate capacities during the course of a normal lifetime. It seems probable, therefore, that the direction and rate of human development are factors that can be and are influenced by a number of variables. Two of the more prominent variables that affect the growth and development are environment and experience.

In growing up, most of us are shaped by a socializing process that is dominated by institutions such as the family, school, church, military experience, and organizations that employ us as adults. Over time, there is a tendency to accept as normal and desirable certain patterns of development that are typical and expected of individuals in our society. Such a process ensures a predictable interaction among adult members of the society.

There is sometimes a price for such socializing process, however; the price is reflected in the human condition of thousands of adults in our society. The creative spontaneity of childhood, the curiosity of preadolescence, and the confidence and motivation of early adulthood are often dulled or destroyed. Many adults in our society accept a substandard existence for themselves because they have been conditioned to doubt their potential. These adults are predictable in their daily behavior because of such conditioning, and their potential contribution to society is severely limited.

These general observations have an important message for school supervisors who work directly with people in an organizational setting. The message is that individuals can only grow and develop to the degree that they are free, or think they are free, to grow and develop. An individual's belief about his or her potential to grow is largely a product of the experiences the person has had and the environment in which they find themselves. Supervisors, because of the helping nature of their role, have the opportunity to influence the kinds of experiences and the environment that affect individuals in school settings. Supervisors can, in short, be a vital ingredient in the development of individual human potential.

Some understandings are useful if the supervisor is to help others to develop. Supervisors must be accepting of others. Specifically, the supervisor must work with individuals wherever they are in their development, and the supervisor must be accepting of the diversity of human beings. A good example of such acceptance is the acknowledgment of differences between individual personalities. While some personality patterns appear more desirable than others in work settings, all personalities have both strengths and weaknesses. Myers has contrasted the effects of two very different sets of personality types in terms of preferences in a work situation (Table 13.1). Note that both introverts and extroverts, for example, possess qualities that are desirable in educational settings.

Human diversity, whether it be in terms of personality, experience, beliefs, or cultural heritage, is a strength if so perceived by the supervisor in a school setting. Acceptance of such diversity is a prerequisite for supervisors if they are to help others grow professionally.

Supervisors also need to clearly understand that a reluctance to enter into growth experiences or a resistance to change is a natural tendency found in *all* persons. Such a tendency is often reinforced by experience, and, for most people, increases with age. Some perfectly logical reasons why people resist change and growth experiences are:

1. *Fear*—The individual has had a previous experience with the change that was unpleasant, or the individual possesses distorted knowledge about the change, or the individual fears failure in attempting the change.
2. *Logical conservatism*—The individual has learned from similar experience that such change is undesirable, or the individual is unable to see how the change will be beneficial in light of his information about the change.
3. *Previous obligations*—The individual sees this change or growth opportunity as in conflict with previous obligations or understandings.
4. *High risk*—The individual assesses that such a change or experience may have a price in terms of lost prestige, status, possession, or so forth that does not warrant the risk of trying.
5. *Lack of identification*—The individual may not be able to see that the change or experience has anything to do with his or her needs.
6. *Awareness level*—The individual may not be able to consider the change or experience because habit or tradition prevent the full analysis of the situation.

All of these reasons for resisting change or new experiences are valid. Supervisors who can accept these reasons for resisting growth opportunities and proposed changes stand a better chance of helping others develop professionally in a work setting.

Another understanding useful to supervisors as they approach the task of releasing human potential in organizations is the complex connection between human motivation and human productivity. Motivation is not simply a matter of things a manager does to influence a subordinate. Rather, motivation is a highly personal thing for individuals that has to do

Table 13.1
Effects of Each Preference in Work Situations

Introverts

Like quiet for concentration.

Tend to be careful with details, dislike sweeping statements.

Have trouble remembering names and faces.

Tend not to mind working on one project for a long time uninterruptedly.

Are interested in the idea behind their job.

Dislike telephone intrusions and interruptions.

Like to think a lot before they act, sometimes without acting.

Work contentedly alone.

Have some problems communicating

Extroverts

Like variety and action.

Tend to be faster, dislike complicated procedures.

Are often good at greeting people.

Are often impatient with long slow jobs.

Are interested in the results of their job, in getting it done and in how other people do it.

Often don't mind the interruption of answering the telephone.

Often act quickly, sometimes without thinking.

Like to have people around.

Usually communicate well.

Feeling types

Tend to be very aware of other people and their feelings.

Enjoy pleasing people, even in unimportant things.

Like harmony. Efficiency may be badly disturbed by office feuds.

Often let decisions be influenced by their own or other people's personal likes and wishes.

Need occasional praise.

Dislike telling people unpleasant things.

Relate well to most people.

Tend to be sympathetic

Thinking types

Are relatively unemotional and uninterested in people's feelings.

May hurt people's feelings without knowing it.

Like analysis and putting things into logical order. Can get along without harmony.

Tend to decide impersonally, sometimes ignoring people's wishes.

Need to be treated fairly.

Are able to reprimand people or fire them when necessary.

Tend to relate well only to other thinking types.

May seem hard-hearted

SOURCE: From Isabel Briggs Myers, *Introduction to Type* (Swarthmore, Pa.: 1970), p. 14. Used with permission.

with their own belief about how to get along in the best manner in a given situation. This has sometimes been called the "principle of psychological advantage," meaning that people will seek values and experiences to the extent that they believe it is safe and possible for them to do so. What will cause an individual to seek a new growth experience is not always obvious or even predictable.

McClelland has identified three major characteristics of self-motivated achievers that shed light on our understanding of human motivation and productivity. The characteristics or "strategies" revealed by major studies are:

1. **Goal-Directed**—These achievers are always setting their own goals and trying to accomplish something. They rarely let life "happen to them," and are quite selective about which goals they commit themselves to.
2. **Moderate Goals**—Self-motivated achievers avoid extremes in selecting goals by gauging what is possible and accepting practical challenges. They avoid tasks that are too difficult because they want to succeed.
3. **Immediate Feedback**—Such achievers rarely engage tasks which are long-term in nature, preferring to know how well they are doing at all times.[1]

Supervisors should realize that these characteristics of self-motivated achievers are, to some extent, universal observations on motivation. Most individuals have preferences, seek success, and like to feel that they are accomplished. For many adults, however, the means to these ends have become elusive as their perceptions of themselves have become clouded by uncontrolled experiences.

A final understanding that supervisors should possess in working with the development of human potential is that most individuals have a considerable amount of hidden creativity which, if unlocked, can make a significant contribution to an organization such as a school. Sometimes such creativity is displayed by a fruitful question, a flash of insight, or an invention. Other times, creativity can be observed by a special adaptiveness such as surviving in a hostile work environment.

It is important that supervisors realize the abundance of creativity that exists among individuals in the adult world. As Combs observes:

> Creativity has long been regarded as a special endowment bestowed on a chosen few. There has been an aura of the mysterious connected with creativity. The word creative has also been subjected to myriad inter-

---

[1] Adapted from David C. McClelland, "The Self-Motivated Achievers," the Gellerman Motivation and Productivity Series, (Rockville, Md.: BNA Films, 1969).

pretations. It has often been used to describe the commonplace, the ordinary, the usual. Traditionally, creativity has been associated with products—paintings, inventions, literary masterpieces, music. Tangible evidence was the criterion—something to see, hold, or hear. Not too much thought was given to the process. We still search for and encourage the tangible, but the concept of creativity has been enlarged to include ideas, decisions, relationships, problem-solving—results of man's cognitive powers. The product, whatever form it may take, would not evolve without the process. The growing realization of the universality of creativity, of man's heretofore unsuspected capacity for creativeness, places the idea of creativity in a new perspective.[2]

While the capacity for creative behavior is more widespread than generally recognized, the amount of displayed creative behavior is quite limited. This is because creativity, especially in a work situation, calls for more than inspiration. It is a set of skills and attitudes that separate creative inspiration from creative performance as Maslow indicates:

We must make the distinction between primary creativeness and secondary creativeness. The primary creativeness or the inspirational phase of creativeness must be separated from the working out and development of the inspiration. This is because the latter phase stresses not only creativeness, but also relies very much on just plain hard work, on the discipline of the artist who may spend half his lifetime learning his tools, his skills, and his materials, until he becomes finally ready for a full expression of what he sees. I am very certain that many, many people have waked up in the middle of the night with a flash of inspiration about some novel they would like to write or a play or poem or whatever and that most of these inspirations never came to anything. Inspirations are a dime a dozen. The difference between inspiration and the final product, for example, Tolstoy's "War and Peace," is an awful lot of hard work, an awful lot of discipline, an awful lot of finger exercises and practices and rehearsals and throwing away first drafts and so on. Now the virtues which go with the second kind of creativeness, the creativeness which results in the actual products, in the great paintings, the great novels, in the bridges, the new inventions and so on, rests as heavily upon the other virtues—stubbornness and patience and hard work and so on, as they do upon the creativeness of the personality.[3]

It can be said that we know little about human potential except that it exists in abundance and can be developed through proper experience and a facilitating environment. The role of the supervisor in encouraging the development of human potential in school settings seems to possess high expectations for the growth of individual talents and capacities, and

---

[2] Arthur W. Combs, ed., *Perceiving, Behaving, Becoming*, 1962 Yearbook (Washington, D.C.: Association for Supervision and Curriculum Development, 1969), p. 142.

[3] A.H. Maslow, "The Creative Attitude," in *The Helping Relationship Sourcebook*, D. Availa, ed. (Boston: Allyn & Bacon, 1974), p. 385.

to provide a leadership that supports such growth. This can best be done if the supervisor (1) accepts human differences and sees them as an asset, (2) understands the reluctance of individuals to enter into growth experiences, (3) realizes that motivation and productivity are a personal phenomenon, and (4) is able to be supportive of initial signs of creativity and growth.

THE POTENTIAL OF A SCHOOL

While it is true that most individuals have great potential for growth and development, the same can be said for schools. Schools are uniquely human organizations, with the real product of education being the interaction of the people. To the degree that there are developing individuals in a school, the school too will also be dynamic. Miles refers to this condition that sometimes happens naturally:

> Schools turn out to be filled with innovative people (each of whom thinks he is a minority). This feature of social systems has been dubbed pluralistic ignorance.[4]

Whether a school as an organization turns out to be a developing, dynamic place need not be an accident. Collectively, people in a school building have the power to control their environment through vision and the ability to choose intelligently among alternatives. Kimball Wiles referenced this condition in describing the task of an agent of change:

> If the change agent wants the change to be lasting, he will bring it about by creating the kind of situation where people can interact in an intelligent manner on problems that concern them.[5]

The task of releasing the potential of an organization as complex as a school is not an easy one. The mosaic of human needs and wants, coupled with the organizational task of educating learners, makes the "engineering" of such a school almost impossible. It is possible, however, to establish conditions that will allow such institutional growth to occur unhampered. Gardner has identified a series of acts that can assist the school in renewal and development. He lists these as "rules" to follow:

1. The organization must have an effective program for recruitment and the development of talent. People are the ultimate source of renewal.

---

[4] Matthew B. Miles, *The Development of Innovative Climates in Educational Organizations*, ERIC, ED 030 971, p. 16.
[5] Kimball Wiles, *Supervision For Better Schools*, 3rd ed. (Englewood Cliffs, N.J.: Prentice-Hall, 1967), p. 281.

2. The organization must have a hospitable environment for the individual. Organizations that have killed the spark of individuality for their members will have greatly diminished their capacity for change.
3. Organizations must have a built-in provision for self-criticism.
4. Organizations must have a fluid internal system, responsive to the problems of the moment.
5. Organizations must have an adequate system of internal communication.
6. Organizations must have a means of combating rigidity in the form of rules and procedures.
7. Organizations must have a way to combat vested interests.
8. Organizations must be oriented to the future, not what has been.[6]

Finally, it is possible to sketch an outline of what a creative, growing, dynamic school might look like. In practice, such a school would have considerable flexibility and would be characterized by:

1. Lots of idea people, open channels of communication, and maximum internal and external contact.
2. An open personnel policy that permits a variety of personality types and persons from all segments of the society.
3. An objective, fact-finding approach to problem solving, assessing ideas and solutions to problems on their merit.
4. A focus on planning and development, as opposed to a commitment to the status quo.
5. Decentralized decision making, placing policy making as close to the problems as possible.
6. A willingness to take risks and calculated chances when necessary.
7. A desire to be unique, developing programs and structures that serve local needs.
8. An acceptance of creativity as a desirable end in education.[7]

INITIATING NEW DIRECTIONS

Recognizing that individuals and organizations have a potential for growth and development is an important first step in changing the role of the supervisor. If the supervisor can tie his or her role to the future, by placing emphasis on those supervisory activities that will promote renewal and growth, the supervisor will assume a unique leadership role in schools. Increasingly, administrative, curricular, and teaching

---

[6] John W. Gardner, "How to Prevent Organizational Dryrot," in *Managing People At Work*, Dale S. Beach, ed. (New York: Macmillan Company, 1971), pp. 12–16.
[7] Adapted from Thomas Sergiovanni and Robert Starratt, *Emerging Patterns of Supervision: Human Perspectives* (New York: McGraw-Hill, 1971), p. 159.

personnel are being forced to address immediate problems that preclude a long-range future orientation. When these traditional concerns are abdicated, a vacuum has been created.

A second and necessary step for supervisors in changing their role to one of leadership in a school district is to become knowledgable about how to release the potential of individuals and organizations. Such knowledge, when directed into the work flow of a school, will become a source of unique power for supervisors.

Initially, the supervisor must recognize that he or she cannot be everything to everybody; that is, the supervisor must limit the type of activities engaged in and seek to establish a theme in his or her daily work. If the supervisor is to be effective, he or she must control work time, identify specific roles, and develop certain themes that will place supervision in a leadership role.

One of the major secrets of being effective in any leadership role is to use time in a wise manner. Given the number of needs in any school or school district, it is easy for a supervisor to become overextended and thereby ineffective in all things. Supervisors need to learn to "bunch" their time and concentrate on achievement of visible acts. Management consultant Peter Drucker has addressed this topic in the following manner:

> If there is one secret of effectiveness, it is concentration. Effective executives do first things first and they do one thing at a time. The need to concentrate is grounded both in the nature of the executive job and in the nature of man. Several reasons for this should already be apparent: There are always more important contributions to be made than there is time available to make them. Any analysis of executive contributions comes up with an embarrassing richness of important tasks; an analysis of executives' time discloses an embarrassing scarcity of time available for the work that really contributes. No matter how well an executive manages his time, the greater part of it will still not be his own. Therefore, there is always a time deficit.[8]

Beyond controlling how time is invested in the job, the supervisor must identify and stick to a limited number of roles. These roles will assist the supervisor in organizing tasks, help identify jobs that do not contribute to a leadership function for supervisors, and eventually suggest themes that others will associate with supervision. In situations where supervisors are able to suggest a job description, these are the types of roles which should be listed:

1. Long-range planning and blueprinting of school programs.
2. Reviewing and synthesizing research for teachers.

---

[8] Peter F. Drucker, *The Effective Executive* (New York: Harper & Row, 1966), p. 100.

3. Disseminating novel ideas and practices.
4. Establishing experimental programs.
5. Demonstrating new techniques and methods.
6. Evaluating instructional systems.
7. Legitimatizing practices through "official" endorsements.
8. Securing funds for new ventures.
9. Preparing new or experimental materials.
10. Coordinating efforts with other educational agencies.
11. Working with classroom teachers.

In developing certain thrusts or themes that are to become the trademark of supervision in a school district, the supervisor must again concentrate on the release of human and organization potential. To the degree possible, such themes should be limited to a few in number and serve as organizers for supervisory projects. Three suggested theme areas, with sample projects that a supervisor might use to promote them, appear below. These themes are not intended to be prescriptive, but rather are examples of the types of areas that the authors believe supervision, as an area of specialization, should pursue.

Research and Development

Many school districts in the United States receive most of their information about school programs, and educational research materials, from commercial salesmen who solicit sales on textbooks, machines, and educational software. This deplorable condition is the result of the absence of a research and development (R&D) component in most public schools. Supervisors who use research and development as a theme for organizing activities must be able to reach teachers with their information. The following activities might be utilized:

Delivering research summaries to teachers by subject area and level on a regular basis. Such summaries should be in easy-to-understand language and speak of behaviors by which teachers might incorporate such new knowledge.

Award minigrants to teachers for ongoing "action research." Such grants should be awarded to answer highly specific instructional questions, or to differentiate the quality of instructional materials.

Special "reward" in-service opportunities for teachers who are part of a cadre of "experimenting" teachers in the district. Such in-services should bring the teachers into close contact with known consultants on a small group basis.

Incentive funds for teachers who are experimenting in their classrooms without external stimulation. Such funds should be rewarded periodically and be based on observation notes following supervisory visits.

Fostering Creativity

While creativity is present in all persons, few educators have a real opportunity to display such creativity in a school setting. Such a condition exists because either initial displays of creativity go unnoticed, or there isn't a system for follow-through on creative ideas in the district. Supervisors can get into the creativity business and make the development of human talent a legitimate concern by activities such as the following:

> Developing an incentive program for better ideas in operating the school. Such awards might range from ten dollars for a money-saving idea to one hundred dollars for a way of making instruction more effective. Awards should be highly visible and be nominated by a committee that is representative of all roles in a school.

Dissemination of a newsletter that features only innovative techniques and practices in the district.

> The organization of ad hoc groups of teachers and other personnel who study problems and make recommendations for policy action to the adminstration. Such groups should be informal, open to all interested parties, and dissolve upon completion of task.

> Developing "leagues of schools" in the district or across district boundaries. Such leagues would sponsor teacher exchanges and other flows of information worthy of dissemination (e.g., effective teaching materials).

> Sponsoring pilot projects that demonstrate or test a novel or creative concept in instruction, evaluation, communication with parents, or other worthy area.

> Idea bombardment of creative notions, insights, or possibilities for improving schools. Such ideas might be delivered through a newsletter, in-service, or organized brainstorming session on certain dates.

Accent on Positivism

In many school districts across the country, teaching has shifted from a profession to an out-and-out occupation. The many social forces that act on schools have reduced teacher freedom, regulated administrative initiative, and defined instructional interaction. The result of these changes has been to restrict introspective articulation by teachers about what actually goes on in schools, and to reduce interest and enthusiasm about school operations. Sadly, the most exciting occupation possible has been transformed into a job that is characterized by fewer and fewer intrinsic rewards.

Supervisors, by the way they define their job, can play a major role in reducing this trend. Activities that feature the positive and give hope and stimulation to teachers and administrators can place the supervisor in a posture of professional leadership. Such activities might include:

Regularly summarizing positive achievements in the school district through a personal letter to individual teachers, administrators, parents, and so forth.

Sponsoring conferences and in-service opportunities for teachers and administrators that feature enthusiastic persons who are having successful experiences in implementing programs.

Developing a "Dear Abby" type of response medium that connects the classroom teacher to the district office. Such a format should specialize in solving small but important personal problems and concerns.

Annually sponsoring a conference on "futurism" in education, bringing new ideas and new hopes to all educational personnel.

The themes that supervisors choose to organize their activities and dictate their roles should be ones with which they feel comfortable. Such themes should be upbeat, positive, and focused on growth and development for individuals and schools. By identifying supervision with the future, supervisors can fill a leadership void that is increasingly present in many school districts. Such a role will be a valued one at a time when knowledgable, informed leaders are desperately needed.

SUPERVISION ACCOUNTABILITY

The types of roles, activities, and themes suggested in this chapter for supervisors may seem to the reader an engima, given the overbearing concern for accountability currently present in the United States education circles. Practically all of the behaviors we suggested are expansionist in nature, calling for new efforts, broadened concerns, and in many cases, the expenditure of additional funds. These suggestions are not irresponsible, but rather present a very different interpretation of the term "accountability," different from one an administrator or a classroom teacher might offer.

When an organization is faced with the need for conservation due to diminishing resources, the most common reaction is to cut expenses and tighten up operations. Pressure from the top filters down through an organization, causing all persons at every level to be more and more cost conscious and frugal in their activity. When the results are measured by ordinary accounting procedures, they usually show a greater performance for the expenditure and the usual interpretation is that such accountability is working.

In human organizations such as schools, such logic is fallible. In educating children, saving cash does not necessarily indicate profit. Such traditional accounting fails to measure what happens to the organization's human assets. If the skills, experience, enthusiasm, or loyalty of humans in an organization like a school are damaged, a short-term gain has been achieved at a long-term cost.

We believe that in many school districts supervision is being restricted in its current role and performance because current conceptions of "accountability" are extremely shortsighted. To wind down school operations into simpler and simpler formats may produce more economical and even more efficient operations, but the traditional accounting procedure has little to do with the purpose of a school. Additionally, such conservatism can be harmful to the school's mission of educating children.

The roles suggested in this chapter are designed to counteract such a "winding-down" process. Supervision is the only role in schools that has a direct concern for the improvement of classroom instruction and, thereby, the upgrading of the educational experience for school children. While administrators, curriculum personnel, and teachers are directly susceptible to pressures that cause them to act more and more conservatively, supervisors sometimes are not. We believe that accountability for the school supervisor demands that he or she continue to act in ways that will improve school programs. In doing so, supervision will inherit a leadership role that is presently being abdicated by other actors in the school organization.

SUMMARY

We feel that supervisors in school settings must act to redefine their role in education. A new role for supervisors must be both unique and functional. It must be one in which the supervisor is perceived as a leader. The promotion of potential in both individuals and organizations is one promising role for supervisors in the future.

Human potential is largely an unknown. This is particularly true in an organizational setting such as a school where human interaction is maximized. Every known indication suggests that individual and organizational performance can be improved through the management of experiences and the environment.

Supervisors are in the unique position to initiate growth and development in school settings. Because their role is changing, they can organize their tasks around themes that will associate supervision with innovative behavior and the future. By concentrating on roles such as long-range planning, disseminating research, establishing experimental programs, demonstrating new techniques, evaluating instructional systems, endorsing practices, securing outside funds, preparing experimental materials, and coordinating efforts with other educational agencies, supervisors can exert positive leadership.

At a time when accountability is forcing other educational leaders to exhibit conservatism, supervisors can become identified with professional leadership. *In tying the role of supervision to the growth of people and schools, supervisors have the best chance to exert influence in improving school instruction.*

Suggested Learning Activities

1. Identify the kinds of potential (capacities and talents) that can be developed in school settings.
2. We identified four understandings that will help supervisors in working with individuals to release their potential. What other understandings should be added to this group?
3. Develop a list of the types of creativity that teachers exhibit in schools today.

Books to Review

Combs, Arthur, ed. *Perceiving, Behaving, Becoming: A New Focus For Education*, 1962 Yearbook. Washington, D.C.: Association for Supervision and Curriculum Development, 1962.

Drucker, Peter R. *The Effective Executive.* New York: Harper & Row, 1966.

Jelinek, James, ed. *Improving the Human Condition: A Curricular Response to Critical Realities*, 1978 Yearbook. Washington, D.C.: Association for Supervision and Curriculum Development, 1978.

Schmuck, Richard, and Miles, Matthew, eds. *Organization Development in Schools.* Palo Alto, Calif.: National Press Books, 1971.

Toffler, Alvin. *Learning For Tomorrow: The Role of the Future in Education.* New York: Random House, 1974.

Indices of Effective Supervision

Since supervision in education is an emerging role, there are no absolute indicators of effectiveness for practitioners. Rather, there are sets of supervisory qualities, understandings, and skills that contribute to successful supervisory practice. The overall role of supervision in school settings is to keep people in communication with one another and to coordinate efforts leading to instructional improvement. We offer the following list of supervisor attitudes and behaviors as indices of effective supervision:

Personal Qualities and Attitudes

The supervisor possesses an educational philosophy that reflects an understanding of the term "education."
The supervisor holds a perception of self as a professional person.
The supervisor maintains an openness to new ideas and practices.

The supervisor possesses an experimental outlook in the attempt to improve educational practices.

The supervisor attempts to accept all individuals for whatever contribution they might make in improving instruction.

The supervisor sees his or her own development as a continuing process.

Understandings and Knowledge Possessed

The supervisor possesses a basic knowledge of human development from birth through adulthood.

The supervisor possesses an understanding of culturally diverse students.

The supervisor possesses a clear definition of supervision—its role, scope of activities, responsibilities and problems.

The supervisor possesses a general knowledge of curricula, nursery school through junior college.

The supervisor possesses a basic knowledge of major disciplines and areas of study including social studies, math, science, language arts, physical education, fine arts, reading, and vocational-technical.

The supervisor possesses an understanding of the cognitive, affective, and psychomotor dimensions of learning.

The supervisor possesses a knowledge of learning theory.

The supervisor possesses a knowledge of social and political forces affecting school planning and management.

The supervisor possesses a knowledge of administrative techniques and organization.

The supervisor possesses a knowledge of effective supervisory practices found in school districts in the United States.

The supervisor possesses an understanding of the problems encountered by classroom teachers as they develop professionally.

The supervisor possesses a knowledge of professional teacher groups and the process of negotiation through collective bargaining.

The supervisor possesses a knowledge of the legislative process for altering educational formats and resource bases.

The supervisor possesses an understanding of the needs of special students found in public schools.

The supervisor understands the potential of creativity and giftedness.

The supervisor possesses an understanding of self-concept and other affective influences on learning.

The supervisor possesses an understanding of accountability issues in planning school programs.

Skills for Improving Instruction

The supervisor can demonstrate a novel teaching technique or procedure.

The supervisor can develop a complete lesson plan.

The supervisor can demonstrate recordkeeping procedures for assessing student progress.

The supervisor can design a learning environment based on expected student outcomes.

The supervisor can diagram models of educational planning, instruction, and evaluation.

The supervisor can define methods of humanizing instruction in classrooms.

The supervisor can demonstrate classroom management techniques.

The supervisor can define individualized instruction in terms of the classroom.

The supervisor can distinguish alternatives for grading/evaluation of students.

The supervisor can assist teachers in assessing their own proficiency in teaching.

The supervisor can assist teachers in planning and implementing research designs focused on changes in curriculum and instruction.

The supervisor can demonstrate the development of teacher-made learning resources such as learning centers, LAPS, and so forth.

The supervisor can demonstrate cooperative teaching and other "teaming" arrangements.

The supervisor can describe testing techniques and limitations.

The supervisor can describe limitations on schools in terms of financial structures, community expectations, personnel resources.

The supervisor can establish programs to test the effectiveness of teaching methods or teaching materials.

The supervisor can identify scheduling alternatives for school programs.

The supervisor can apply cost analysis techniques such as zero-based budgeting.

The supervisor can establish criteria for a system-wide needs assessment.

The supervisor can establish criteria for a teacher evaluation program.

The supervisor can conduct short- and long-range planning for instructional improvement.

The supervisor can prepare applications for funds for research projects or special programs of instruction.

The supervisor can develop an effective public relations program for the school district.

The supervisor can identify persistent instructional problems.

The supervisor can establish criteria for assessment of instructional materials.

The supervisor can develop a method of involving teachers in developing goals and objectives for instruction.

The supervisor can plan an in-service experience for new teachers or teachers who are not experienced in the district.

The supervisor can translate research findings into a form that is meaningful to classroom teachers in terms of their instruction.

The supervisor can diagnose attitudes of the community toward schools.

The supervisor can demonstrate skill in writing and editing professional materials.

The supervisor can evaluate a school instructional program for strengths and weaknesses.

The supervisor can conduct an interaction analysis of classroom teaching.

The supervisor can use resource networks such as ERIC to solve problems and find relevant materials for teachers.

The supervisor can identify and catalog resources for classroom teachers by subject.

The supervisor can counsel individual teachers during a fifteen-minute "help" session.

The supervisor can cite methods of facilitating communication in small groups.

The supervisor can establish a learning climate in a school building.

The supervisor can assess requests made for the purchase of instructional materials.

The supervisor can listen effectively to others who may make significant contributions to improving instruction.

The supervisor can disseminate information on current innovations and developments in instruction.

The supervisor can open channels of communication that will allow crossing of grade levels and discipline structures.

The supervisor can provide vision for long-range instructional improvement.

The supervisor can secure and disseminate research studies that contribute to understanding pupils, subject matter, motivation, or other relevant instructional considerations.

The supervisor can encourage teachers to participate in pilot programs.

The supervisor can identify professional development opportunities for teachers.

The supervisor can select consultants that meet the in-service needs of participants.

While such lists of supervisory practices are almost limitless, it should be recognized that supervisors become effective over time. You are encouraged to develop from this list a five-year professional development program for practicing school supervisors.

CASE HISTORY ONE

Guiding Renewal of an Elementary
Language Arts Program

Supervisors in many school districts have a wide range of tasks to perform. This is particularly true of elementary school supervisors who often are responsible for instruction in many content areas. This case study involves the work of an elementary supervisor who was asked by the superintendent to work with teachers to review the district language arts program.

A preliminary survey of conditions in the district left the supervisor puzzled about how to proceed. Each of the district's seven elementary schools was using a different adopted reading text or reading program. A history of competition among the schools for scores on the district-wide testing programs caused teachers and principals within buildings to be defensive about their programs. There was no existing vehicle for communication among language arts teachers in the school district.

The supervisor, whom we shall call Jo, requested that a steering committee be established to study the language arts program in the school district and develop plans for its renewal. A total of thirty teachers, principals, librarians, and parents were appointed to the Language Arts Review Committee and a first meeting was scheduled.

When members of the steering committee arrived for their first meeting in the old band room, they found coffee, cookies, and chairs arranged in small informal circles. Jo started the meeting by reviewing the conditions that brought them together. The district was interested in learning whether the present language arts program was the best one that could be provided. The superintendent had appointed a steering committee comprised of leaders in the district in the area of language arts. Their task was to study the existing program and make recommendations for improvements.

During the first session, Jo reviewed for the committee her own findings in looking at the existing program in the district. Among those findings were:

1. A variety of reading programs produced by commercial publishers were being used in the district elementary schools. While all of these programs had merit, such a condition was causing some problems in the case of student transfers from school to school, and in the vertical articulation of the curriculum in the upper grades.

2. The overall pattern of material acquisition and use in the district was not favorable. Buying materials in small lots for special programs was expensive and materials were not generally interchangeable.

3. Because teachers were specializing in particular reading programs, it was becoming increasingly difficult to transfer them from school to school to meet shifting population needs in the city.

4. Scheduling in-service opportunities for language arts teachers in the district was difficult because each school had unique system needs.

5. Overall evaluation of the language arts program was impossible due to the differing skills being taught by the reading programs and the unique expectations of each reading program.

6. Curriculum renewal, in the past and at present, was a reactive process of choosing between commercially-prepared programs rather than developing the program most appropriate for the children of the city.

At this point, Jo called for a break and allowed members of the newly-formed steering committee to talk among themselves. Upon calling the group back together, reactive comments were solicited and a brainstorming session was held to "play with ideas" at this point. The first meeting adjourned after an hour with the resolution to formalize the group's ideas about a good language arts program next time they meet.

At the second meeting of the committee, Jo noticed a change in attitudes and patterns of interaction. While the teachers from different schools were no longer strangers, teachers from the same school tended to cluster together. Initial conversations could be overheard voicing concern for the meaning of this review at their school. Jo began the meeting by reviewing the problem they were addressing: What is a good language arts program and how should the district improve present programs? Jo then reviewed briefly the conditions she had noted at the first meeting. Finally, she identified some needs, being careful to accommodate the rising anxiety among committee members:

1. To communicate to other language arts teachers in the district how we will proceed on this review.
2. To identify optimum conditions in our district for a language arts program.
3. To develop a plan for reviewing the language arts program in the district.
4. To monitor the renewal efforts as they take place.

The agenda for the second meeting with the steering committee was twofold: (1) To generate ideas about what constituted a "good" language arts program, and (2) to generate a general model of how the group might proceed.

In continuing their brainstorming sessions from the previous meeting, the group began to share ideas about what comprised a "good" language arts program. Separate lists generated on the blackboard revealed two areas of thought

Content of Language Arts Programs

Reading	Drama	Poetry
Literature	Oral Expression	Phonics
Spelling	Listening	Humor
Creative Writing	Library Skills	Debate
Handwriting	Language Experience	Movies
Grammar	Critical Thinking	Psycholinguistics
Study Skills	Speech	

Indicators of a Good Program

Has a variety of materials and options
Meets individual needs
Teaches specific skills

Motivates teachers and pupils
Provides diverse, meaningful situations for skill practice
Is consistent and sequential
Fosters creativity and self-awareness
Is integrated into the total school curriculum
Fosters independence and builds self-confidence
Provides a means to identify each child's needs and progress
Is taught in a single block of time
Grows from regular meetings of a building's teachers

Following a break during which the steering committee members could exchange opinions about the two generated lists, Jo introduced two possible models that might guide the committee's efforts (Figure B.1). In both models the committee would start with an awareness of their role and mission, but beyond that point there would be a focus on either an "ideal" program toward which they might work or a "remedial" model, which would focus on the removal of deficiencies. Jo described that the models would operate like this:

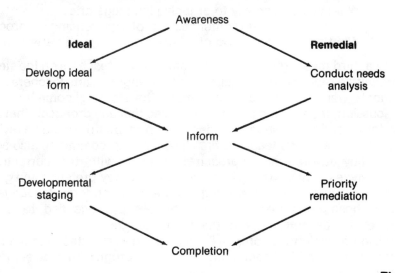

Figure B.1
Curriculum Development
2 Approaches

Ideal Model

The group would continue to brainstorm and define the best possible language arts program available regardless of costs, conditions, or other factors that might affect the attainment of such a program. They would present that model to the district decision-makers and seek permission to plan for the accomplishment of the program. The program would be attained in stages, constantly developing the language arts program closer to the ideal form agreed upon by the steering committee. Over a period of time the ideal form might be attained.[1]

Remediation Model

The group would conduct a fairly thorough needs assessment of ongoing programs in the district, thereby identifying the greatest problem areas. The group would present a plan to the district decision-makers to eliminate those problems through action. Remediation steps would be prioritized and a program of improvement initiated. Eventually, all problem areas would be removed or neutralized, bringing the present program to a desired condition.

In addition to outlining these two basic approaches, Jo listed five questions for the steering committee members to consider prior to the next scheduled meeting. Those questions were:

1. What is language arts?
2. What is language arts for?
3. What is the best way to organize language arts?
4. How should students differ because of experiencing the program?
5. What are the indicators of a successful language arts program?

At a third meeting held later the same month, teachers on the steering committee reported that other classroom language arts teachers in their schools were asking questions about the steering committee. After discussion, the steering committee agreed that any proposals that might be forwarded to the superintendent or school board should be reviewed by all language arts teachers first. The steering committee also agreed that they favored an approach that dealt with the correction of deficiencies. Finally, the group decided that they preferred the generic term, *communication skills*, to the more common term, *language arts*. With those corrections in mind the group proceeded to develop guidelines for the renewal of the district program.

Using a "weighting formula," the steering committee identified eight indicators of an ideal communications skills program. Those eight items were:

An Ideal Communications Skills Program

Is consistent and sequential
Is integrated into the total school program
Meets individual needs
Teaches specific skills
Provides diverse, meaningful situations for skill practice

---

[1] For a complete description of this approach see Jon Wiles, "Developmental Staging: In Pursuit of Comprehensive Curriculum Planning," *Middle School Journal* 6 (February 1975): 6–10.

Motivates teachers and students
Fosters creativity and self-awareness
Has a variety of materials and options

Using these eight indicators as working guidelines, the steering committee then broke into small groups to:

1. Contrast an acceptable program having such indicators with an ideal program.
2. Identify questions which, when answered, would indicate the presence of the indicator in the communications skills program.

Work on these tasks over the next two steering committee meetings produced two documents. First, each of the eight indicators was given a narrative that more fully described the item. Second, a set of questions was developed into a questionnaire that could be used to solicit feedback from other language arts teachers in the district. An example of a short narrative was:

A Good Communication Skills Program Should be Consistent and Sequential

A consistent and sequential communications skills program has a well-planned, district-wide scope and sequence chart that is usable and used. It could travel with the child from grade to grade. A usable scope and sequence chart would list materials to facilitate teaching. A district skills bank could be developed to accompany the chart.

To progress in a consistent and sequential manner would take strong coordination between all grade levels within a building. Part-time teachers might serve in a coordinator capacity to ensure this, or three district reading coordinators, one at primary, one at middle, and one at upper level, might serve to expedite the program.

A sequential communications skills program identifies when mastery, competence, and exposure of skills should take place, and provides proper evaluation to determine the mastery of skills. Also important are means for review and reinforcement of skills. It is important that the record keeping be reasonable and not a detriment to the teacher.

Language arts needs to be a program of consistent progression district-wide. Materials for such a progression need to be accessible to all teachers.

Using the same indicator, questions soliciting information from other language arts teachers via a questionnaire were:

1. Do teachers in your building satisfactorily coordinate their communication skills instruction between grade levels?
2. Are available instructional materials identified with specific skills and levels?

3. Is the district cumulative record written so that teachers can interpret and use information?
4. Are communications skills reinforced periodically throughout the year?

Following development of a narrative for each working indicator of a quality program in language arts, steering committee members returned to their schools and administered the committee-developed questionnaire. Directions for the questionnaire to all regular language arts teachers in the district read as follows:

> The Communication Skills Evaluation Committee has, through a series of idea exchanges, developed eight indicators of an ideal communications skills program. The following narrative is a compilation, in rough form, of what we mean by an *ideal program* and some of the attributes of each criterion.
>
> Our next step in evaluating the District Communications Skills Curriculum is to determine how our present program compares to our indicators of an ideal program. Your Communications Skills Committee representative will be asking you questions that will help you with this comparison. Your answers to the questionnaire will tell us the areas of our curriculum which need the most help. All comments and suggestions are most welcome and will be included in future deliberations.

The response of language arts teachers in the district to the committee's questionnaire was basically positive. Although there were some reservations about the nebulous quality of the specific question, the teachers responded with opinions that appeared in both narrative and quantitative form. Examples of responses which were narrative include the following:

> I don't feel I'm failing the students with our current program. But our current program is completely different; hence, many "no" answers on the questionnaire. I feel the questionnaire is geared toward a language block, which does sound great. The questionnaire is really rough on what is happening now—and over the years!!
>
> As far as I know this district has no identifiable sequence of communication skills. There exists no timetable for assessing expected competency in skills areas. If competency-based education becomes a reality, we would have to build a standardized schedule and sequence for all skills. Am not aware of existence of such a scope and sequence. We need such a structure.
>
> I feel uninformed. I have no insights into other programs in other schools in the district.

In addition to documenting the opinions and perceptions of teachers from all schools in the district concerning the existing language arts program, the questionnaire provided an analysis of opinion that could be presented in percentage form. Among the strongest indicators of opinion about the language arts program from all language arts teachers in the district were the following items:

Question	Percent "no"
Is there a district-wide plan for skill acquisition in communication skills?	93%
Is there district agreement about when competency in each communication skill should be achieved?	95%
Are teachers given planning time to develop programs for differing individual abilities?	90%
Does the district have a cumulative report card that provides adequate information about placement and mastery of specific skills?	85%

As the steering committee met to analyze the returned questionnnaires and share reports of informal feedback, it was evident that most teachers in the district believed that the present program in communication skills could be improved. Resistance to the steering committee's efforts seemed to be restricted to fears that existing reading programs that were succeeding might be compromised by the development of a district-wide plan. The steering committee decided that Jo, as language arts supervisor, should go before the school board to report findings and seek an endorsement for proceeding to develop a district plan.

At the next meeting of the school board, Jo presented a report of the committee's work over the past six months. The eight indicators of quality and their descriptors were reviewed. Findings of the teacher question-naire were described. A description of possible next steps for the steering committee were presented. The school board accepted the report and suggested that the Communication Skills Steering Committee continue to function and develop plans for the improvement of programs in the language arts.

In meeting again with the committee, Jo explained that the board favored the continuation of their efforts and would provide the resources necessary for the development of a district-wide plan. After a lengthy discussion, the steering committee decided the best way to proceed was to develop an elementary skills continuum for the entire district. The steering committee was assigned to various grade levels with the task of working with teachers to develop a list of those skills thought appropriate to each grade level.

At the end of a two-month period, each grade level subcommittee of the Communication Skills Steering Committee met and reported on its list of skills. A consultant from a nearby university was brought in to help the steering committee "flow chart" its skill continuums. An example of communication skills identified for the first grade in the school district is shown on the following pages.

SKILLS CONTINUUM

Flow Chart
Grade One

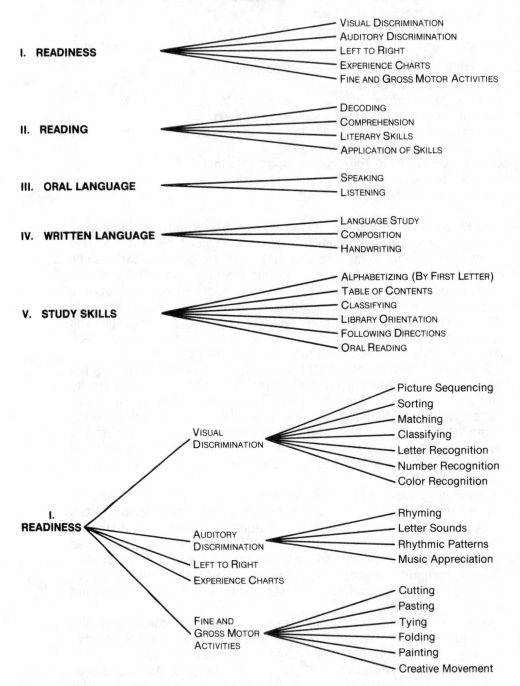

I. **READINESS**
- VISUAL DISCRIMINATION
- AUDITORY DISCRIMINATION
- LEFT TO RIGHT
- EXPERIENCE CHARTS
- FINE AND GROSS MOTOR ACTIVITIES

II. **READING**
- DECODING
- COMPREHENSION
- LITERARY SKILLS
- APPLICATION OF SKILLS

III. **ORAL LANGUAGE**
- SPEAKING
- LISTENING

IV. **WRITTEN LANGUAGE**
- LANGUAGE STUDY
- COMPOSITION
- HANDWRITING

V. **STUDY SKILLS**
- ALPHABETIZING (BY FIRST LETTER)
- TABLE OF CONTENTS
- CLASSIFYING
- LIBRARY ORIENTATION
- FOLLOWING DIRECTIONS
- ORAL READING

I. **READINESS**

VISUAL DISCRIMINATION
- Picture Sequencing
- Sorting
- Matching
- Classifying
- Letter Recognition
- Number Recognition
- Color Recognition

AUDITORY DISCRIMINATION
- Rhyming
- Letter Sounds
- Rhythmic Patterns
- Music Appreciation

LEFT TO RIGHT

EXPERIENCE CHARTS

FINE AND GROSS MOTOR ACTIVITIES
- Cutting
- Pasting
- Tying
- Folding
- Painting
- Creative Movement

302

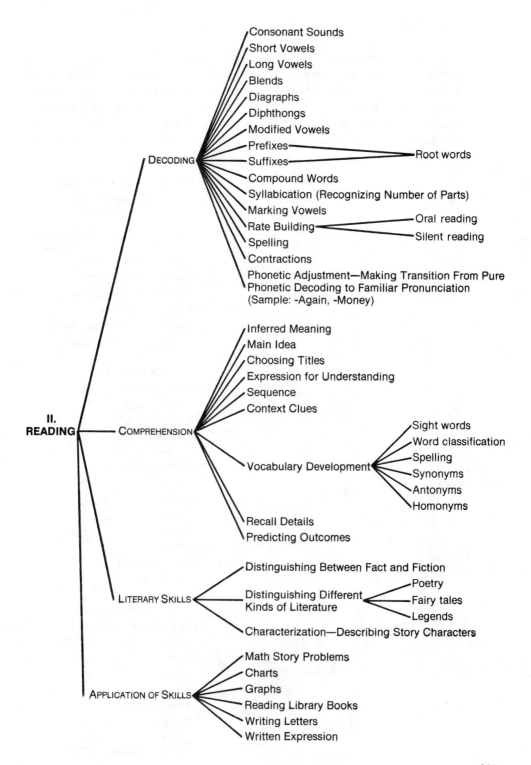

**II.
READING**

DECODING
- Consonant Sounds
- Short Vowels
- Long Vowels
- Blends
- Diagraphs
- Diphthongs
- Modified Vowels
- Prefixes — Root words
- Suffixes — Root words
- Compound Words
- Syllabication (Recognizing Number of Parts)
- Marking Vowels
- Rate Building — Oral reading / Silent reading
- Spelling
- Contractions
- Phonetic Adjustment—Making Transition From Pure Phonetic Decoding to Familiar Pronunciation (Sample: -Again, -Money)

COMPREHENSION
- Inferred Meaning
- Main Idea
- Choosing Titles
- Expression for Understanding
- Sequence
- Context Clues
- Vocabulary Development
  - Sight words
  - Word classification
  - Spelling
  - Synonyms
  - Antonyms
  - Homonyms
- Recall Details
- Predicting Outcomes

LITERARY SKILLS
- Distinguishing Between Fact and Fiction
- Distinguishing Different Kinds of Literature
  - Poetry
  - Fairy tales
  - Legends
- Characterization—Describing Story Characters

APPLICATION OF SKILLS
- Math Story Problems
- Charts
- Graphs
- Reading Library Books
- Writing Letters
- Written Expression

303

Once the steering committee had developed a schema of the communications skills program for the school district through the use of a master flow chart, they were ready to initiate a major curriculum renewal effort. To be accomplished during the coming year was the analysis of various programs currently in use, the selection of materials to be standardized, and the development of an evaluation component to

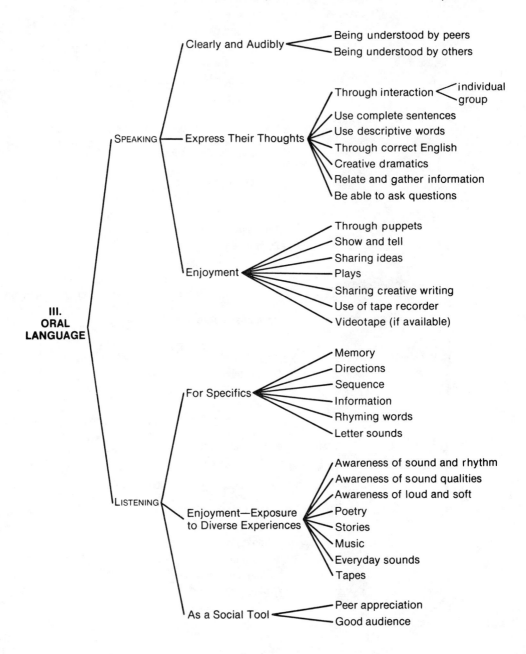

assess improvement efforts. An outline of this supervisory effort to renew a language arts program, along with the skills employed by the supervisor in this effort, is presented below. Some questions about the effort are also presented for further reflection and consideration.

Primary Steps in Renewal Effort	Skills Used
Survey of conditions in language arts	Tracing system of language arts by asking questions and reviewing existing data
Establishing a vehicle for change	Suggesting and helping to select a steering committee
Planning for initial meeting	Setting a climate for meeting, developing a rationale for group work, setting an agenda, leading small group discussion
Developing of documents and recordkeeping devices	Summarizing decisions made, keeping records of group efforts
Gaining consensus of those involved in change effort	Administering questionnaire, summarizing teacher responses, presenting findings

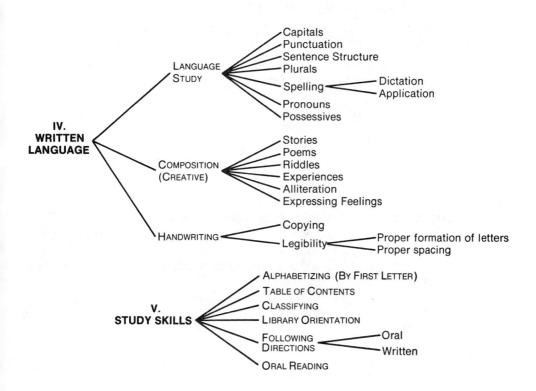

Gaining endorsements required for action	Making formal presentation to school board, fielding questions about effort, suggesting directions to school board
Developing systematic procedure for changing	Organizing groups and developing grade level skills, hiring of consultant to "flow chart" a change blueprint
Analyzing existing program	Using grade level skills to assess present programs and materials, developing an evaluation system to guide change effort
Planning and initiating changes	Translating change needs into action steps

Questions about Case History One

1. In this case study, was the role of the supervisor basically one of an authority figure forcing changes, or a nondirective and facilitating helper? List actions that suggest either role.

2. How was Jo able to keep the steering committee on task when anxiety about changing began to rise?

3. What should Jo have done if the school board had not endorsed this renewal effort?

4. Can you outline a more effective way in which Jo might have approached this change effort?

CASE HISTORY TWO

Conversion to a Middle School

Sometimes supervisors are placed in the role of curriculum developers. In this case, a supervisor who conducted a study of instruction in a junior high school anticipated that a middle school format might be more appropriate for meeting the instructional needs of preadolescents. Upon approaching the superintendent, the supervisor was given the task of investigating the possibility of conversion to a middle school. A task force of principals, teachers, and parents was formed to look at this new program.

At the first meeting of the task force the supervisor, Mike, outlined the background of events leading to the initiation of the study. Over a period of time, the curriculum of the junior high school had proven less than effective in serving the diverse learners in the intermediate grades. While the academic program appeared sound, the physical, social, and emotional needs of students were not being met. These other needs, Mike suggested, were interferring with, and sometimes preventing, normal classroom instruction. Mike presented the following national statistics he had found during a preliminary survey of alternative programs:

> The second greatest cause of deaths among teenagers (after accidents) is suicide.
> Approximately one-half of all persons arrested for serious crimes in this country (rape, murder, robbery) are juveniles. Juveniles, ages 7–18, have become this nation's most crime-prone group.
> Twenty percent of all U.S. births are to teenagers. An estimated 11 million teenagers are sexually active; 600,000 illegitimate babies were born to girls between 10–18 last year, 15 percent to girls between 10–13.
> One child in six in public schools comes from a broken home.
> Forty-five percent of all couples in America divorce.
> Last year 45 million Americans moved.
> 4.6 million Americans moonlighted last year—the largest number in our country's history.
> Alcoholism is increasing dramatically among teenagers.

"While such statistics may not represent our community," Mike stated, "they do indicate that there are some serious problems among youth between childhood and adulthood." Many of the problems stem from a lack of supervision by parents at home and from the failure of other agencies in society to accept such responsibility. In his own study of educational alternatives to deal with such problems, Mike reported that he had come upon the middle school concept.

At this point, a building principal from a local junior high school raised his hand and asked whether Mike felt that the school was responsible for taking care of general social ills? Mike responded that the problems he had outlined had educational implications. In this district, for instance, the following conditions can be documented:

1. Achievement rates are slowed considerably during the age range from 10–14, particularly in the basic skills.
2. Interest levels related to school and school subjects show a gradual decline.
3. The inclination to drop out of school among eventual dropouts surfaces during this developmental period. Such attrition has serious implications for a school district experiencing a decline in enrollment.

Mike proceeded to outline the "middle school philosophy." Middle schools are reformed intermediate schools that attempt through administrative and curricular reorganization to provide a balanced program for preadolescent learners. By "balanced" it is meant that the school program addresses the physical, social, intellectual, and emotional needs of the students. Parity in program emphasis is given to personal development, skills for continued learning, and utilization of knowledge. Three basic assumptions are at the heart of the middle school approach:

1. Preadolescents have special needs that identify them as a unique group within the K-12 continuum.
2. Transition from childhood to adolescence requires an environment with an organization that is designed to meet those special needs.
3. Transition from the elementary school to the high school should be a gradual and personalized process.

Following Mike's presentation, the task force asked numerous questions about the middle school. Mike outlined some reading materials presently found in the district curriculum library that would be informative. A bibliography of readings was given to each task force member, and the next meeting was scheduled for the following week.

During the ensuing week most task force members were able to do some reading about the middle school concept, and interest was high as the group reconvened. In a discussion during the first half-hour, it became clear that the middle school, in the literature, was indeed a complex school design. Among the innovations found through reading were flexible scheduling, team-teaching, individualized instruction, nongradedness or multiage grouping, diversified learning materials, skills continuums, counseling programs, and other administrative and curricular arrangements. When the group decided to take a break, considerable anxiety and frustration were evident.

Upon returning from the break Mike asked the group how they might best proceed to develop a plan for conversion to the middle school. After some discussion it was decided that the literature should be surveyed again to determine the most common middle school arrangements. It was also noted that middle schools appeared to be individually unique, reflecting community and student needs. Two study groups were formed from the task force members—one to extract a composite middle school from available descriptions, and another to formulate a series of questions about students in the local school district that needed answers. With those assignments, the task force scheduled another meeting and concluded the session.

The third meeting of the task force was structured to hear and respond to the two reports from the subcommittees. The subcommittee on common middle school organization presented the following findings.

Originally middle schools were organized around grades 5–8 because research showed that 95 per cent of all students enter a pubescent period during the corresponding ages of 10–14 years. A recent university study had revealed, however, that most middle schools are grade 6–8 programs.

Middle schools come in all shapes and forms but have in common the use of the student as the planning criteria. This is in contrast to the traditional junior high school that simply defines the curriculum in terms of content or subject mastery. In using student development as a focus for school planning, the middle school attempts to personalize the educational process through various techniques and innovations. Among the most common arrangements are flexible schedules, interdisciplinary planning and teaching, a beefed-up guidance program, and an exploration component in the curriculum.

In reading about middle schools, the subcommittee reported, it was obvious that the school plan is adapted to local community needs and resources; no two middle schools appear exactly alike. Additionally, the middle school curriculum is not fixed, but is always seen as emerging or developing. The idea of the middle school, only fifteen years old, is exciting, the committee concluded.

The second subcommittee report on intermediate students in the district was considerably shorter. The committee had sought school records that might indicate the kinds of questions that needed to be asked about the preadolescent learner. They were shocked to find few records available on this student group; it seemed that the students changed too fast during this period to allow close recordkeeping. The committee then had turned its attention to the formulation of some basic questions. Among them were:

1. What is the purpose of the existing intermediate program in our district?
2. In terms of pupil outcomes, what is expected from the current intermediate program?
3. What are the attitudes of students, teachers, and parents toward the existing intermediate program?
4. What is the achievement level of students experiencing the existing intermediate program?
5. In what ways is the existing intermediate program meeting the individual and personal needs of the students?
6. What data exists to document the needs and interests of students in the intermediate program?
7. What statistics are available to pinpoint problem areas in the existing intermediate program?
8. How is the existing intermediate program working to coordinate its efforts with other social agencies?
9. How is the intermediate program coordinated with the elementary and high school programs?

Before the close of that evening's meeting, Mike asked the task force what they thought needed to be done at this point. The group was unanimous in recommending some sort of needs assessment that would gather substantive data about students in the intermediate grades in the school district. The group also thought that some sort of teacher consensus was needed to identify long-term goals for intermediate education in the district. Mike volunteered that he would work to find a way to gain such information.

During the next two weeks, Mike and his secretary searched for existing needs assessments, student interest inventories, and measures of school program effectiveness. Combining eight documents, a manageable needs assessment instrument was developed. Addressing the need for a device to provide value consensus, Mike modified a Phi Delta Kappa card-sorting technique to deal with questions related to the intermediate years. At a meeting of the subcommittee, both the needs assessment instrument and card-sort measure for prioritizing values were approved. Over a period of two weeks, task force members collected data in their schools.

Because the data collected were substantially more than anticipated by the task force, data analysis was perceived as a problem. Mike requested from the superintendent that the entire task force be released from teaching duties for two days to assess their findings. The request was honored and after two days a report was issued by the task force:

> Preliminary findings of the Middle School Task Force, based on data gathered by a needs assessment and an opinionnaire administered in all schools, indicate the need for a major renewal of the intermediate programs in this school district. It is the belief of this committee that the district should study and adopt some of the practices found in the middle school model of intermediate education. Such a change would suggest a more comprehensive and personal program of education for our intermediate students. During the coming semester the Task Force will be developing a plan by which this district can begin to modify programs and practices leading to this end. We welcome the input of all teachers, parents, students, and administrators in this effort.

Among the major deficiencies identified through the needs assessment that related to the curriculum of the existing intermediate program were:

1. Teaching-learning time is excessively fragmented.
2. There is relative isolation of teachers within classrooms.
3. In-service programs are severely weak and irrelevant.
4. The report card doesn't reflect the present curriculum.
5. Transportation for field trips is expensive or unavailable.
6. Students of unequal ability are given the same assignments in most classrooms.
7. Learning materials are inadequate given the diversity of individual student needs.

8. Social promotion of academically deficient students is common.
9. Teacher planning time is uncoordinated and irregular.
10. Many students are not fully participating in the school program.

Among the points where consensus was in evidence, as reflected by the card-sort opinionnaire, were the following:

1. We want to provide a program where our students can learn to utilize knowledge in their everyday lives.
2. We want to provide a program where students master social skills basic to full participation in society.
3. We want to provide a program where students learn and utilize study skills.
4. We want to provide a program conducive to the educational development of students regardless of differences or capacities.
5. We want to provide a program with a wide range of exploratory activities for socializing, interest development, and use of leisure time.
6. We want to provide a program that gives each student access to personal guidance and counseling.
7. We want to provide a program that allows for the maximum development of individual creativity.
8. We want to provide a program that stimulates career awareness in students.
9. We want to provide a program free from undue pressures and unrealistic academic expectations.
10. We want to provide a program that guarantees a secure transition from the elementary years to the high school years.

Using both the concerns drawn from the needs assessment, and the desires drawn from the opinionnaire card-sort, the Middle School Task Force is developing a full report on the potential of middle school education during this semester. Major chapters of the report will be:

1. Rationale for the Middle School
2. The Middle School Student
3. The Teacher in the Middle School
4. Program Design for Middle School Education
5. Organization of the Middle School
6. Instructional Materials and Resources
7. In-service Training Needs for Middle School Teachers
8. Evaluation Criteria for Middle Schools

Accompanying this report will be a "companion" management system to guide the conversion of the school district to the middle school concept. It is hoped that within three to five years Mike's district will join thousands of other districts that have made the commitment to a program of education focused on the preadolescent learner.

Below you will find an outline of this supervisory effort to lead conversion to the middle school. Also identified are the supervisory skills employed to promote this effort. Finally, some questions are presented for further reflection.

Preliminary steps to a Conversion	Skills Used
Identifying persistent problems	Informing superior of problem area and gaining a commitment to deal with problem
Forming a task force to study the problem	Selecting and orientating the task force
Gathering and presenting data for structuring thought about problem	Researching key statistics and summarizing in meaningful form
Clarifying the scope of task force responsibility	Drawing major implications for schooling and program design
Presenting alternatives or choices for action	Researching possible alternatives and providing materials for further study
Designing a plan for action	Forming two study groups to propose action taken
	Hearing recommendation of two study groups
Gathering data for decision-making	Identifying questions to be answered. Developing a questionnaire and opinionnaire (card-sort)
Collecting and analyzing data	Organizing data collection in schools via task force
	Obtaining release time for task force to analyze data
Identifying needs to be addressed	Listing deficiencies
Developing plan for meeting identified needs	Organizing comprehensive study of middle school plan with a companion management plan for implementation

Questions about Case History Two

1. In this case the supervisor became an advocate for a solution to the

problem quite early. Is there anything wrong with such a posture of activism in public education?

2. Early in this effort Mike used "social statistics" to impress upon the task force the seriousness of the problem. Could the supervisor have taken another approach to this situation?

3. In this case, the supervisor experienced little resistance to his push for conversion to a middle school format. Where would you normally have expected resistance to be found and why? How would your expectations affect such actions as determining the composition of the task force?

4. Outlining the major steps of this supervisory action, where might you expect the effort to break down (e.g., no release time for the task force to analyze data)? Can you project alternative actions for each potential breakdown anticipated?

5. How might parents and students have been involved in this particular supervisory action?

CASE HISTORY THREE

The High School Attrition Problem

For many supervisors in the high school, a dilemma exists in regard to defining effective instruction. Is the measure of good teaching what the instructor teaches, or is it what the student actually learns because of the instruction? In this case the supervisor, Barbara, has been asked to visit the classroom of a math teacher who is deeply troubled by the failure rate at the high school.

Upon arriving at the teacher's classroom, Barbara observed a learning space characterized by considerable clutter and extensive activity. Students were everywhere in the room, engaged in project work, small group work, and independent study. The teacher, Ms. Harmon, was roaming about the room attending to the various students in a variety of ways; encouraging, showing, telling, and listening. After fifteen minutes the bell sounded ending the school day, and the supervisor and teacher sat down for a conference.

Ms. Harmon opened the meeting by apologizing for the untidiness of her room and the noise level present when the supervisor entered. She hastened to add, however, that this was her style of teaching, and she believed that such individual attention to students was crucial. Her real concern, she confided, was that other teachers didn't approve of her methods. She was also most anxious about how her students would do on year-end standardized achievement tests.

Ms. Harmon went on to tell Barbara that she believed something was very wrong with the way math was being taught in the high school. Instruction was directed toward the advanced students, many students were failing, and most teachers simply lectured to students instead of involving them in the exciting world of applied mathematics. The conference closed with Barbara promising to look into grading patterns at the school.

During the next week Barbara did in fact review the grading patterns at the high school. Her preliminary review turned up some startling information. Nearly 20 percent of the students at the high school were leaving school prior to grade 11. Failure rates for freshman and sophomores were running as high as 47 percent in some math, science, and English classes. Grading patterns beyond grade 10 were regular, bell-shaped distributions. Even more disturbing, an unusually high proportion of minority students were leaving school or experiencing poor academic evaluations.

After reviewing the records, Barbara met with the building principal to share her findings and concerns. The principal voiced surprise over the supervisor's findings and offered to make all records available for a complete analysis. Barbara suggested that it would be useful to involve teachers at the school in the analysis and requested that a meeting be set up during an upcoming in-service day. A date and time for the session were set. Barbara sent a brief note to Ms. Harmon informing her of the actions being taken.

On the day of the meeting all of the high school's 90 teachers filed into the auditorium to attend the session. Barbara was brief but firm in outlining her concerns about the pattern of evaluation in the school, and asked for the support of the teachers in conducting an in-depth inquiry. She suggested that each department identify two teachers who might assist in the assessment of data and in making recommendations. She asked that these names be forwarded to the building principal by the following week.

On the appointed date the supervisor returned to the school and met with the principal to collect the names of those teachers who would assist in the study. The principal was apologetic, explaining that only two departments had forwarded names and that several protests had been recorded through the teacher professional organization. The major reservation on the part of the teachers, the principal explained, was a fear that their academic standards were being challenged.

After returning to her office, Barbara considered possible alternatives for action. She could, of course, drop the issue and work only with Ms. Harmon and others trying to meet the needs of students. She might also go to the superintendent to gain his advice and the endorsement of authority. She could proceed with the study as if a full study council had been appointed. She could work through the professional organization.

That evening Barbara reviewed a number of textbooks on supervision looking for an answer to her problem. In one such book she found the following statement:

> Lacking the defined role and official sanction understood both "above" and "below" the image he has of his own position, he falls into giving direct personal assistance to teachers, especially the beginners, the isolated, the incompetents, and the malcontents. These are the ones most responsive to supervisory direction which lacks authority. Such teachers are also the most visible to supervisors—that is, the most easily diagnosed.[2]

Barbara decided to try once more to reach the teachers in the high school.

The next week Barbara spent three days in the high school talking with teachers about student evaluation. She found that they were not generally aware of the overall picture, and tended to view evaluation as a judgmental process, rather than a diagnostic/prescriptive device. She was also able to identify some teachers who were interested in learning more about grading and willing to consider new ways to teach students who lacked high aptitude or academic motivation.

Returning to the principal, the supervisor requested the student records and had them analyzed by her own staff back at the district office. A summary of the findings were mailed to each teacher at the high school along with an invitation for special in-service opportunity on the topic of alternative learning and teaching styles. To provide such an in-service program, Barbara amended her own budget and requested an extra appropriation from the superintendent to pay for the release time of teachers interested in attending the session.

Three weeks later, twenty-nine teachers from the high school met in a two-day workshop that explored alternative teaching and learning formats. A special consultant presentation was made on the topic of mastery learning. Mastery learning is an educational system that promotes the idea that 90–95 percent of all students can master objectives normally reached by only "good students." In order for this to happen, teachers must orient their teaching to the achievement of objectives, as opposed to seeing their job as separating the good students from the poor students by testing and evaluation.

Following the workshop, Barbara administered a questionnaire to the participants asking whether they would like to have further training in such areas as scheduling for more learning time, using divergent materials in the classroom, diagnosing prerequisite skills, and understanding culturally different students. The returned questionnaires

---

[2] L. Craig Wilson, et al. *Sociology of Supervision: An Approach to Comprehensive Planning in Education* (Boston: Allyn & Bacon, 1969), p. 19.

indicated that there was sufficient interest in these topics for additional in-service assistance.

Having scheduled four additional workshops for the remainder of the year, the supervisor then turned her attention to the kinds of practices found in the high school. From among the twenty-nine teachers who had attended the workshop. Barbara identified sixteen teachers who were trying new techniques. Working with the principal, Barbara was able to schedule the teachers' classes in such a manner that they shared the same students in many cases. A research pilot study was established that compared performance of students in classes with these sixteen teachers to those in classes with all other teachers. After one semester of observation the following appeared true:

1. Students in the sixteen experimental classes had more positive attitudes toward learning.
2. Students in the sixteen experimental classes had higher grade point averages in the subjects studied.
3. Fewer students in the sixteen experimental classrooms indicated a desire to quit school at the end of the year.

At the end of the school year all students in the school were given a battery of standardized examinations in English, mathematics, science, and reading. Preliminary analyses of the data suggested that students in the experimental classrooms performed as well as students in standard classrooms.

As the school year concluded, Barbara was busy working with the sixteen teachers to establish a "buddy program" with the other teachers who had attended the workshops but were not involved in the study as experimental teachers. The supervisor hoped that through an organized program of sharing, the teaching practices of the sixteen could be spread to the other willing teachers. Using such a "multiplication method," Barbara hoped to have half the high school teachers trying the new methods within one year. Meanwhile, she would continue to collect data on student achievement, attendance, attitudes, and retention as a means of supporting her experimental teachers' efforts.

An outline of this supervisory effort to address the problem of student attrition at the high school follows. Also identified are supervisory skills employed to promote this effort. Finally, some questions are presented for further consideration.

Preliminary Steps to Address the Problem	**Skills Used**
Identifying problem at teacher conference	"Actively listening;" suspends judgment until data available

Reviewing problem area	Researching area and drawing preliminary conclusions
Sharing findings with colleagues and superiors	Meeting with building principal to seek assistance; requesting meeting with all teachers
Establishing formal review of the problem	Planning major assessment of student evaluation at high school
Confronting logistical problem	Accepting teachers' resistance; seeking resources from supervision texts
Re-establishing procedures	Visiting high school teachers to build a consensus of opinion
Implementing strategy for changing	Planning and establishing invitational in-service experience; securing special release time for volunteers
Establishing baseline evaluation of change effort	Developing research study of sixteen experimenting teachers and their students
Directing change effort	Expanding experimental methods through "buddy system," enlarge study of high school students and evaluation practices

Questions about Case History Three

1. In the original observation of Ms. Harmon, Barbara refrained from making verbal observations about the condition of her classroom. Was this the right thing for the supervisor to do?

2. The supervisor found that in some math, science, and English classes failures were running as high as 47 percent of the students. Is this figure excessive in today's public school classrooms at the high school level?

3. After her efforts to involve the teachers in a study of evaluation practices were rejected, Barbara retreated to her office to study the situation. Should she have taken more immediate action?

4. Can you describe the strategy that the supervisor is pursuing to deal with the situation?

5. What is the exact role of the research study in Barbara's overall plan?

6. How might the supervisor improve on this series of action?

Because supervision in educational settings is not a clearly defined role, supervisory procedure and techniques are often improvised. The school supervisor must often find his or her own way in meeting and solving day-to-day problems. For this reason, supervisors should be aware of resources available to them and know how to retrieve such resources in an efficient and timely manner. This appendix seeks to introduce those who are new to supervision to the wealth of resources presently available to school supervisors.

Major organizers for this appendix include newsletters, information services, directories, reference books, annotated bibliographies, consulting organizations, research and development centers, films, and professional organizations. In addition, we list those institutions of higher education that currently hold national accreditation (NCATE) at the doctoral level in the area of instruction or curriculum and supervision.

NEWSLETTERS

ASCD News Exchange
Association for Supervision and
  Curriculum Development
1701 K Street, N.W. (Suite 1100)
Washington, D.C. 20006

Department of Classroom Teachers
News Bulletin
National Education Association
1201 16th Street, N.W.
Washington, D.C. 20036

Educational Product Report
Educational Products Information
   Exchange Institute (EPIE)
386 Park Avenue, South
New York, N.Y. 10016

Educational Researcher
American Educational Research
   Association (AERA)
1126 16th Street, N.W.
Washington, D.C. 20036

Education Recaps
Educational Testing Service
Princeton, New Jersey 08540

Education U.S.A.
National School Public Relations
   Association
1201 16th Street, N.W.
Washington, D.C. 20036

NASSP Newsletter
National Association of Secondary
   School Principals
1201 16th Street, N.W.
Washington, D.C. 20036

National Elementary Principals
National Elementary Principals
Department of Classroom Teachers
1201 16th Street, N.W.
Washington, D.C. 20036

SLANTS
School Information and
   Research Service (SIRS)
100 Crochett Street
Seattle, Washington 98109

INFORMATION SERVICES

ERIC (Educational Resources Information Center)

ERIC is a network of information centers by topic area established by the U.S. Office of Education. ERIC disseminates research findings and other resource materials found effective in developing school programs. The holdings of the nineteen clearinghouses are abstracted in *Research in Education*. All documents in this journal are available in either hardcopy or microfiche from:
   ERIC Document Reproduction Service
   National Cash Register Company
   4936 Fairmont Avenue
   Bethesda, Maryland 20014
Individual ERIC clearinghouses, by topic, are listed below:

Adult Education
Syracuse University
Syracuse, New York 13210

Counseling and Personnel Services
University of Michigan
Ann Arbor, Michigan 48104

Disadvantaged
Teachers College
Columbia University
New York, New York 10027

Early Childhood Education
University of Illinois
Urbana, Illinois 61801

Educational Administration
University of Oregon
Eugene, Oregon 97403

Educational Facilities
University of Wisconsin
Madison, Wisconsin 53703

Educational Media and Technology
Institute for Communication
  Research
Stanford University
Stanford, California 94305

Exceptional Children
The Council for Exceptional
  Children
Arlington, Virginia 22202

Junior Colleges
University of California at
  Los Angeles
Los Angeles, California 90024

Higher Education
George Washington University
Washington, D.C. 20006

Library and Information Sciences
University of Minnesota
Minneapolis, Minnesota 55404

Linguistics
Center for Applied Linguistics
Washington, D.C. 20036

Reading
Indiana University
Bloomington, Indiana 47401

Rural Education and Small Schools
New Mexico State University
Las Cruces, New Mexico 88001

Science Education
Ohio State University
Columbus, Ohio 43221

Teacher Education
American Association of Colleges
  for Teacher Education
Washington, D.C. 20005

Teaching of English
National Council of Teachers
  of English
Champaign, Illinois 61820

Teaching of Foreign Languages
Modern Language Association
  of America
New York, New York 10011

*Vocational and Technical
  Education*
Ohio State University
Columbus, Ohio 43210

OTHERS

*National Middle School
  Resource Center*
120 East Walnut Street
Indianapolis, Indiana

*SRIS (School Research
  Information Service)*
Phi Delta Kappa Research
  Service Center
Eighth and Union Streets
Bloomington, Indiana 47401

National Audiovisual Center
National Archives and
  Records Service (GSA)
Washington, D.C. 20409

DIRECTORIES

*Directory of Educational
  Information Services*
Division of Information Technology
  and Dissemination
Bureau of Research
U.S. Office of Education
Washington, D.C.

*Directory of Special Libraries and
  Information Centers*
Gale Research Company
The Book Tower
Detroit, Michigan 48226

The Education Index (authors and titles in education)
The H.W. Wilson Company
950 University Avenue
New York, New York

Encyclopedia of Associations
Gale Research Company
The Book Tower
Detroit, Michigan 48226

The Directory of Publishing Opportunities
Academic Media
Cordura Corporation
32 Lincoln Avenue
Orange, New Jersey 07050

Current Index to Journals in Education (CIJE)
CCM Information Corporation
909 Third Avenue
New York, New York 10022

REFERENCE BOOKS

Dictionary of Education
Edited by Carter V. Good. New York: McGraw-Hill, 1959. Definitions of educational terminology.

Digest of Education Statistics
Available from U.S. Government Printing Office, Washington, D.C. 20402. A statistical abstract of American education activity.

Encyclopedia of Educational Research
Fourth ed., edited by Robert L. Ebel. New York: Macmillan, 1969. Describes research findings on broad range of topics in education.

National Society for the Study of Education Yearbook (NSSE)
Published by the University of Chicago Press. An in-depth treatment of an educational concern each year. More information from NSSE, 5835 Kimbark Avenue, Chicago, Illinois 60639.

The World Yearbook of Education
Available from Harcourt, Brace, and Jovanovich, New York. Provides articles on various topic areas in education by year.

ANNOTATED BIBLIOGRAPHIES

Self Development Aids for Supervisors and Middle Managers, Personnel Bibliography Series 34. Library, Washington, D.C.: U.S. Civil Service Commission, 1970.

ERIC Abstracts: *A Collection of ERIC Document Resumes on Inservice Education for Staff and Administrators.* Washington, D.C.: American Association of School Administrators, 1970.

ERIC Abstracts: *Linking Schools and State Education Departments to Research and Development Agencies.* Eugene, Oregon: ERIC Clearinghouse on Educational Administration, 1971.

ERIC Abstracts: *A Collection of ERIC Document Resumes on Politics and Power Structure: Influence on Education*. Washington, D.C.: American Association of School Administrators, 1969.

ERIC Abstracts: *A Collection of ERIC Document Resumes on Collective Bargaining and Negotiations in Education*. Washington, D.C.: American Association of School Administrators, 1969.

Havelock, Ronald G.; Huber, Janet; and Zimmerman, Shaindel. *Major Works on Change in Education: An Annotated Bibliography and Subject Index*. Ann Arbor, Mich.: Center for Research on Utilization of Scientific Knowledge, University of Michigan, 1969.

Hall, John S. *Implementing School Desegregation: A Bibliography*. Eugene, Oregon: ERIC Clearinghouse on Educational Administration, 1970.

Hahn, Marshall. *Review of Research on Creativity*. Minneapolis, Minn.: Research Coordinating Unit in Occupational Education, 1968 (ED 029 090).

ERIC Abstract: *A Collection of ERIC Document Resumes on Human Relations in Educational Administration*. Washington, D.C.: American Association of School Administrators, 1969.

CONSULTING ORGANIZATIONS

Regional Educational Laboratories

Throughout the United States there are private, nonprofit educational corporations created by the 1965 Elementary and Secondary Education Act. Through contracts with the U.S. Office of Education, these regional laboratories attempt to link research and development programs with practice in the schools of their respective regions. Each REL has a theme that is identified with the addresses below:

Appalachia Educational Laboratory (AEL)

Theme: Rural education/ Communication media

Appalachia Educational Laboratory
P.O. Box 1348
1031 Quarrier Street
Charleston, West Virginia 25325

Center For Urban Education (CUE)

Theme: Urban education

Center For Urban Education
105 Madison Avenue
New York, New York 10016

Central Atlantic Regional Educational Laboratory (CAREL)

Theme: Fine arts for early childhood and elementary age

Central Atlantic Regional Educational Laboratory
1200 17th Street, N.W.
Washington, D.C. 20036

Central Midwestern Regional Educational laboratory (CEMREL)

Theme: Mathematics/Aesthetics/Learning disabilities

Central Midwestern Regional Educational Laboratory
19646 St. Charles Rock Road
St. Ann, Missouri 63074

Eastern Regional Institute for Education (ERIE)

Theme: Elementary education

Eastern Regional Institute for Education
635 James Street
Syracuse, New York 13203

Educational Development Center (EDC)

Theme: Research at all levels

Educational Development Center
55 Chapel Street
Newton, Massachusetts 02160

Far West Laboratory For Educational Research and Development (FWLED)

Theme: Teacher education/Communication systems/Early
education

West Regional Laboratory
One Garden Circle
Hotel Claremont
Berkeley, California 94705

Mid-Continent Regional Educational Laboratory (McREL)

Theme: Teacher behavior/Inner-city education

Mid-Continent Regional Educational Laboratory
104 East Independence Avenue
Kansas City, Missouri 64106

Northwest Regional Educational Laboratory (NWREL)

Theme: Small Schools/Cultural differences/Instructional leadership

Northwest Regional Educational Laboratory
400 Lindsay Building
710 Southwest Second Avenue
Portland, Oregon 97204

Southeastern Educational Laboratory (SEL)

Theme: Disadvantaged learners

Southeastern Educational Laboratory
3450 International Blvd.
Suite 221
Atlanta, Georgia

Southwest Educational Development Laboratory (SEDL)

Theme: Intercultural education

Southwest Educational Development Laboratory
800 Brazos Street
Austin, Texas 78701

Southwestern Cooperative Educational Laboratory (SWCEL)

Theme: Communication arts/Adult education/Indian education

Southwestern Cooperative Educational Laboratory
117 Richmond Drive, N.E.
Albuquerque, New Mexico 87106

Southwest Regional Laboratory for Educational Research and Development (SWRL)

Theme: Research-based instructional systems

Southwest Regional Laboratory for Ed. Research and Development
11300 LaCienega Blvd.
Inglewood, California 90304

Upper Midwest Regional Educational Laboratory (UMREL)

Theme: Design of educational environments

Upper Midwest Regional Educational Laboratory
1640 East 78 Street
Minneapolis, Minnesota 55423

IDEA (Institute for the Development of Educational Activities, Inc.) Charles F. Kettering Foundation, Dayton, Ohio

IDEA has three missions:
1) Research on educational change
2) Promotion of innovative educational programs
3) Information and services

Research for Better Schools, Inc. 1700 Market Street, Suite 1700, Philadelphia, Pennsylvania 19103

Promotion of educational opportunities for individualizing and humanizing education at all levels

RESEARCH AND DEVELOPMENT CENTERS

Center for the Advanced Study of Educational Administration
1478 Hendricks Hall
University of Oregon
Eugene, Oregon 97403

Concerned with the planning capacity of schools and providing information which will aid educational decision-makers.

Center for the Study of Evaluation
Graduate School of Education
University of California
144 Hilgard Avenue
Los Angeles, California.
    Concerned with the development of techniques useful in the evaluation of instructional programs in school settings.

National Center for Career Education
612 Eddy Street
Missoula, Montana (University of Montana).
    Concerned with retrieval, assessment, and dissemination of career education curricula from throughout the United States.

Stanford Center for Research and Development in Teaching
Stanford University
770 Welch Road
Palo Alto, California 94304
    Concerned with research on teaching and the promotion of educational practices that support excellence in teaching.

Research and Development Center in Teacher Education
College of Education
University of Texas,
Austin, Texas 78712
    Concerned with teaching effectiveness and interdisciplinary inquiry into the practices of teaching.

FILMS AND MEDIA

A large number of professional films relate to the area of supervision, but we feel that one group of films is superior to all others for training purposes. The following films are produced by BNA Communications Inc., 9401 Decoverly Hall Road, Rockville, Maryland 20850, and, while expensive, do an outstanding job of addressing critical supervision concerns:

PRACTICE OF SUPERVISION Series (Gellerman)
    Planning, Organizing and Controlling, Part I (21 minutes)
    Planning, Organizing and Controlling, Part II (21 minutes)
    Planning, Organizing and Controlling, Part III (20 minutes)

ADVANCED SUPERVISION Series (Gellerman)
    Managing in a Crisis (Beckhard) (30 minutes)
    Working With Troubled Employees (Levinson) (30 minutes)
    Controlling Absenteeism (Gellerman) (30 minutes)

TWO-PERSON COMMUNICATION Series (Berlo)
    Gathering Good Information: "Get 'em up, Scout" (25 minutes)
    Seeking Understanding and Acceptance: "Try to tell it like it is" (30 minutes)
    Building a Working Team: "Let's get engaged" (28 minutes)
    Maintaining the Organization: "How far can I trust you?" (30 minutes)
    Helping People Develop: "Don't tell me what's good for me" (30 minutes)

MANAGEMENT BY OBJECTIVES Series (Humble)
    Focus the Future (25 minutes)
    Management by Objectives (27 minutes)
    Defining the Manager's Job (21 minutes)
    Performance and Potential Review (23 minutes)
    Management Training (23 minutes)
    Colt—A Case History (24 minutes)

ORGANIZATION RENEWAL Series (Lippitt)
    Growth Stages of Organizations (25 minutes)
    Confrontation, Search and Coping (25 minutes)
    Individuality and Teamwork (25 minutes)
    Coping With Change (25 minutes)
    How Organization Renewal Works (25 minutes)

MANAGERIAL GRID® Series (Blake-Mouton)
    The Managerial Grid in Action (30 minutes)
    The Grid Approach to Conflict Solving (30 minutes)

MOTIVATION AND PRODUCTIVITY Series (Gellerman)
    Strategy for Productive Behavior (Introduction) (20 minutes)
    Motivation Through Job Enrichment (Herzberg) (28 minutes)
    The Self-Motivated Achiever (McClelland) (28 minutes)
    Understanding Motivation (Gellerman) (28 minutes)
    Theory X and Theory Y: The Work of Douglas McGregor
    Part I, Description of the Theory (25 minutes)
    Theory X and Theory Y: The Work of Douglas McGregor
    Part II, Application of the Theory (25 minutes)
    Human Nature and Organizational Realities (Argyris) (28 minutes)
    The Management of Human Assets (Likert) (28 minutes)
    Motivation in Perspective (Conclusion) (20 minutes)

MOTIVATION TO WORK Series (Herzberg)
    The Modern Meaning of Efficiency (25 minutes)
    KITA, or, What Have You Done for Me, Lately? (25 minutes)
    Job Enrichment in Action (25 minutes)
    Building a Climate for Individual Growth (25 minutes)
    The ABC Man: The Manager in Mid-Career (25 minutes)

EFFECTIVE COMMUNICATION Series (Berlo)
    Avoiding Communication Breakdown (24 minutes)
    Meanings Are in People (24 minutes)
    Communication Feedback (24 minutes)
    Changing Attitudes Through Communication (24 minutes)
    Communication Management's Point of View (24 minutes)

EFFECTIVE EXECUTIVE Series (Drucker)
  Managing Time (25 minutes)
  What Can I Contribute? (25 minutes)
  Focus on Tomorrow (25 minutes)
  Effective Decisions (25 minutes)
  Staffing for Strength (25 minutes)

EFFECTIVE ORGANIZATION Series (Gellerman)
  Assessing Management Potential (Bray) (25 minutes)
  Management by Participation (Marrow) (30 minutes)
  Pay for Performance (Kay) (30 minutes)
  Making Human Resources Productive (Myers) (31 minutes)
  Team Building (David) (30 minutes)
  Confronting Conflict (Davis) (30 minutes)

Free preview centers for all of these BNA films are located the following cities:

Atlanta
  2996 Grandview Avenue
  Atlanta, Georgia 30305
  (404) 233-5435
New York
  711 Third Avenue
  Room 313
  New York, New York 10017
  (212)490-1647
Chicago
  10400 West Higgins Avenue
  (Near O'Hare International
  Airport)
  Rosemont, Illinois 60018
  (312) 297-6320
Cleveland
  Cleveland, Ohio
  (216) 234-7300
Phoenix
  Phoenix, Arizona
  (602) 279-0770
Los Angeles
  3460 Wilshire Boulevard
  Suite 804, Wilshire Center
  Los Angeles, California 90010
  (213) 380-1653
Rockville
  9401 Decoverly Hall Road
  Rockville, Maryland 20850
  (301) 948-0540

Additional films of high quality for supervisory training can be rented or purchased from the National Audio Visual Center, National Archives and Records Service, General Services Administration, Washington, D.C. 20409. Examples of titles available through this source are:

Techniques of Decision Making (01256/DB)
Successful Supervision of Handicapped Employees (000755/DB)
Basic Report Writing (008096/DB)
Equal Opportunity and Affirmative Action (005692/DB)
Arbitration of a Grievance (005153/DB)
People, Not Paper (010370/DB)

Other films, videocassettes, audiocassettes, books, and workbooks are available through professional organizations.

PROFESSIONAL ORGANIZATIONS

Association for Supervision and Curriculum Development (ASCD)
National Education Association (NEA)
Phi Delta Kappa (PDK)
National Elementary Principals Association (NAESP)
National Association of Secondary School Principals (NASSP)
American Educational Research Association (AERA)

Among other functions, these professional organizations produce excellent journals that allow educators to communicate with one another over a broad range of concerns. The following journals are thought to be valuable resources for those persons engaged in supervision work:

Academy of Management Journal
American School Board Journal
Educational Administration Quarterly
Educational Forum
Educational Leadership
Educational Technology
Elementary School Journal
Harvard Educational Review
Journal of Research and Development in Education
Journal of Secondary Education
Learning Magazine
Management Review
NASSP Bulletin
National Elementary Principal
Phi Delta Kappan

Psychology Today
Review of Educational Research
School Review
Sloan Management Review
Teacher
Theory Into Practice

PROFESSIONAL DEVELOPMENT PROGRAMS

There comes a time for most supervisors when there is a need for formal training provided by universities and colleges. While some 1,367 colleges and universities prepare teachers, and 554 possess national accreditation at some level, only 94 institutions are nationally accredited (NCATE standards) at the doctoral level in the areas of curriculum and/or supervision. While such accreditation does not insure a quality education for those seeking professional development at this level, accreditation does insure certain standards in human and material resources that make up such programs. For this reason, we have chosen to list these institutions holding National Council for Accreditation of Teacher Education at the doctoral level in supervision (as of the twenty-fourth listing) by state:

Alabama

    Auburn University
    University of Alabama

Arizona

    Arizona State University
    University of Arizona

Arkansas

    University of Arkansas

California

    University of California—Berkeley
    University of the Pacific
    University of Southern California

Colorado

    Colorado State University
    University of Colorado—Boulder
    University of Denver
    University of Northern Colorado

Connecticut

    University of Connecticut

Florida

    Florida Atlantic University
    Florida State University
    University of Florida
    University of Miami

Georgia

    Atlanta University
    Georgia State University
    University of Georgia

Illinois

    Loyola University of Chicago
    Northern Illinois University
    Northwestern University
    Southern Illinois University
    University of Illinois—Urbana

Indiana

    Ball State University
    Indiana University
    Purdue University

Iowa

    Drake University
    University of Iowa

Kansas

    Kansas State University
    University of Kansas

Kentucky

    University of Kentucky

Maryland

    University of Maryland

Massachusetts

    Boston College
    Boston University
    Harvard University
    University of Massachusetts

Michigan

    Michigan State University
    University of Michigan
    Wayne State University
    Western Michigan University

Minnesota

University of Minnesota—Minneapolis

Mississippi

Mississippi State University
University of Mississippi

Missouri

University of Missouri—Columbia
University of Missouri—Kansas City

Montana

University of Montana

Nebraska

University of Nebraska

New Jersey

Rutgers University

New Mexico

University of New Mexico

New York

Fordham University
New York University
State University of New York—Albany
State University of New York—Buffalo
Syracuse University
Teachers College, Columbia
University of Rochester

North Carolina

Duke University
University of North Carolina—Chapel Hill
University of North Carolina—Greensboro

Ohio

Bowling Green State University
Kent State University
Ohio State University
University of Akron
University of Cincinnati
University of Toledo

Oklahoma

Oklahoma State University
University of Oklahoma

Oregon

> University of Oregon

Pennsylvania

> Lehigh University
> Pennsylvania State University
> University of Pittsburgh
> Temple University

South Carolina

> University of South Carolina

South Dakota

> University of South Dakota

Tennessee

> George Peabody College for Teachers
> Memphis State University
> University of Tennessee, Knoxville

Texas

> North Texas State University
> Texas A&M University
> Texas Tech University
> University of Houston
> University of Texas, Austin

Utah

> Brigham Young University
> University of Utah
> Utah State University

Virginia

> University of Virginia
> Virginia Tech University

Washington

> University of Washington
> Washington State University

West Virginia

> West Virginia University

Wisconsin

> University of Wisconsin, Madison

Wyoming

> University of Wyoming

Finally, we offer as a resource ten of *Murphy's Laws*. These laws can be traced back to an earlier proposition known as Dill's Law of Random Perversity and are food for thought for anyone charged with the responsibility of supervision:

If anything can go wrong, it will.
Nothing is as easy as it looks.
Everything takes longer than you think.
Left unto themselves, things tend to go from bad to worse.
It always costs more than first estimated.
It is easier to get involved in something than to get out of it.
Every solution breeds new problems.
If you're feeling good, don't worry—you'll get over it.
It is impossible to make everything foolproof because fools are so ingenious.
The more complex the idea or technology, the more simpleminded the opposition.

The Authors

Jon Wiles

Jon Wiles received his Ed. D. in curriculum and instruction from The University of Florida. His present position is professor of education at The University of Montana. Dr. Wiles has served as a classroom teacher, curriculum director, professor of education, and dean of a college of education. As an educational consultant, he has worked with schools in over twenty states and seven foreign countries.

Dr. Wiles is the author of three additional books: *Curriculum Planning: A New Approach* (1974), *Planning Guidelines For Middle School Education* (1976), and *Curriculum Development: A Guide To Practice* (1979). He has also authored numerous articles in professional education journals.

Joseph Bondi

Joseph Bondi, professor of education, The University of South Florida, received his doctorate in education from The University of Florida. Dr. Bondi has both teaching and administrative experience in public schools on elementary and secondary levels and has served as chairman of the Department of Curriculum and Instruction during his college teaching at The University of South Florida.

Dr. Bondi has authored or coauthored eight texts in education and is the author of numerous articles in professional journals. He has served as president of the Florida Association for Supervision and Curriculum Development and as a member of the Board of Directors and Executive Council of ASCD. He is active in other professional associations and has been a consultant in curriculum development to school districts in forty-five states and Canada.

Name Index

Subject Index